CAMBRIDGE LIBRARY COLLECTION

Books of enduring scholarly value

Slavery and Abolition

The books reissued in this series include accounts of historical events and movements by eye-witnesses and contemporaries, as well as landmark studies that assembled significant source materials or developed new historiographical methods. The series includes work in social, political and military history on a wide range of periods and regions, giving modern scholars ready access to influential publications of the past.

West African Countries and Peoples, British and Native

This book, first published in 1868, became the best-known work of medical officer and writer James Africanus Beale Horton (1835–1883), who was born in Sierra Leone to parents of Igbo descent. He was chosen by the British to train as an army medical officer and attended King's College, London, and Edinburgh University. He returned to West Africa and published his doctoral thesis, which was a medical topography of the region; subsequent works called for health reforms. *West African Countries*, however, went beyond medicine. In it Horton refutes the derogatory racial theories about Africans rife in Victorian Britain and its empire, and he examines the possibility of self-government and how it might function in Sierra Leone and other territories in West Africa, foreshadowing the decolonisation that took place almost one hundred years later.

Cambridge University Press has long been a pioneer in the reissuing of out-of-print titles from its own backlist, producing digital reprints of books that are still sought after by scholars and students but could not be reprinted economically using traditional technology. The Cambridge Library Collection extends this activity to a wider range of books which are still of importance to researchers and professionals, either for the source material they contain, or as landmarks in the history of their academic discipline.

Drawing from the world-renowned collections in the Cambridge University Library, and guided by the advice of experts in each subject area, Cambridge University Press is using state-of-the-art scanning machines in its own Printing House to capture the content of each book selected for inclusion. The files are processed to give a consistently clear, crisp image, and the books finished to the high quality standard for which the Press is recognised around the world. The latest print-on-demand technology ensures that the books will remain available indefinitely, and that orders for single or multiple copies can quickly be supplied.

The Cambridge Library Collection will bring back to life books of enduring scholarly value (including out-of-copyright works originally issued by other publishers) across a wide range of disciplines in the humanities and social sciences and in science and technology.

West African Countries and Peoples, British and Native

And a Vindication of the African Race

JAMES AFRICANUS BEALE HORTON

CAMBRIDGE UNIVERSITY PRESS

Cambridge, New York, Melbourne, Madrid, Cape Town,
Singapore, São Paolo, Delhi, Tokyo, Mexico City

Published in the United States of America by Cambridge University Press, New York

www.cambridge.org
Information on this title: www.cambridge.org/9781108028592

© in this compilation Cambridge University Press 2011

This edition first published 1868
This digitally printed version 2011

ISBN 978-1-108-02859-2 Paperback

WEST AFRICAN COUNTRIES AND PEOPLES.

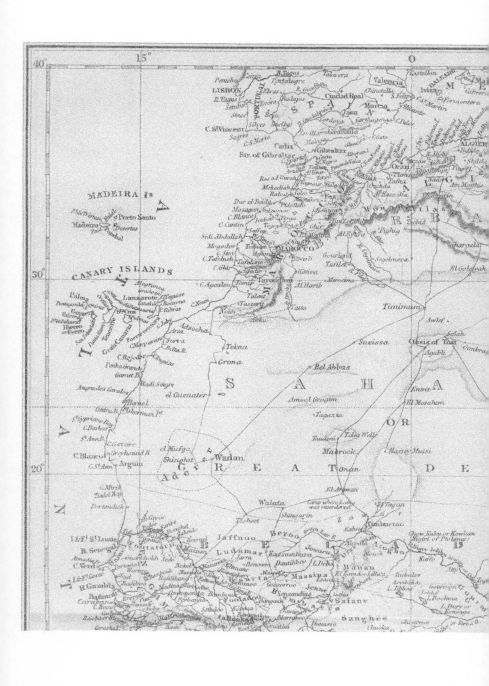

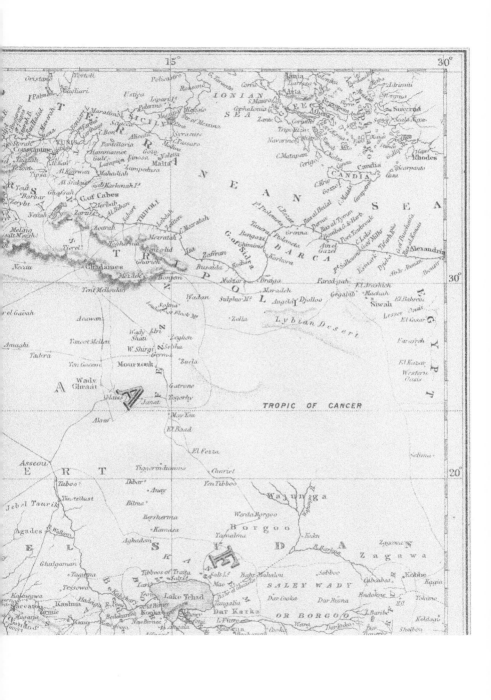

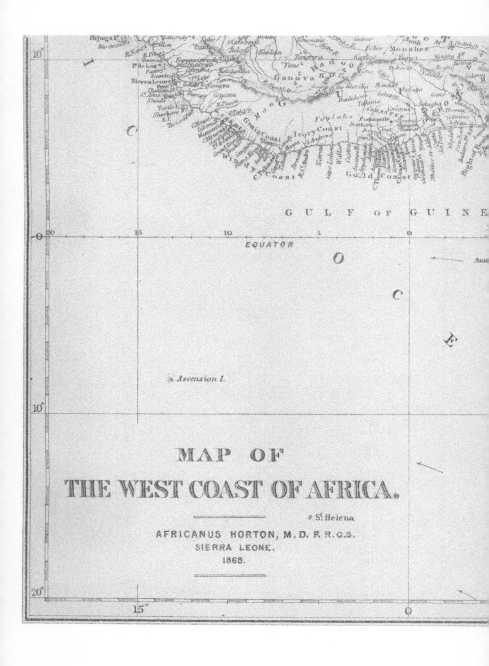

MAP OF
THE WEST COAST OF AFRICA.

o St Helena

AFRICANUS HORTON, M.D. F. R.G.S.
SIERRA LEONE.
1868.

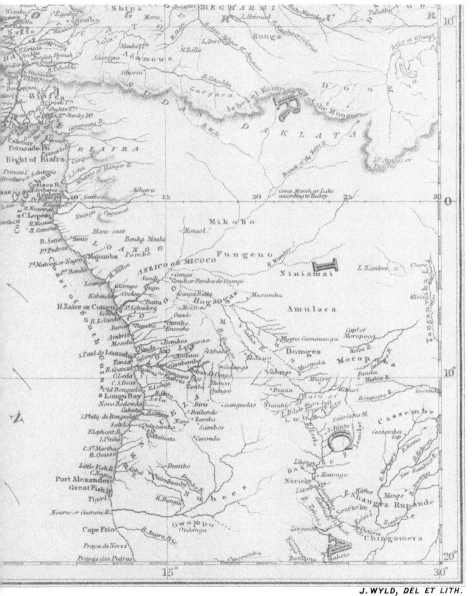

J. WYLD, DEL ET LITH.

WEST AFRICAN

COUNTRIES AND PEOPLES,

BRITISH AND NATIVE.

WITH THE

REQUIREMENTS NECESSARY FOR ESTABLISHING THAT SELF
GOVERNMENT RECOMMENDED BY THE COMMITTEE OF
THE HOUSE OF COMMONS, 1865 ;

AND A

VINDICATION OF THE AFRICAN RACE.

BY

JAMES AFRICANUS B. HORTON, M.D.Edin., F.R.G.S.,

AUTHOR OF "PHYSICAL AND MEDICAL CLIMATE AND METEOROLOGY OF THE WEST COAST OF
AFRICA," "GUINEA WORM, OR DRACUNCULUS," ETC., ETC., ETC.

STAFF ASSISTANT-SURGEON OF H.M. FORCES IN WEST AFRICA; ASSOCIATE OF KING'S COLLEGE, LONDON;
FOREIGN FELLOW OF THE BOTANICAL SOCIETY OF EDINBURGH; CORRESPONDING MEMBER OF
THE MEDICAL SOCIETY OF KING'S COLLEGE, LONDON; MEMBER OF THE INSTITUTE
D'AFRIQUE OF PARIS, ETC., ETC., ETC.

"Africa ought to be allowed to have a fair chance of raising her character in the scale
of the civilized world."—EMPEROR OF RUSSIA.

LONDON:

W. J. JOHNSON, 121, FLEET STREET.

1868.

LONDON: W. J. JOHNSON, PRINTER, 121, FLEET STREET.

TO

THE REV. HENRY VENN, B.D.,

PREBENDARY OF ST. PAUL'S CATHEDRAL, HONORARY SECRETARY OF THE CHURCH MISSIONARY
SOCIETY, ETC., ETC.,

AS A

SLIGHT MEMENTO

OF APPRECIATION FOR HIS UNTIRING ZEAL TOWARDS THE DEVELOPMENT
OF THE MORAL, SOCIAL, AND CHRISTIAN ADVANCEMENT OF
THE AFRICAN RACE;

AND AS AN

ACKNOWLEDGMENT OF MANY PERSONAL KINDNESSES RECEIVED,

This Work

IS MOST RESPECTFULLY DEDICATED

BY

THE AUTHOR.

CONTENTS.

PART I.

WEST AFRICAN COUNTRIES AND PEOPLES, AND THE NEGRO'S PLACE IN NATURE.

PART II.

AFRICAN NATIONALITY.

CONTENTS.

PREFACE.

It must appear astounding to those who have carefully and thoughtfully read the history of England in connexion with the subject of the African race, when its greatest statesman, so long ago as 1838, stated in Parliament the endeavours his Government had been making to induce the various continental and transatlantic ones to put down slavery, that the abolition of that institution in the Southern States of America should have produced so much bile amongst a small section in England; who, although they have had undeniable proofs of the fallacy of their arguments, and inconsistency of their statements with existing facts, have formed themselves into an association (*sic* Anthropological Society) to rake up old malice and encourage their agents abroad to search out the worst possible characteristics of the African, so to furnish material for venting their animus against him. ' Its object,' as has been stated, ' is to prove him unimprovable, therefore unimproved since the beginning, and, consequently, fitted only to remain a hewer of wood and drawer of water for the members of that select society.' It would have been sufficient to treat this with the contempt it deserves, were it not that leading statesmen of the present day have shown themselves easily carried away by the malicious views of these negrophobists, to the great prejudice of that race.

It is without doubt an uphill work for those who have always combated that vile crusade of prejudice, especially when considering themselves at the point of putting a crowning stroke to the superstructure which had taken them years to erect, to find the foundation undermined by rats of a somewhat formidable size, and therefore requiring a renewed and a more unassailable structure. One of the anthropological myths is to prove that, up to the age of puberty, the negro can combat successfully, and even show a precocity superior to that of the more enlightened race of a temperate climate, but that after this period, which corresponds to the closing of the sutures, he is doomed—a limit is set upon his further progress. But to prove more convincingly that this malign statement is fallacious, let those who are interested in the subject refer to the Principals of the Church Missionary College, Islington; King's College, London; and Fourah Bay College, Sierra Leone; where full-blooded Africans, who have had the complete development of their sutures, have been under tuition, and they will then be able to form an opinion from unbiassed testimony. I do not for a moment attempt here to prove that, as a whole, a race whose past generations have been in utter darkness, the mental faculty of whose ancestors has never received any culture for nearly a thousand years, could attempt to compete successfully in their present state with one whose ancestors have successively been under mental training and moulding for centuries. To think so would be to expect an ordinary-bred horse to have equal chances in a grand race with a thorough-bred one. But I say that the African race, as exemplified by the results of enterprises in Western Africa, if put in comparison with any race on the face of the globe, whether Caucasian, Mongolian, Teutonic, Celtic, or any other just emerging from a state of barbarism, as they are, will never be found a whit behind. But to draw deductions by comparing their present state with the civilization of the nineteenth century is not only absurd, but most unphilosophical.

Even Captain Burton, the *noli me tangere* of the African race, the greatest authority in the present school of English anthropologists (their vice-president), who, from his writings, has led everyone to believe that he has a fiendish hatred against the negro, whilst animadverting in all his works on Western Africa, in the most unmistakably malicious language, on the impossibilty of improving that race he so hates, forgot himself in one place, and exclaimed, as to their intellectual superiority, ' There are about 100 Europeans in the land ; amongst these there are many excellent fellows, *but it is an unpleasant confession to make,* the others appear to be inferior to the Africans, native as well as mulatto. The possibility of such a thing had never yet reached my brain. At last, in colloquy with an old friend upon the Coast, the idea started up, and, after due discussion, we adopted it. I speak of *morale*. In intellect the *black race is palpably superior, and it is fast advancing in the path of civilization.*' The first and last *italics* are ours.

But these anthropologists have still worse designs for Africa, since we find them seriously arguing in their meetings and proclaiming in the public press that the Mohammedan religion, in all cases where Western Africa is concerned, should supplant that of Christianity ; that the belief in the False Prophet is substantially better than the belief in Christ for the African. And when we see the chief of them suiting his actions to his words, kneeling in the presence of the native population every morning with his face towards the rising sun, bowing and making signs, in the attitude and after the fashion of a true believer in Mohammedanism; when, I say, we see such men seriously arguing that polygamy is the natural and more genial institution, and monogamy not, and laying aside and totally ignoring the biblical revelation, what else can the negro expect but a complete falsification of every circumstance relating to his race ?

I believe and firmly hold, that it is not by Mohammedanizing the inhabitants of Western Africa according to the present school of anthropologists, that they can or will be civilized; and I maintain that no civilization would take root and bear fruit except that based on the principles of the Christian religion; and that the people had far better remain as they are, than to have any other religious belief except the Christian introduced and propagated amongst them. I, amongst a great many others, appreciate every European element that enters Western Africa, whether in the capacity of merchants or pioneers of civilization, or in that of missionaries; and whilst I hail their efforts, respect their talents, and revere the civilization they are capable of imparting, I will never permit any unjust abuse, any unfounded diatribe against the African race, to be ruthlessly lavished on them without repelling or exposing the calumny. I am aware that such explicit and independent statements as are contained in this work, do not tend to advance a man's worldly interest; but if they tend to expose the weak and one-sided opinions of those who take every opportunity to advance theories about Africa and the Africans contrary to the truth, and if they lead to the better appreciation of, and a proper application of means to meet the growing wants and requirements of Her Majesty's West African Settlements, I shall feel sufficiently repaid for my labours.

This work has been divided into three parts :—

Part I. An endeavour is made to disprove many of the fallacious doctrines and statements of anthropologists (detrimental to the interests of the African race) from existing facts.

I commenced by giving a detailed account of the various phases of existence found among the uncivilized nations of Western Africa; and then proceeded to consider the various forms of Government met with on the Coast, and, among others, that of the Republic of Liberia. In the subsequent chapters I endeavoured, from personal observations and by quotations from the writings of various authors, to disprove those mischievous doctrines which have been promulgated to the detriment of the growing races of Western Africa. As conformation forms the sheet anchor of many of their arguments I have endeavoured to prove that a race of the most perfect Caucasian type would degenerate according to the influences brought to bear on the undeveloped and delicate structure of the infant; and that when once a deformity has become established, the laws of physiology have shown that it has a tendency to perpetuate. Adopting this view, the present conformation of the negro race can be traced to natural causes, depending most materially on the pernicious mode of managing the young, who undergo every degree of compression or distortion. During infancy, when firmly secured on the back of its nurse for several hours daily, the soft, yielding, undeveloped tissues of the infant undergo various degrees of distortion, which ultimately form, after some generations, a permanent type; capable, however, of great improvement by careful manipulation of the young. That this is the most fruitful source, may be traced in the number of forms found in typical tribes, having the same origin, but variously brought up; and I will prove my point, by quoting from the writings of the most determined African hater—the Vice-President of the Anthropological Society. Captain Burton, in describing the Egbas of Abeokuta, writes, 'never have I seen such villainous crania and countenances as amongst the seniors of Abeokuta. Their calvaria, depressed in front and projecting cocoa-nut like behind, the absence of beards, the hideous lines and wrinkles that seamed and furrowed the external parchment, and the cold unrelenting cruelty of their physiognomies in repose, suggested the idea of the eunuch torturers so common in Asia.' Yet this very same author, whilst describing this same tribe, located only a few miles south of Abeokuta, where they might be expected to be still worse, writes thus: ' The race—the Egbadoes or Lower Egba—is distinctly negroid, without showing the characteristics of the full-blooded negro. The skin is of a dark dilute copper, sometimes black, whilst several of the chiefs are almost light coloured. When the eyelashes and brows are plucked, the eye is fine. . . . The lips are not thick, but the gums are blue, and the teeth are by no means improved by the process of chewing. . . . Their diet is poor, their climate poorer; calisthenics are unknown; they are not boxers or runners, like the people of Nufie, and even gymnastics, except tumbling, are little practised. *What*,' he exclaimed, ' *can, then, account for the beauty of their conformation ? '* If we examine closely the doctrines of modern anthropologists, as exhibited by the published works of Hunt, Burton, &c., it will be evident that by a little manipulation of the young we might be able to make two brothers of the same African parentage of two distinct Huntean or Burtonean races, one of the typical Huntean Congo negro, and the other of Burton's negroid race.

Part II. refers to the Self-government of Western Africa, according to Resolution 3 of the House of Commons Committee—viz., 'that the object of the policy of the Government should be to encourage in the natives the exercise of those qualities which may render it possible for it more and more to transfer to them the administration of all the goverments, with a view to our ultimate withdrawal from all, except, perhaps, Sierra Leone.'

Taking advantage of this declaration, a stanch friend of African advancement has remarked that the ambition of Great Britain in these days is to see her colonies attain, one by one, to the position of wealth and power, and to form themselves into nations. It is her desire 'to have independent nations, once her feeble offspring, associated with her in the great work of the world's natural development and the spread of Christian civilization;' whilst her whole aim is 'to raise the nations of Africa from the debased and degraded state to which they have fallen, both morally and physically, to free them from the bloody and demoralizing influence of beastly superstition: from polygamy; from domestic slavery; from the paralysing effects, as regards productive industry, of customs and institutions which, by the insecurity they create, as well as the licentious and foolish extravagance they prescribe and encourage, prevent the creation of that capital by which alone the works necessarily attendant on civilization can be executed.' In the chapters included in this part of the work, I have endeavoured to point out the benefit Western Africa has received through British rule; and the condition of the people—whether or not they are in that position in which they can be left to govern themselves—as well as their relation to the civil authorities.

Part III. relates to the requirements of the various colonies. If the Third Resolution, above quoted, meant at all what it seems to indicate, the various subjects considered in Part II. will show the lamentable deficiency, in many material points, in the moral and social condition of the people, and the necessity for speedy and valuable reforms in the institutions of the various colonies. In Part III. I have endeavoured to lay down a few of the numerous absolute requirements of the colonies, and which Resolution 3 makes imperative. But I have overstepped the ordinary limits of a preface, and, consequently, on leaving my readers, I hope the following pages, although, I fear, full of imperfections, will convince them that the Africans are not incapable of improvement; but that by the assistance of good and able men they are destined to figure in the course of time, and to take a prominent part in the history of the civilized world.

AFRICANUS HORTON, M.D.,
Staff Assist.-Surgeon.
(Native of Sierra Leone.)

ROYAL VICTORIA HOSPITAL, NETLEY,
December, 1867.

PART I.

WEST AFRICAN COUNTRIES AND PEOPLES;

AND

THE NEGRO'S PLACE IN NATURE.

CHAPTER I.

DESCRIPTION OF THE ORIGINAL AND UNCIVILISED STATE OF THE NATIVE TRIBES.

THE hypothesis based on the ingenious demonstrative analogies of the manners, customs, and tenets of the inhabitants at present occupying this globe, as compared with those of a few centuries ago, may be safely regarded as a truism—viz., that mankind by the knowledge of metallurgy and other useful arts emerge from a primitive state of barbarism, and have gradually brought to themselves the benefits of a civilised life. Of this primitive state or mythic epoch but little is furnished us in history, and very little is actually known; but from analogical references we are led to believe the speculative traditions of the ancient Romans,* that 'mankind, as the state of political community now exists, advance from a rude and helpless state to the formation of political society;' and entirely disapprove of the Greek mythological legend, that 'mankind emerge from a state of innocence and bliss.'†

Bearing in mind the foregoing, it will be my province to prove

---

* Æschylus Prou. 451—515 ; Diod. i. 8 ; Lucian, Amore, c. 33, 34.
† Hesiod, Op. et Di. 109 ; Ovid, Met. i. 88—112.

the capability of the African for possessing a real political Government and national independence; and that a more stable and efficient
Government might yet be formed in Western Africa, under the
supervision of a civilised nation, in conformity with the present
Resolution of the Committee of the House of Commons.

In viewing the map of West Africa, and tracing out those
political communities which are not due to the agency of more
civilised politicians, we affirm that there are amongst them fixed and
established Governments, although rude and barbarous; that the
obedience to the supreme power in many cases is implicit, the right
of property is enforced by adjudicature; and, although the power
of the supreme head has been used with extreme despotism, as in
Dahomey and Ashantee, yet still it is as truly a political Government as that of France or England. By nature the African is a
social being, possessing the capacity of commanding and obeying,
and that type of improvement which advances as the reason is
cultivated, which are the essential elements both of a political
Government and a political community; and therefore Africans bear
no relation whatever to those gregarious species of animals—apes,
monkeys, &c.—to which some fantastic writers have likened them.

Examining Western Africa in its entirety, we find it to be composed of a number of political communities, each ruled by a national
Government, formed in many cases of distinct nationalities occupying determined territory; but some national communities are broken
up into innumerable fractional sections, governed by rebel chiefs, or
satraps; others depend upon a political body whose sovereign chief
rules over life and property; and others, again, are under well-
regulated civilised government. But in order to develop among
these different nationalities a true political science, it is necessary
that the inhabitants should be made acquainted with the useful
arts, and the physical conditions which influence other more civilised
and refined political Governments.

What, it may be asked, are the different forms of government
now in existence on the West Coast of Africa?   The two principal
forms are the monarchical and the republican.

In the purely native community we observe the recognition of
power, in many cases, vested in a single individual, variously called

by the different tribes, but to which we apply the name of *basileus*, or king; surrounded by a number of headmen, who pledge themselves to do his will. Some of these *basileus*, such as those of Ashantee and Dahomey, have implicit power over life and property, and therefore are held in dread by their subjects. Of the tribes who are governed by these autocrats we may well apply the language of Merivale,* when speaking of the Asiatic races, that ' they have acquiesced in their own immemorial despotisms to which they have been abandoned. To them the names of liberty and equality, invoked in turn by their neighbours, are unintelligible; their sympathies are centred always in men, and not in government.' A desperate and successful warrior, such as an Owoosookorkor, a Mahbah, and a Gezo, commanded all their devotions, and for them the ' foundation of laws lay in the bosom of the autocrat.'

Among other political native communities we find that in some the form of government resembles very closely a limited monarchy —in others a democracy, in which all the caboceers or head men stand almost on equal terms. Among those tribes who are goaded with religious tenets and infinitesmal rites and ceremonies, who believe implicitly in the supernatural powers of their fetish and medicine man, whom they suppose to have the power of communicating with the world of spirits, and using their agency in human affairs, the population are subject to a spiritual despotism not easily comprehended by civilised nations. In matters of great interest, in many cases a whole nation assemble together for deliberation; but the counsels of the aged, from their experience, especially when backed by previous sage advice and reputation of wisdom, a sober and thoughtful deportment, and a vigorous and energetic character, generally decide the will of the multitude. The authority of a chief is hereditary, but this hereditary descent differs materially from that in civilised countries; the individual to whom the succession falls being, not the eldest son of the chief, but the son of his sister; and this is accounted for by the plurality of wives which each man maintains. But men who have shown themselves to possess great tact, courage, and strength in time of war, although

---

* History of the Romans under the Empire, Vol. ii. p. 141.

they might have been originally slaves, may in time of peace arrogate to themselves such predominant influence, that they soon create themselves chiefs (such as the present King of Denkera on the Gold Coast).

Not being acquainted with letters, they have no history, and are absolutely ignorant of events for any long period beyond the memory of their head men; successive events once out of sight are for ever lost; they pass away like the spectres in a phantasmagoria, leaving no other trace behind them than a dreamy recollection of some distant circumstances that had taken place. They satisfy the curiosity of their generation by the aged among them giving the oral narration of legendary tales, heroic myths, vague traditions, &c., descriptive of deeds of wonder at an uncertain and undated antiquity, and which forms the only channel by which their ' thoughts can be transmitted from one country and one age to another.' Not knowing anything of the useful arts, their Governments are feeble and unenterprising, and their military organization impotent and inefficient; amongst the higher classes in some of them the head wives occupy important positions in the domestic circle, whilst all the other women occupy a degraded position.

Proper legislative science is entirely unknown to them; they possess no means by which a continuous and profitable revenue can be brought into their imperial coffers; no proper determination of political causes, and, consequently, no established principle which might be made to form a guide to the Legislature in the making of new laws or the alteration of old ones, and thus for ages they have shown no improvement in the executive administration; and possess no proper legal status, and no generalized principle of international law. There is an entire absence of any domestic history amongst them. By them a society is never contemplated, either in its constituent elements or mutual relations; in its private recesses or habitual intercourses. A fact, an anecdote, a speech, or remark, which would illustrate the condition of the common people, or of any rank subordinate to the highest, is considered too insignificant to intrude upon a relation which concerns only grandees and ministers, thrones and imperial powers. Some towns there are which are governed entirely by chiefs, who exercise an uncertain rule over the inhabitants—who are regarded more as a father of the community than a political head; some of them are nomadic in their nature, but others constitute themselves into a political society of the most primitive order.

The Bakalai tribe, for example, are particularly distinguished for their roving character, and this is principally caused by their great fear of death. ' They never stay long in one place. A Bakalai village is scarcely built—often the plantations have not borne fruit the first time—when they feel impelled to move. Then everything is abandoned; they gather up what few stores of provisions they may have, and start off, often for great distances, to make, with infinite pains, a new settlement, which will be abandoned in turn; sometimes after a few months, though occasionally they remain a year or two, and even more, in the same place.' In localities where they can carry out commercial speculations they remain for a few years, but yielding at times to their natural propensity they shift from one place to another about one or two miles distant.

With those in this primitive state of ignorance and poverty we observe their chief occupation to consist in the cultivation of a small plot of ground, where they plant various species of cereals, besides squash, casada, pumpkins, yams, sweet potato, and several sorts of edible fruits. Not being in connexion with civilised nations, their agricultural instruments consist of large shells, sharpened sticks, or rude iron hoes, all consequently of a barbarous nature. They make baskets and mats from the fibre and hard outer-covering of the bamboo. Their dress is very scanty, and in many instances consists of a small piece of plaited straw placed as a frontal covering. They know no intoxicating liquor except the palm wine, the product of nature, after it has been kept for several hours to undergo fermentation; they amuse themselves by rude dances, consisting of severe athletic pantomimic gymnasium, per-formed with the hands and feet, accompanied with the clapping of hands, and rude dramatic recitations of the bystanders, or musicians.

They carry on warfare with clubs, bow and arrows, and stones, and their system always is to surprise their enemy. Each warrior and hunter (in some cases) manufactures for himself his weapons and his implements; his war-clubs of hard and heavy wood, wrought and ornamented with great ingenuity; his bows shaped and polished; his arrows pointed with flints, shells, or sharp bones, which serve as cutting instruments. They reckon by the number of the 'moon,' and by the occurrence of some remarkable events; they fell large trees by fire, and in all things exhibit great rudeness and extreme simplicity.

Some, such as the *Fans*, show considerable ingenuity in the manufacture of iron. In their country, interior of the Gaboon, iron ore is found in considerable quantity, cropping out at the surface. To obtain the iron, they 'build a huge pile of wood, heap on this a considerable quantity of the ore broken up, then come with more wood,' and apply fire to the whole; wood is continually being thrown into it until the ore becomes fluid, when it is allowed to cool down, and cast iron is obtained. To temper and make it malleable, 'they put it through a most tedious series of heating and hammerings, till at last they turn out a very superior article of iron and steel,' which is much better than the trade quality brought out from Europe. Of this they make their knives, arrowheads, and swords. They reverence their charms and fetishes, and believe in witchcraft; some are cannibals, and others make very disagreeable enemies, by being very energetic, warlike, fierce, and possessing great courage and ingenuity.

Among those tribes who have made some onward step in the career of civilization we observe that agriculture is supported by regular labours at the proper season, the produce of which they bring to European markets, to exchange for useful implements, cotton goods, and rude luxuries; they weave a kind of cotton or fibre cloth, which they employ as wearing apparel and for exportation, and some of it is much prized, even by Europeans, for the dexterity of the workmanship; and a particular rough kind (Bandy cloth) forms an important medium of commerce in Western Africa. The inhabitants collect themselves in large and populous towns, with the idea of strengthening their powers of defence, as in Abeokuta. Some, as the Fantees (Cromantees), in whose region gold forms the medium of commerce, are fully aware of its value, and possess a knowledge of the means of working it into various trinkets and articles of domestic importance. In war they have some knowledge of pitched battles, but the great point in their tactics in war is to take their enemies by surprise; each warrior carries his own provisions, consisting of the production of the land; they possess no commissariat, but are allowed by the chieftain to go out foraging in the enemies' country. They employ guns and powder, cutlasses and swords, and are very furious in their first attacks, killing every one before them, women and children not excepted. After this impulsive passion in attack has been satiated, the women are taken prisoners, and if attractive are received in the domestic circles as wives; the men and children are held in slavery, and in some instances the lives of the former are terminated by a horrible death. They consider war as the most honourable and glorious occupation for men, and they carry it on in the hope of conquest and plunder, or for revenge. The heads of the great chiefs who may be slain are carried on poles as trophies of war. Among the Ashantees, when a chief is killed in war his body is buried in a selected and marked spot, concealed from their enemies, and on their return they exhume the body, well wash it, and carry it to the territorial mausoleum. If they return from a successful expedition, they are met and escorted to its last home by the women and children, singing songs of praise, glory, and welcome. Fishing and hunting form also a part of their pursuits, and in many cases they excel in these to an appreciable degree. In North-Western and Central West Africa, the regions of the Gambia and Sierra Leone (as also in Dahomey), the inhabitants are accustomed every summer to set fire to the bush, and thus consume the grass and underwood, giving the country an open appearance.* But in other parts there are large, dense forests, impenetrable to man, and with difficulty penetrable to the larger quadrupeds.

Some of the languages of the tribes are harsh and guttural, such

---

* 'The burning of the grass in Mandingo,' says Mungo Park, 'exhibits a scene of terrific grandeur. In the middle of the night I could see the plains and mountains, as far as my eyes could reach, variegated with lines of fire; and the light reflected on the sky made the heavens appear in a blaze. In the day-time pillars of smoke were seen in every direction, while the birds of prey were observed hovering round the conflagration, and pouncing down upon the snakes, lizards, and other reptiles which attempt to escape the flames. The annual burning is soon followed by a fresh and sweet verdure, and the country is thereby rendered more healthy and pleasant.'

as the Jollofs and Calabars; others are soft and mellowy, as the Mandingo, Teminemeh, and Fantee; and others again are palatal, as the Accra, Awoonah, and Dahomey. The trading propensity is most extensively developed among every tribe; in their native state money, as a coin, is unknown to them; in many places cowrie shell is the prevailing medium—as from Accra to the Niger; in Bonny and Calabar, iron bar; in the Gambia and Senegal and the Casa-mangs, native-made cloth, called *bandy cloth;* in Fantee, Bassa, Abanta, Apollonia, Ashantee, and Soosoo, gold; in some places, however, domestic slaves form the principal article of barter. Although advanced to some degree of civilization, some of these tribes indulge in witchcraft and various superstitious rites and ceremonies. The sickness of a chief might lead to the death of many harmless persons; a professed sorcerer is summoned to find the cause or the individual who has bewitched him; ' this he does by inspecting the inside of a mystic fowl, which has been killed and split into two parts. Blackness or blemish about the wing is supposed to denote treachery in children or kinsmen; in the backbone, it convicts mother and grandmother; in the tail, it accuses the wives; and in the thighs, the concubines; in the shank or feet, it condemns the common slaves. Some are so entirely dominated by the super-stitious ideas of their country that even after they have been for years under Christian teaching and civilising re-agents, they look back with a sort of veneration and fear on some of the heathenish customs of their fatherland. In these semi-savage countries the inhabitants believe that the religious devotees are in league with disembodied spirits, who transfer to them such supernatural powers that they are recognized by every one to have the good fortune of weaving the web of human fate; and these pretenders carry them-selves with such striking dignity of look and action, such undoubt-ing confidence, at the same time evincing such strength of language and energy of purpose, that these weak-minded people are involun-tarily compelled to cherish a deep veneration for those pre-tensions to supernatural knowledge, and always to hold them in reverential awe. In those places where religion and knowledge have made some progress, as in the seacoast towns of a part of the Gold Coast, these devotees are regarded with hatred and horror, but in those parts where a higher degree of knowledge is attained, they are regarded in the true light of impostors, and expelled wheresoever they come with their pretensions.

Polygamy is very common among all the population who can afford it; marriage is a sort of contract, by which the father or parent receives a certain amount for the daughter, who at first meets with a great deal of attention and fondling, and in a few months sinks into the state of a domestic slave.* Some of the tribes are subject to violent gusts of temper, but are plain and open-hearted, such as the Egboes, along the banks of the Niger; whilst others, such as the Yorubas, have a happy power of exercising a strict command over their passions. As a rule, the tribes in Western Africa are very hospitable to strangers, generous, sociable, and obliging; in some cases honest, harmless, faithful, kind, and affec-tionate to each other, and would, if needs be, share their last meal with a companion,† but in many cases they are tyrannical to their

* 'The Fan marriages,' says Du Chaillu, ' are very rude, but are an occa-sion of great jollity. Of course the husband has to buy his wife, and the shrewd father makes a bargain with him as well as he can, putting on a good price if the man's love is very ardent. . . . When a wedding is in prospect, the friends of the happy couple spend many days in obtaining and laying in great stores of provision, chiefly smoked elephant meat and palm wine. They engage hunters to keep up the supply, and accumulate enough to feed the great numbers who are expected to come. When all is ready, the whole town assembles, and without any ceremony, but merely as a public sale, as it were, the father hands his daughter to her husband, who has generally already paid her price.'—'*Adventures in Equatorial Africa*,' page 86.

† Lawrence, in his Lectures delivered in the Royal College of Surgeons, says : ' Many of the dark races, although little civilised, display an open-ness of heart, a friendly and generous disposition, the greatest hospitality, and an observance of the point of honour, according to their own notions, from which nations more advanced in knowledge might often take a lesson with advantage. They possess a natural goodness of heart and warmth of affection.'

' The negroes,' says Adamson, in his visit to Senegal in 1754, ' are sociable, humane, obliging, and hospitable, and they have generally preserved an in-estimable simplicity of domestic manners. They are distinguished by their tenderness for their parents, and great respect for the aged ; a patriarchal virtue which, in our days, is too little known.'

' The feelings of the negroes,' says a French writer, ' are extremely acute. According to the manner in which they are treated they are gay or melan-choly, laborious or slothful, friends or enemies. When well fed and not maltreated they are contented, joyous, and ready for every engagement, and the satisfaction of their mind is painted in their countenance. Of slaves. Many of them, the Egboes and Mandingoes for example, will never forget kindness or benefits, but will never forgive an injury done them. The women work hard in the field and in selling, and they are the great supporters of the domestic circle. Divorce is at the pleasure of the husband; if the wife divorce herself, her parents are required to return the purchase money or dowry given to them at marriage. Their wives and slaves are in some cases their only property, a man's standing being estimated by the number of his wives. The Mohammedan portion have rude mosques for the celebration of their religious ceremonies, while others resort to dark groves and thick forests.

Some of the tribes make canoes from the trunk of the silk cotton-tree, *the bombax*, which they hollow out and afterwards burn; those on the river Gambia make their canoes out of the mahogany tree, which is very strong and durable, resisting the action of the powerful rays of the sun, which, with the effects of the water, easily destroys other boats. They mould their rude cooking utensils— water-pot, plates, and dishes—from the clay of the land, and cut out their spoons and combs from different kinds of wood.

The unmarried women in some countries, as from the Gold Coast to the Gaboons, are allowed with little or no restraint to follow the bent of their inclination; in other parts they are tolerably continent. The male sex are by no means remarkable for continence, which cannot be expected in places where domestic slavery is in vogue. The men having so many wives do not show a very profound liking for their children, but the affection of the mother is unbounded. Personal cleanliness is a chief trait in the character of most tribes; gambling forms part of the amusement of some; they practise several athletic games, such as wrestling, boxing, and running for sport and exercise. In some tribes they build large stockades of

benefits and abuses they are extremely sensible, and against those who injure them they bear a mortal hatred. On the other hand, when they contract an affection to a master, there is no office, however hazardous, which they will not boldly execute to demonstrate their zeal and attachment. They are naturally affectionate, and have an ardent love for their children, friends, and countrymen. The little they possess they freely distribute among the necessitous, without any other motive than that of pure compassion to the indigent.'—' *Hist. des Antilles*,' p. 483.

wood or mud, which on examination exhibit undeniable evidence of design and labour.

After the death of a near relative, in some tribes, there is great moaning, weeping, and lamentation; but among others, as is the practice on the Gold Coast, as soon as the funeral party returns from the graveyard they are regaled with champagne and other wines and with spirits; a dancing party is invariably given, either in the same evening or a few days afterwards, in the house of the deceased, the chief mourner being the chief dancer.

In a few isolated spots the chastity of the young female is carefully watched by the priests of the country, and the girls are known by peculiar names; in the Sherbro and Quiah countries they are called ' *Boondoo girls*,' and in Adogme and Crobboe ' *Fetish girls*.' they are kept under strict surveillance, no intrusion is permitted; a discovery of any irregularity is attended with a heavy fine, slavery, or even death on the part of the male. After remaining for some years, varying from two to six, certain rites are performed by the priests, and they are then allowed to return to their homes. In some countries, such as Ningo and Prampram, there is an annual custom which is practised for a week; during this period the most sacred matrimonial bond can with impunity be invaded by any man, even before the eyes of the husband, who dares not make the least remonstrance. At this period free licence is given to every man and woman, except the Fetish girls, and the most horrible abominations are continually being practised.

12

CHAPTER II.

THE ORIGIN, DANGERS, AND PROGRESSIVE DEVELOPMENT OF THE LIBERIAN REPUBLIC.

In the Colonies the monarchical form of Government in substance is observed; the different political heads are English, French, Dutch, and Spanish. The French occupy Senegal, Grand Bassa, and the Gaboons; the Dutch, a portion of the Fantee Territory; and the Spanish, Fernando Po. It is not my intention here to touch on the political bearings of these several Governments on the Coast, but only of that in whose interest we are principally concerned—viz., the English, who occupy the Gambia, Sierra Leone, Cape Coast (or the greater part of the Gold Coast), and Lagos.

The only exception I feel bound to make is as regards Liberia, the first self-governing civilised black community on the West Coast of Africa. This country is a Republic.

Under the auspices of the Colonization Society of America,* a

* In the Rev. G. F. Fox's memoir of the Rev. Mr. Hoffman, the following interesting account of the origin of the Liberian Republic is recorded :—

The Colony of Liberia had its origin in the sympathy felt by a small section of people in the United States for the African race, and in a strong desire which prompted them to colonize the free negroes of America on the soil of their ancestors ; thus at the same time removing them from the scorn and downtrodden condition which they endured in the United States, and likewise opening out to them a new field of enterprise, which might develop their latent powers, and afford them scope for self-government and self-improvement, especially with a view to the future evangelization of Africa.

Hence there sprung into existence in the year 1816, in the United States, an organization known as the Colonization Society, the professed object of which was to enable free American negroes to emigrate to the Coast of Western Africa, by the purchase of land, and the furnishing them with such pecuniary assistance as was needful. Thus was founded the Colony of Liberia, which extends along the coast of Western Africa, from 4° 15′ to 7° north latitude, its northern extremity being bounded by the Galinas river, near Sherbro Island. From the commencement, neither the Colonization Society, nor the colony planted by it, has ever had any direct connexion with the Government of the United States, but during its earliest colony of American liberated negroes was formed in the Kroo coast. For the first twenty-five years they had no independent national existence; political power over the people was held by the

days, it engaged the sympathy and substantial help of the United States Government, in consequence of the deep interest which President Monroe took in the scheme, and which he was enabled to gratify by reason of the capture at that period of some slaves by United States ships of war; for the Government having declared the slave-trade to be piracy, had taken vigorous steps towards its suppression, and when slaves were recaptured the question arose, What must be done with them? The practical answer which President Monroe rendered to this question was to make the newly-selected Colony of Liberia the depôt for liberated slaves, which furnished him with a plausible reason to justify his sending over agents of the Government and vessels of war, to co-operate with the agents of the Colonization Society in effecting a settlement of the first emigrants. This timid and feeble body proceeded to Sierra Leone in the year 1819-20, and from thence to the Island of Sherbro, which proved a very unhealthy spot, where they obtained a temporary and most unsatisfactory settlement from a treacherous Prince. Failing in their attempt to get land on the Sherbro river, the agents of the Government and the Colonization Society proceeded to Cape Mesurado; here, after much difficulty, they made a purchase of territory from the natives, and built a town which, in honour of the President of the United States, was called Monrovia.

Subsequently, settlements were effected at Grand Cape Mount, forty miles north-west of Monrovia, and south-east at the Junk, Bassa, and Sinoe rivers, distant twenty, forty, and one hundred and twenty miles from Cape Mesurado. The towns at these places were named Robert's Port, Marshall, Buchanan City, and Greenville.

Such was the origin of Liberia, founded exclusively by persons of colour from the United States, under the guidance and with the pecuniary assistance of the Colonization Society. Not being, however, a colony of the United States, some form of political government was requisite. During the infancy of the colony a Governor was appointed by the Colonization Society; but in the year 1845, when considerable progress had been made in the consolidation of the colony, they felt themselves to be in a position to assume the responsibilities of self-government, and at that period, having liberated themselves from the control of the Colonization Society in Washington, they proceeded to organize a Government upon the model of the United States, which was to consist of a President, a Senate, and a House of Representatives; a fundamental condition being that its members must consist of persons of African, or, more strictly speaking, of negro blood.

Monrovia was made the capital, where the Government is administered, and where suitable public buildings have been erected—viz., two separate halls for the Senate and House of Representatives, a residence for the President, and other Government buildings. * * *

All the functions of a well-organized Government are administered in the Colony; powers of taxation, both internal and by Custom-house duties, are exercised; and though a standing army is not kept up, yet in cases of emergency the colonists have formed a temporary army under the administration and pay of the Government. * * *

But in addition to this there sprang up another colony, quite indepen-

Society, who appointed white agents as Governors, 'suggested, formed, or sanctioned such laws as governed them, paid their Government officers, erected their public buildings, and constructed their public works ; leaving to the people no other care than that of educing from the soil or other sources their own private living, and of protecting themselves against the onset of their savage neighbours.' The Government was carried on without their assistance, their natural wants were always supplied, and there was not the least opportunity afforded them for the development of that 'large-heartedness and public spirit which is the life of nascent communities.' Difficulties arose between the Liberians and the foreigners as the territory increased, which produced a disruption in the political tranquillity between the Government and the colonists ; the people by their representatives met in convention to consider this important matter, and in thirty days presented to the

dent of Liberia, called Cape Palmas, situated 250 miles lower down the coast than Monrovia, and which was founded by the Maryland Colonization Society in the years 1834 and 1835. It, like Liberia, remained for some years under the control of American administration, but eventually followed the example of its neighbour, and became an independent state, under the name of Maryland in Liberia, and elected the Hon. J. B. Drayton as President. The natives, however, residing in the neighbourhood, and within the bounds of the territory of the colony, refused to recognise the authority of the new Government. A collision arose, which resulted in the removal of 1,500 of the natives from the point of land called Cape Palmas, which they had hitherto occupied in common with the colonists.

These natives, united with other allies, so strengthened themselves, and organized such a formidable opposition, as to repel a serious attack of the colonists, hemming them in so as to make their situation critical in the extreme.

In this predicament, the states of Maryland in Liberia, that is to say, the colonists of Cape Palmas, appealed to the Republic of Liberia for aid. Assistance was promptly sent, consisting of soldiers headed by ex-President Roberts ; and the natives, being no longer able to face the joint forces, were the more readily brought to terms. Everything was soon settled by negotiation, and the Colony at Cape Palmas was formally annexed to Liberia as one of the counties of the Republic. From this date Liberia was divided into four counties—viz., Mesurado, Bassa, Serise, and Maryland. The distance between the extreme points—viz., from Cape Mount to Kabla on the Hora river—is 300 miles. The line of coast, however, claimed by the Republic extends above and below these points, so as to make in all above 500 miles, although not more than 600 square miles are as yet occupied by the colonial population and their descendants.

world a Constitution and a Declaration of Independence. 'Liberia was declared to be a free, sovereign, and an independent state.'

It will be necessary to take a retrospective view of the early colonists of Liberia, and compare them with the inhabitants of the other part of the coast; and then we may be able to prove how far these are capable of self-government. 'The foundation of Liberia,' writes the Rev. W. Blyden, M.A., Professor in the Liberian College, in an able pamphlet,* 'was laid under circumstances peculiar in the history of the world. The emigrants were urged to these shores by motives far different from those which led to the founding of other colonies. They were not a restless people, who, finding their advancement to wealth and honour in their native country too slow for their ambitious and enterprizing minds, resolved to accelerate their dilatory fortunes beneath a foreign sky. They were not persons who had once been in a condition of opulence and splendour, and who, having fallen by luxury and extravagance into penury and disrepute, sought new scenes to repair their shattered fortunes. They were not politicians adhering to some new principle in politics deemed by them all-important, and seeking some new field for its untrammelled exercise and fair development. They were not the victims of religious persecution, fleeing from the horrors of an enthralled conscience. No. Had they belonged to any of these classes, they might, perhaps, have contented themselves with cultivating small farms, and reaping slow gains; they might have taken fresh courage, and by patient industry restored measurably their dilapidated fortunes; they might have changed their political or theological views, rather than brave the dangers and undergo the privations of founding a home and residing in a country proverbial for its unhealthy and dangerous climate. But they belonged to none of these classes. They were a peculiar people. They were those who themselves, or whose ancestors had been, in the providence of God, suffered to be carried away from heathenism into slavery among a civilised and Christian people.' Being therefore slaves or their descendants,

* Our Origin, Dangers, and Duties. The Annual Address before the Mayor and Common Council of the City of Monrovia, July 26, 1865.

they could not rise among slaveholders; force of circumstances
kept them hopelessly down. 'They felt the depression, they saw
its causes; they felt the deteriorating effects of these causes upon
their minds and the minds of their children. And they thus found
that it was useless to contend against these unfavourable influences.'
It was hopeless to contend against such mighty difficulties. A
home, therefore, was necessary for them where they could enjoy
the rights and immunities of a civilised life, and a settlement on the
West Coast of Africa was then fixed upon. 'They left the land
of their birth . . . with hearts heavy and distressed . . . forced
by irresistible circumstances from their native country in their
poverty and ignorance, to seek a home where to be of African
descent would involve no disgrace.' With this element, then, the
Republic of Liberia was formed.

The inhabitants now elect their own President and Representatives
in a National Congress, according to a constitution framed on the
principles of the American Republic. They 'display a degree of
intelligence in managing their affairs highly creditable to their
ability, and calculated to rebut the insinuations which have sometimes been put forth by the enemies of freedom, as to the supposed
mental inferiority of persons of African descent.'

The Liberian Government had its trials and difficulties to en-
counter, but experience has proved that they are perfectly competent to carry on their own Government; and having mastered a
great many of the vicissitudes and drawbacks which a Government
brought to existence in the form in which they have been brought
must expect to meet with, they bid fair to occupy an important
place in regenerated Africa.

But it was necessary that they should have made limited scientific
experiments on the subject-matter of many branches of their
political science, not for the purpose of determining abstract truth,
but of establishing every portion of their executive administration
on a firm and healthy footing. Being a new political assembly,
when once they have chosen the subject of their experimentation,
they should gradually examine and note the true relation of each
phenomenon as it presents itself, its true political causation, and
what influence, ordinary and extraordinary, it has on the body

politic of the nation; for when once a practical mistake has been made which acts extensively on the institutions and affects their political economy, it acts like an ' electric affinity with the rotten parts of the social fabric, and dissolves them by combin tion.'

Thus the Liberian statesmen have not long ago fallen into a grave error in the practical experiment which they made in their financial department. The materials employed were sound and valuable, but they were not used with that due correction and allowances which are essential for material success. They issued during one of their political crises a certain limited amount of paper currency, which was easily redeemable by the Government. The political success of this provisional experiment operated so greatly on their better judgment that, instead of acting like the pilot steering a vessel through an unknown and dangerous channel, the Executive launched out an excessive number of this medium. Mark the results; the greenbacks fall to a great discount—the strength of the Government is tried—it finds itself incapable of supporting the crisis; its paper issues now become its weakest point, and as, by the mechanical aphorism, nothing is stronger than its weakest point, so they find that no effort of theirs is capable of preventing a crisis:—

Multa quæ nunc ex intervallo non apparent bellum aperiet.*

The merchants receive the notes from the people at a fearful discount, and pay them to the Government for duty and taxes at their full nominal value; the specie being exported to foreign countries, none is to be found in the State exchequer; and all Government *employés* are paid in greenbacks.

For the last twenty years the people of Liberia have enjoyed an independent political existence. Experiments have been assiduously made in the various branches of the political affairs of the nation, and at present the constitution, as it now stands, is found to be lamentably deficient in many points of vital importance to the State; and however sacred and venerable the document may be, the national existence and prosperity demand that it should receive a

* Livy, xxviii., 44.

thorough revision. The first point requiring amendation, as recorded by Mr. Blyden, is the increase of the Presidential term of
office. At present it is limited to two years only. This term is so
short that the President, instead of devoting his attention and
ability to measures that will develop and advance materially the
prosperity of the State, is tempted to direct his administrative power
to electioneering expedients. The President, instead of becoming an
able statesman, becomes an electioneer; the body politic of the
nation suffers most severely; the whole nation consequently do not
sufficiently pride themselves on their President; they do not sufficiently venerate him as the sovereign power of the whole nation, and
thus in the election of a new President, party feelings run high, the
President is traduced in the most violent manner by the opposite
parties, his most laudable undertakings are scoffed at and greatly
misrepresented, and the whole nation is convulsed for a time by
violent political conflicts. That the President ought to be elected
for a longer period is self-evident; a period of six years should be
the minimum term of office, and he should not be immediately re-
eligible.

Again, by the constitution, after the election of a President, a
period of eight months is allowed to elapse, namely, from May to
January, before the new President can be inaugurated. The consequence is pernicious to the nation, as the defeated President has
ample opportunity of carrying out such party views and adverse
plans as suit his purpose.

A third amendment necessary in the Liberian constitution is
to remove what is found to be a prolific source of mischief
in a large republic, and still more so in a small but rising State,
such as Liberia—viz., the power conferred upon the President
of dismissing Government *employés* indiscriminately at his pleasure.
Mr. Blyden shows the deteriorating effect of this power when it was
first introduced into America, and how manifold and all mischievous
the consequences have been; indeed, so great has been the evil
resulting from its introduction, that in 1859, he says, the fact that a
man holds a removeable Government office is a presumptive
evidence that he is either an adventurer, an incompetent person, or
a scoundrel. The evils are threefold—First, 'Few men can obtain

any skill or experience in their offices, and the official capacity of the civil service must be deplorably impaired. Secondly, every man, knowing that he has only a four years', or, at most, and by every exertion, an eight years' tenure of office, will be inclined to feather his nest as fast and as daringly as he can. Thirdly, it renders it impossible for men of intelligence, ability, and virtue, who wish for a reasonable permanence and a decent independence, to become servants of the State.' If in America, where there are thousands of men of ability, education, and experience in political matters, the experiment is found to work so badly, how much worse must it be for the small State of Liberia, where the Government ought to concentrate around it the best abilities of the land. We hope that the national Representatives in the House of Assembly will not consider themselves helplessly bound to each item of a constitution which their political existence and scientific experiments have proved to be practically unsuited to the national prosperity and advancement, but make such amendments as shall place their executive administration on a better and far healthier foundation.

CHAPTER III.

EXPOSITION OF ERRONEOUS VIEWS RESPECTING THE AFRICAN.

THE British portion of the Government of Western Africa is in a transition state, and it is Her Majesty's Principal Secretary of State for the Colonies to whom we must now look as the guardian of the practical policy of the Colonies of Western Africa in its internal and foreign relations ; and now that we have been carried through the distress, danger, difficulty, and doubts attendant on the late Parliamentary Committee,* every African who deserves to have his nationality based upon a stable footing, must regard him as the statesman, whom we might liken to the steersman at the helm of a ship, who, by his attentive and vigilant observations, will guide the national policy to a successful end. We hope that ere long a constitutional foundation will be erected which will greatly improve the system of government on the Coast, and that the natives will be really and properly brought up to self-government.

The new laws and measures which the Government, according to the resolutions of their Committee,† are now about to enact

---

*Select Committee of the House of Commons on Africa (Western Coast), nominated March 3, 1865 : The Right Hon. E. Cardwell, Secretary of State for the Colonies ; Mr. Chichester Fortescue, Under Secretary of State for the Colonies ; Sir Francis Baring ; Lord Stanley ; Mr. Seymour Fitzgerald ; Sir John Hay ; Mr. Charles Buxton ; Mr. W. E. Forster ; Mr. Gregory ; Mr. Cheetham ; Mr. Cave ; Mr. C. B. Adderley ; with power to send for persons, papers, and records. Five to be a quorum. Members subsequently added to the Committee : The Marquis of Hartington, Mr. Henry Seymour.—*African Times,* Vol. iv., p. 114.

† *Resolutions of the House of Commons Committee on Western Africa :—*

1. That it is not possible to withdraw the British Government wholly or immediately from any settlements or engagements on the West African Coast.

2. That the settlement on the Gambia may be reduced by M'Carthy's Island, which is 150 miles up the river, being no longer occupied ; and that the settlement should be confined as much as possible to the mouth of the river.

3. That all further extension of territory, or assumption of government, or

giving to the educated natives experience in the form of government, ought to form an important step in the advance of African
history; they can, however, only be regarded for the present as
provisional and tentative experiments until confirmed by proofs of
practical success. It will be the place of the local executive authorities to watch carefully and cautiously their operation, reporting
faithfully on their progress, so that correct data may be drawn. It
was by similar reports furnished to the American Colonization Society, that they were subsequently led to transfer all authority to
the inhabitants, thus virtually giving them a nationalty.

In order that these propositions may be operative and effective,
it is necessary that a proper executive machinery should be provided to give that impulse to native industry, to encourage that
habit of independence and business, to excite that interest amongst
the inhabitants of each locality for public affairs and political
education, which seems to have been an intention of the majority of
the members of the late Committee.

Those who have gone to such extremes in opposition to the
views entertained by Mr. Cardwell,* Mr. Charles Buxton, Lord

---

new treaties offering any protection to the native tribes, would be inexpedient;
and that the object of our policy should be to encourage in the natives the
exercise of those qualities which may render it possible for us more and
more to transfer to them the administration of all the Governments, with a
view to our ultimate withdrawal from all, except, probably, Sierra Leone.

4. That this policy of non-extension admits of no exceptions as regards new
settlements, but cannot amount to an absolute prohibition of measures which,
in peculiar cases, may be necessary for the more efficient and economical
administration of the settlements we already possess.

5. That the reasons for the separation of West African Governments in
1842 having ceased to exist, it is desirable that a Central Government over all
the four settlements should be established at Sierra Leone, with steam communication with each Lieutenant Government.

6. That the evidence leads to the hope that such a central control may be
established, with considerable retrenchment of expenditure, and, at the same
time, with a general increase of efficiency.

7. That in the newly-acquired territory of Lagos, the native practice of
domestic slavery exists still to a certain degree, although it is at variance with
British law; and that it appears to the Committee that this state of things,
surrounded as it is by so many local difficulties, demands the serious attention
of the local Government, with a view to its termination as soon as possible.—
African Times, vol. v., p. 6.

* Speech in the House of Commons, Tuesday, February 21, 1865.

Alfred Churchill,* and many others, as to run down the capacity of the African race, and liken them to the anthropoid apes, ought to know that the African, in common with the most enlightened people, may be impelled by events into philosophical speculations; and this is proved by the existence of a written language amongst them, designed entirely by themselves. The origin of this language, if their legend is reliable, was in the wonder excited by some messengers of the Quiah tribe carrying a letter from an educated person of a more civilized nation to an individual at a distance, the reading of which conveyed to him the information of what had taken place in their own town. Possessing clearly a philosophical turn of mind, they became curious to discover the contrivance which so struck their observation; and from that time began to put in writing on leaves and barks of trees the language of their country.

Well might Colonel D'Arcy, the late Administrator of the Government of the Gambia, in his Blue Book Report for 1865, write, with equal truth and justice: 'After many years of intercourse with the race [African] I cannot see in the African any incapacity for civilization; on the contrary, I am convinced that the liberated Africans contain in themselves all the elements of a commercial people. If Adam Smith's theory is pronounced orthodox, that it is to the principle of parsimony we owe our capital, and again to capital we owe our comforts and enjoyment, we certainly have this desideratum in the African, who is for the most part a parsimonious citizen, ambitious to rise in the world, and consequently to save and amass. They remind me much of the Banians in Eastern cities, whose personal expenditure is *nil*, but whose trade speculations are mighty and adventurous; but refinement passes over these half-civilized bigots, as the air of heaven over a stagnant lake, and they are as we find them in 1757; whereas the liberated African is perhaps rather too eager to adapt our laws to his immediate advantage before he can possibly understand them.' The gallant Colonel thus forcibly concludes: 'As it takes three generations at home to make an English gentleman, so likewise

* Speech in the House of Commons, Tuesday, February 21, 1865.

does it take three generations to make an intelligent, well-educated African gentleman.'

But the anthropologists of these days will not view the African race, whether educated or uneducated, with a calm, quiet, and unprejudiced mind; could they but do so they would involuntarily come to the conclusion that these people, even in their native rudeness, where they have nothing to stir up the latent powers of improvement in them but the book of nature, whose pages, truly, are filled with objects of wonder and admiration, do, in many cases, show signs of possessing wonderful powers of observation; and when once they acquire the necessary information respecting natural objects by habits of patient attention, which must be the inevitable result, when those powers are brought into play, they are indelibly riveted in their memory.   Too true, the majestic trees of the forest, covered with their evergreen foliage of a thousand variegated colours; the numerous gay tropical birds with beautiful plumage; the solitary and melancholy grandeur of many of the scenes with which they are surrounded; the magnificent rivers which run through their country; the ocean, in all its forms of sublimity and terror; the tremendous rocks which resound with the ceaseless roar of the billows, and the numerous shells which stud the shores of their country, form in a scientific point of view but a small portion of their consideration, from their seeming insignificance, and from a want of scientific knowledge in the beholders; yet still, the brillant stars, the splendid midday sun, the resplendent full moon, and the terrific tornado, with its thunder and lightning, all call into exercise the peculiar disposition and talents of their mind.

They calculate figures in their memory to an extent which would surprise the most practised mathematician, without using any mechanical means for their aid.   Thus an unlettered liberated African, whom I knew and repeatedly questioned, could calculate within an incredibly short space of time any amount of pennies, halfpennies, or farthings, reducing them to pounds, shillings, and pence.   Some keep for years the debit and credit side of their account in their memory with great accuracy.

This confirms the account of Dr. Rush of a negro slave in Maryland, Fuller by name, who could neither read nor write, but who showed extraordinary quickness in mental calculation. He was at one time asked in company, for the purpose of trying his powers, how many seconds a person had lived who was seventy years and some months old; he gave the answer in a minute and a half. On reckoning it up after him in figures, the result was slightly different from his calculation, 'Have you not forgotten the leap years?' he interrogated. On supplying this omission, the answer agreed exactly with the number they obtained.

Barbot, in his large work on Africa, remarking on the acuteness of the uncivilized Africans, said 'The blacks have sufficient sense and understanding; their conceptions are quick and accurate; their memory possesses extraordinary strength. For, although they can neither read nor write, they never fall into confusion or error, in the greatest hurry of business and traffic. Their experience of the knavery of Europeans has put them on their guard in transactions of exchange; they carefully examined all our goods piece by piece, to ascertain if their quality and measure were correctly stated, and showed as much sagacity and clearness in all these transactions as any European tradesman could do.'

In an *Essay on Colonization*, written by Walstrom, speaking of the acuteness of the African race, he said, 'Though on the whole passion is more predominant in the African character than reason, yet their intellects are so far from being of an inferior order, that one finds it difficult to account for their acuteness, which so far transcends their apparent means of improvement.'

If we compare these testimonies with some of the statements made by but too many of the witnesses in the House of Commons Committee, we must confess, to say the least of it, that the objects of these latter were to suppress what was right and just, and to expose those things which were bad and ludicrous.

Under the above considerations, it is necessary that we should premise that the framers of the ordinance regulating the form of Government now to exist in Western Africa should not expect to meet perfection in the working of their plans; since it is a well-known fact that no Government can be copied from a plan. Our Legislature, therefore, must receive with caution the report of the ill-disposed, who will magnify any seeming failure in their scheme,

and should reply to them in the words of Lord Holland : ' Attempts
to form a perfect constitution have uniformly failed, and those institutions have thriven best which have sprung out of the necessity
of the occasion. Constitutions are, in fact, productions that can
neither be created nor transplanted; they are the growth of time,
not the invention of ingenuity; and to frame a complete system of
government depending on habits of reference and experience, is an
attempt as absurd as to build a tree or to manufacture an opinion.

' The chief objection to a constitution complete in all its parts is
that in the course of the last twenty years the experiment has been
tried under various circumstances, and among different people, and
that in no one instance can it be said to have succeeded. A constitution so drawn raises expectations which are not easily realised,
and the disappointment produces either indifference to all law, or,
on the contrary, a fresh endeavour, by the exaggeration of every
principle of liberty and the subversion of every practical provision
in the constitution, to attain an ideal perfection, of which, perhaps,
no human society is capable. Securities are devised against dangers
which never exist, and inconveniences are soon felt which were not
foreseen, and which no means are left for providing against. These
difficulties must be submitted to, or, if removed, the alteration
shakes the confidence of the public in the stabilities of law, the
fundamental nature of which has been represented to them as their
only security.' *

It cannot be denied by even the most casual observer that the
British portion of Western Africa has made a very rapid stride in
improvement since Sierra Leone has been formed. Fancy a lot of
slaves—unlettered, rude, naked, possessing no knowledge of the
useful arts—thrown into a wild country, to cut down the woods
and build towns; fancy these ragged, wild natives under British,
and, consequently, civilised influences, after a lapse of a few
years, becoming large landowners, possessing large mercantile
establishments and money, claiming a voice in the legislative
government, and giving their offspring proper English and foreign
education; and dare you tell me that the African is not susceptible

* " Sketch of a Constitution for the Kingdom of Naples," 1815.

of improvement of the highest order, that he does not possess in himself a principle of progression and a desire of perfection far surpassing many exising nations—since it cannot be shown in the world's history that any people with so limited advantages has shown such results within fifty years.

In 1818, the immortal Clarkson, in the Congress of *Aix-la-Chapelle*, exhibited certain articles of native African manufacture to the Emperor of Russia, whilst endeavouring to secure support in the suppression of the slave-trade; viewing the articles, the Emperor said, ' You astonish me; you have given me a new idea of the state of these poor people; I was not aware that they were so advanced in society. The works you have shown me are not the works of brutes, but of men endued with natural and intellectual powers, and capable of being brought to as high a degree of proficiency as any other men. *Africa ought to be allowed to have a fair chance of raising her character in the scale of the civilized world.*'

' They have not,' it must be admitted, as a learned author remarked, ' contributed much towards the advancement of human art and science, but they have shown themselves willing and able to profit by these advantages when introduced among them. The civilization of many African nations is much superior to that of the aborigines of Europe during the ages which preceded the Goths and Swedes in the north, and the Romans in the southern parts. The old Finnish inhabitants of Scandinavia had long, as it has been proved by the learned investigations of Rütis, the religion of Fetishes, and a vocabulary as scanty as that of the most barbarous Africans.' From ages immemorial they lived without government, laws, or social union; in all matters of domestic or political importance each individual was the supreme arbiter of his own actions; ' and they displayed as little capability of emerging from the squalid sloth of their rude and merely animal existence. When conquered by a people of Indo-German origin, who brought with them from the East the rudiments of mental culture, they emerged more slowly from their pristine barbarism than many of the native African nations have since done. Even at the present day there are hordes in various parts of Northern Asia whose heads have the form belonging to the Tartars, to the Sclavonians, and other

Europeans, but who are below many of the African tribes in civilization.'

But with these potent facts in evidence we find that Captain Burton* and many others† have unblushingly advanced the *theoreticum absurdum*, the jejune and barren generalization or apophthegm, that British civilization and Christian influences have demoralised the native African—that, in fact, these institutions were the chimera of a mistaken philanthropy ; whilst the very advance of the Africans is a positive proof that they make it their principle that their great and leading object should be to ' illustrate the provision made by nature in the principles of the human mind and in the circumstances of man's external situation, for a gradual and progressive augmentation in the means of national wealth; to demonstrate that the most effectual plan for advancing a people to greatness is to maintain that order of things which nature has pointed out,' by encouraging the development of the useful arts, of agriculture, of education in the masses, which will be produced by the governed having a voice in the governing body, and which will lay in the minds of the rising generation a solid foundation of the fundamental principles of political government.

But the committee of the House of Commons, in the summary of their resolutions, seemed to throw some disparaging remarks on the good effects of missionary operations on the native African;—' the success,' say they, ' of education of the liberated Africans at Sierra Leone seems questionable.' This resolution was deduced from evidence which cannot withstand the test of criticism. Whilst the missionaries assert the success with strong proofs, supported by other able evidence, such as that of the Governor of the colonies and the Commissioner sent by the Colonial-office expressly to report on colonial affairs, the committee seemed to be guided rather by the evidence of a few interested mercantile gentlemen, who excluded all consideration of the age of the colony, and certainly did not, as impartial observers would have done, look at the now existing improve-

---

* " Wanderings in West Africa," p. 267.

† Lord Stanley, Speech in the House of Commons, Tuesday, Feb. 21, 1865. Dr. Hunt " On the Negro's Place in Nature," p. 57. Carl Vogt, "Lecture on Man."

ment in all its different phases. These witnesses belonged to a country where civilization exists in perfection, and where for the last eighteen hundred years the arts and sciences have been gradually but securely advancing, and they forgot that the country which they now see, and the inhabitants which form the subjects of their observations and report, have only been under civilizing assistance within the last fifty years, which was the only time (and, in many cases, less than that) occupied in bringing them from a state of utter barbarism to that of semi-civilization, in which they are now. They also forgot that the number of civilizing agents were so extremely small, in comparison with the bulk of the liberated population, that they were as one to three or four thousand; and Mr. Harris showed that he was extremely narrow in his views when he stated in his evidence that the result of missionary labours upon the natives is not so effective as it ought to be. It would be as absurd to attempt to compare the civilization of Britain fifty years after the landing of Julius Cæsar with the civilization of Rome, then in the zenith of her prosperity, as to attempt to compare the result of civilization of a savage, barbarous race of Africa, during fifty years' feeble attempts at civilization, with the civilization of the nineteenth century in England. And, in fact, if the comparison be made between the degree of improvement exhibited by the two countries, history informs us that the present degree of improvement exhibited by the liberated Africans under missionary influence far exceeds that of Britain under Roman influences during a similar period of time.

At the early establishment of the colony of Sierra Leone, ere the Emancipation Act was promulgated, and captured negroes liberated from slave ships were introduced there, the Maroons and settlers formed the black civilised inhabitants of the colony; they were by nature a bigoted, self-opinionated race, who had been driven from Nova Scotia. They looked down with contempt on the liberated Africans, or 'nata' as they called them, and would not condescend to link their blood with theirs, nor would they attempt to impart to them the smallest portion of the education which they had received; and the spirit of exclusiveness ran rampant among them. The European merchants and Government officials befriended them, and chose their mistresses from among their daughters whom the parents would have thought degraded by *marrying* the poor Government apprentice or liberated African ; in the course of time marriages of consanguinity took place amongst them; a race sprang up less healthy and less energetic than the preceding, and a fearful mortality was the consequence; while the liberated Africans proved to be capable of far greater powers of improvement than they were, and in turn looked down on them but more in pity and compassion than in disdain.

The missionaries, during these periods, in their laudable exertions for good, still persevered in their arduous work, although discouraged by many of their countrymen, and without material assistance from the Government ; and now, within so short a period, they have brought up a race of men for whom destiny has mapped out an important mission in Africa.

I claim the existence of the attribute of a common humanity in the African or negro race ; that there exist no radical distinctions between him and his more civilised *confrère ;* that the amount of moral and intellectual endowments exhibited by him, as originally conferred by nature, is the same, or nearly so, as that found amongst the European nations; and it is an incontrovertible logical inference that the difference arises entirely from the influences of external circumstances.   Truly—

Natura una et communis omnium est.

This dictum has been the theme of many writers in different ages. Sir William Temple,* in his essay upon the ' Origin and Nature of Government,' thus expresses himself: ' The nature of man seems to be the same in all times and places, but varied like their statures, complexion, and features, by the force and influence of the several climates where they are born and bred, which produce in them, by a different mixture of the humours and operations of the air, a different and unequal course of imaginations and passions, and consequently of discourses and actions.'

Aristotle propounded the same idea in his Rhetoric †:—

Ὅμοια γὰρ ὡς ἐπι το πολυ τὰ μέλλοντα τοῖς λελονόσι.

' There are certain physical appetites,' says Sir Cornewall Lewis,

* Works, Vol. ii., p. 29, ed. 8vo.
† Rhet. ii., 20 'sec. 88.

' certain moral sentiments, certain intellectual faculties, which are common to the entire human race, assuming the body and mind to be in a normal state. The desire of food, the sexual passions, the feeling of revenge, anger, fear, jealousy, sympathy, compassion, pride, expectation, disappointment, the love of pleasure, the dislike of pain, are shared by all men.'

I might adduce a great many examples to prove that the natural tendency of the now civilised European was exactly the same as the natural tendency of the now uncivilised African ; but I shall here only give a simple proof to show that this is not dissimilar to that of the ancient inhabitants of Britain. The inhabitants of the Gold Coast and other parts, to this day, paint their bodies with exquisite taste and beauty, although it is now gradually falling into disuse. History informs us that these were the wants and desires of the first inhabitants of England; and Dr. Johnson, in his ' Life of Sir F. Drake,'* has said : ' It is observable that most nations amongst whom the use of clothes is unknown paint their bodies. Such was the practice of the first inhabitants of our own country. From this custom did our earliest enemies, the Picts, owe their denomination. As it is not probable that caprice or fancy should be uniform, there must be doubtless some reasons for a practice so general, and prevailing in distant parts of the world which have no communication with each other.'

In the pages of history we find it recorded, by a no less reliable historian than Cicero, that the ancient Britons went about most scantily clothed ; they painted their bodies in fantastic fashions, ' offered up human victims to uncouth idols, and lived in hollow trees and rude habitations.' As regards the amount of development of their intellectual and moral faculties, we are told by the same writer that the ugliest and most stupid slaves came from England; and so degraded were the Britons considered in Rome, that he urges Atticus, his friend, ' not to buy slaves from Britain on account of their stupidity and their inaptitude to learn music and other accomplishments.' His own words are comprised in the following : Britannici belli exitus expectatur : constat enim aditus insulæ esse

---

* ' Life of Sir Francis Drake.' Works, Vol. vi., p. 347.

munitos murificis molibus; etiam illud jam cognitum est, neque argenti scrupulum esse unum in illâ insulâ, neque ullam spem prædæ nisi ex mancipiis; ex quibus nullos puto, te literis aut musicis eruditos expectare.*

The tone in which Cæsar speaks of the ancient Britons is no less contemptuous, for he calls them 'a nation of very barbarous manners;' he says that 'most of the people in the interior never saw corn, but live upon milk and flesh and are clothed with skins. He further remarked in another place : "In their domestic habits they are as degraded as the most savage nations. They are clothed with skins, wear the hair of their heads unshaven and long, but shave the rest of their bodies, except their upper lip, and stain themselves a blue colour with wood, which give them a horrible aspect in battle.'

Remarking on the foregoing, Dr. Prichard observes that 'the ancient Britons were nearly on a level with the New Zealanders and Tahitians of the present day, or, perhaps, not very superior to the Australians.' He in another place also remarked that 'of all Pagan nations the Gauls and Britons appeared to have had the most sanguinary rites. They may well be compared in this respect with the Ashanti, Dahomians, and other nations of Western Africa.'

Now let us ask would it be consistent with reason, with common sense and justice, with humanity, for Tacitus, Cæsar, or Pliny, to have condemned the British island and the British nation to an eternity of Bœotian darkness—'to be the officina of hereditary bondage and transmitted helplessness?' And yet if we read some of the testimonies in the late Parliamentary Report (1865) and most of the writings of the members of the Anthropological Society, we find that the negro race, from some supposed moral and intellectual inferiority, are condemned by men who, in many respects, can be regarded as generous and honourable, to live in perpetual ignorance, misery, and barbarity, forgetting that as the present untutored negroes appear to them,

'Just such [their] sires appeared in Cæsar's eyes.'

The late Sir George Cornewall Lewis, in his '*Treatise on*

* Epist. Ad. Atticum 1, iv. Epist. 16.

Politics,' has laid down a general aphorism, which might be well
applied to the forthcoming measures of the Government—viz., that
when the average and predominant operation of a political form
or institution is good, it may yet be frustrated by the badness of
those who use it. We hope, therefore, that we shall not have to
liken the persons on whom the execution of the scheme of the
Government depends to the tools of a refined maker placed in
the hands of a clumsy or ignorant artisan; since they may, from
their moral defects, convert wholesome food into poison through
the want of skill, intelligence, patience, and habits of sustained
attention and mutual forbearance; while the denier of African
advancement will not look to them as the cause of the failure, but
will entirely throw aside the legal maxim—

> Quilibet præsumitur bonus, donec probetur contrarium—

and lay the whole blame, unheard, on the incapacity of the African
race to support such a Government.

It cannot be expected that this tentative legislative improvement will give unalloyed satisfaction in all the different governments on the Coast. It may produce displeasure amongst those
who from 1842 had independent action, which has become a time-
honoured custom to them; and we do not blame them, since habit
is second nature; but they must remember that no legislative
changes could be made without producing some inconvenience, and
it is only by these means that they can progress in their
political history, and advance in civilization; that the world
would have been stationary through successive generations had
no changes taken place; and that the greatness of England is
dependent on the gradual and successive changes in her political
economy; and we must recommend to them the words of Lord
Bacon in his ' *Essay on Innovation* '*—' It is true that what
is settled by custom, though it be not good, yet at least it is fit,
and those things which have long gone together are, as it were,
confederate within themselves; whereas new things piece not so
well, but though they help by their utility, yet they trouble by
their inconformity; besides they are, like strangers, more admired

* 'De Augmentis,' Vol. viii., p. 375.

and less favoured. All this is true, if time stood still; which contrariwise would so sound, that a froward retention of custom is as turbulent a thing as an innovation, and they that reverence too much old things are but a scorn to the new.' As well as that of Niebuhr*—' The noblest and most salutary forms and institutions, whether in civil or moral societies, when bequeathed from generation to generation, after the lapse of centuries will prove defective. However exquisitely fit they may have been when they were first framed, it would be necessary that the vital power in States and Churches should act instinctively, and evince a faculty of perpetually adapting itself to the occasion.' Man is a dissatisfied animal, and his *nisus*, or natural tendency, is to improve the *status quo*. But notwithstanding this progressive tendency which always actuates him, the colonists must rest satisfied now with what they have obtained, and wait patiently until the time when their improvement will necessitate the adoption of a better and a more independent form of Government; then their rulers will consider the means best fitted for the attainment of this end, and what practical, not ideal, form of Government will be best suited to their condition; whether the republican or monarchical.

* ' History of Rome,' Vol. i., p. 622.

D

CHAPTER IV.

FALSE THEORIES OF MODERN ANTHROPOLOGISTS.

I MUST say a few words on some grave errors in generalization which men of science with restricted observation have arrived at respecting the capacity of progression in the African race. Thus it has been argued that their physical and mental peculiarities have undergone no change since they were first observed by civilized nations. 'The type,' says Sir George Cornewall Lewis, 'is as unchanged as that of the greyhound, since the time of the Romans.'* Hume, in his Essay on 'Natural Characters,'† says that, 'There scarcely ever was a civilized nation of that complexion (negro), nor even any individual eminent either in action or speculation. . . . In Jamaica, indeed, they talk of one negro as a man of parts and learning, but it is likely he is admired for slender accomplishments, like a parrot who speaks a few words plainly.'

A witty writer, the late Dr. Knox, of Edinburgh, believes that the races of men, particularly the negro, as they were several centuries ago, still continue to be now; and that despite of Christian influences and other civilizing agencies bearing on their rude and savage character, they will still continue to be. Although there might be something suggestive and interesting in this anti-theological scientific doctrine propounded in his ' *Fragment of the Races of Men;*' yet still we deprecate in the strongest terms the main points of his arguments. Resting them on what has been discovered in Egypt, he maintained that ' on the banks of the Nile still wandered in considerable numbers the descendants of men who built the Pyramids and carved the Sphinx and Memnon. On the tombs of Egypt, the most valuable of all existing records, there stands the Negro, the Jew, the Copt, the Persian, the Samaritan, nearly as we

---

* 'Treatise on Politics,' Vol. ii., p. 432.
† Hume 'On Natural Character,' Part i., Essay 21.

find them still. Different races of men are sketched on the walls of the tomb opened by Belzoni, showing that the characteristic distinctions of races were as well marked three thousand years ago as now. The negro and other races existed there as they are at present, or if a pure race has appeared to undergo permanent change when transferred to a climate differing from its own, such change will be found on closer inquiry to be delusive.'

Now it must be acknowledged that the damaging influences to which the negro race has for centuries been subjected, have not been favourable to the improvement of their condition, nor in any way raising their minds to a higher species of cultivation; trampled under foot by perpetual despotism, enslaved from one generation to another, inhabiting the most wretched hovels that it is possible for humanity to exist in, deprived of every means of education or of witnessing the conquests of arts and science, pent up as it were within the circumference of their own towns and villages, *not daring to travel even a few miles without an escort for fear of being captured and sold as slaves*, can there be the least doubt in the minds of the unprejudiced that their present unimproved condition is the natural sequence of the operation of these powerful demoralizing re-agents? True it is that certain peculiarities which are characteristic of a nation can be traceable for generations, however greatly admixture and other external influences may have operated on their general character; but to insist on the broad dogma that no changes have taken place in the races of men, or even animals, as far back as historical evidences can be traced, is to insist on what is opposed to nature; and none but the unreflecting can be carried away by so sweeping a doctrine. Dr. Knox regards everything to be subservient to race; and his arguments are brought forward to show that the negro race, in spite of all the exertions of Exeter Hall, or as his commentators most sneeringly call them, the 'broad-brimmed philanthropy and dismal science school,' will still continue as they were. To him, as he says, 'Race is everything—literature, science, art—in a word, civilization depends on it. . . . With me race or hereditary descent is everything, it stamps the man.'

Of late years a society has been formed in England in imitation of the Anthropological Society of Paris, which might be made of great use to science had it not been for the profound prejudice exhibited against the negro race in their discussions and in their writings. They again revive the old and vexed question of race, which the able researches of Blumenbach, Prichard, Pallas, Hunter, Lacépéde, Quatrefages, Geoffroy St. Hilaire, and many others, had years ago (as it was thought) settled. They placed the structure of the anthropoid apes before them, and then commenced the discussion of a series of ideal structures of the negro which only exist in their imagination, and thus endeavour to link the negroes with the brute creation. Some of their statements are so barefacedly false, so utterly the subversion of scientific truth, that they serve to exhibit the writers as perfectly ignorant of the subjects of which they treat. The works of Carl Vogt, ' *Lectures on Man ;*' of Dr. Hunt, ' *Negroes' Place in Nature ;*' and of Prunner Bey, ' *Mémoire sur les Negres,* 1861,' contain, in many respects, tissues of the most deceptive statements, calculated to mislead those who are unacquainted with the African race.

M. Prunner Bey rests his description on observations of the most narrow nature confined to Egypt; his ' *Mémoire* ' on the negro race, which has been made so much of, and which forms the key-stone for writers on negro formation in these days, was made on slaves, who for the last two thousand years have been subjected to the most damnifying degradation by their most austere Mohammedan masters ; yet still this description is held up as *the standard.* We can, therefore, account for his opening fallacy: ' The stature of the negro approaches the middle size. . . . I know of no instance of dwarfism among negroes ; though the monuments of Egypt show that there were dwarfs among negroes at a very remote epoch. . . . Obesity is exceptionally found in the males of high rank and more frequently in women.' Now, from the above statement it would appear that there are no dwarfs among the negroes, and in fact those who quote or comment on his statement affirm that to be the case, which is a great mistake; there are very likely none amongst the serfs of Egypt, whilst before me now, in Jamestown, Accra, on the Gold Coast, there are three dwarfs, and in every part of the West Coast I have met with them, except in the Gambia. Obesity he considers not to be a common thing

among the negroes, and certainly not amongst those in Egypt; as
the negroes there follow the general rule in mankind, that obesity
is found among the rich, indolent, well fed, and little-to-do inhabitants, and not generally among slaves.

Of Dr. Hunt we must truly state that he knows nothing of the
negro race, and his descriptions are borrowed from the writings of
men who are particularly prejudiced against that race; his absurd
pro-slavery views, as contained in his pamphlet, would perhaps have
suited a century ago; but all true Africans must dismiss them
with scorn.

Carl Vogt, in his lectures, takes the worst specimen of a hundred
and fifty different negro races, such as the Austral negro, who
exhibits the worst possible form, to compare with the best
specimen of the proud Caucasian race—the Germans, and the
skull of the great mathematician, Gaus, the standard; at the
same time depriving the negro race of some of its best specimens, the Mandingoes and Kaffirs, as these would not suit his purpose. His descriptions are, therefore, one-sided, erroneous, and most
deceptive.

Quatrefages has given the following most able statement as his
views respecting the difference between man and animals. He says:
'Shall we find the characters of the human kingdom in the intellectual capacity? Certainly, the comparison of the mental development of man with the rudimentary intelligence of even the most
gifted animals, never suggested itself to me. The interval between
brute and man is in this respect so great that a perfect difference
between them was admissible. But this is no longer tenable. The
animal does possess intelligence, and though their fundamental
capacities are less developed, they nevertheless exist; the animal
feels, wills, remembers, deliberates, and the correctness of his
judgment seems frequently miraculous; whilst the very errors
which the animal corrects give evidence that its judgments are not
the mere results of a blind and necessary impulse. We, moreover,
observe great inequalities in the various groups of animals. Thus,
among the vertebrata, we see that birds much excel fishes and
reptiles, but are much inferior to mammals. It would, therefore,
not be surprising if among the latter we were to find some animal

possessing a much higher intelligence; this would only be a progress, but no fundamentally new phenomena.

'What we observe of intelligence in general applies also to his highest manifestation—language. Man, it is true, alone possesses articulate language; but two classes of animals possess voice. They, like ourselves, produce tones which express feelings and thoughts, and which are not only understood by individuals of the same species, but even by man. The hunter learns quickly to understand what is called the language of birds and beasts; nor does it require a long apprenticeship to distinguish their sounds of love, passion, pain, or alarm. This kind of language is no doubt very rudimentary, consisting, it might be said, of mere interjections, but it is sufficient to establish the mutual relation of these creatures. But does this language differ fundamentally from that of man by the mechanism of its production, its object, and its results? Anatomy, physiology, and experience teach that it does not; here also we find a progress, an immense development, but nothing absolutely new.

'Finally, as regards the qualities of the heart, which partly depend on instinct and partly on intelligence, we find their manifestations in the animal as we find them in the man. The animal loves and hates; it is known how greatly many of them are attached to their young, and how strong is the instinctive hatred with which some animals pursue each other. It is known how the congenital faculties may be further developed by training. We also find among our domestic animals individual characters, as we find among men. We all know how docile and good-natured some dogs are, and how vicious and irritable others. Man and brute resemble each other, perhaps, most as regards character.

'Where then shall we find this something new which is absent in the animal and belongs exclusively to man, and which would justify the establishment of a separate kingdom? In order to overcome this difficulty we shall follow the naturalist, and examine all the characters of the being to which we are to assign a place. We have hitherto directed our attention chiefly to the organic, physiological, and intellectual characters of man; we must now consider him in his moral aspect; here we find the fundamental features which have as yet escaped our notice. We find in every society possessing a language sufficiently developed to express abstract ideas words designating virtue and vice, good or evil. Where language fails in this respect we find opinions and habits which plainly show that the notions exist, though not expressed in the vocabulary. Even among the most savage peoples and tribes to which by general consent is assigned the lowest rank in humanity, we see public or individual actions performed, which show that man recognizes something above what is physically good or evil. Among nations further advanced the whole political economy rests upon this basis.

'The abstract idea of moral good and evil thus exists in every human society; nothing leads us to suppose that it also exists in animals; here, then, we have the first character of the human kingdom. In order to avoid the word conscience, which is frequently taken in too restricted a sense, I call morality that quality which furnishes man with the above notions, just as we term sensibility that quality which perceives impressions.

'There are other allied conceptions which are found in all, even the smallest and most degraded societies of man. Everywhere man believes in another world different from ours, in mysterious beings of a higher nature which must be feared or worshipped, in a future life after the destruction of the body; in other words, the notions of a Deity and a future life prevail generally as those of good and evil. However faint these ideas may be, they everywhere give rise to important facts. From such notions arise a number of habits and usages which, even among the most savage peoples, are the equivalents of the greater manifestations among civilized peoples.

'Never has anything similar or analogous been observed in animals; we find, therefore, in the existence of these conceptions a second character of the human kingdom, and designate the sum of the qualities which furnish man with these notions—religiousness.'

But Carl Vogt scoffs at the religious conception of Quatrefages, as difference between man and animals, and accounts for the nonexistence of the idea in the latter from the supposition that man forms ideas concerning certain phenomena which he cannot fathom, which animals through their inferior mental capacity take no consideration of. 'The idiotic Cretan,' says he, 'takes no notice of thunder; the simple-minded in ignorance of causes fears it; the heathen imagines a thunder-god; the Christians also believe that God speaks in thunder; whilst the intelligent man produces himself thunder and lightning, when provided with proper apparatus. This is the usual march of religious ideas, and I know of no sufficient reason for endowing the human race with religiousness as an exclusive quality.'

Whilst admitting that negro children, in schools, have shown intellectual capacities in no point behind the white child, he emphatically states that after puberty, and the closing of the sutures, and the 'projecting of the jaws,' the intellectual faculties become stationary, the individual, as well as his race, is incapable of further improvement. 'The grown-up negro,' he writes, 'partakes, as regards his intellectual faculties, of the nature of the child, the female, and the senile white. He manifests a propensity to pleasure, music, dancing, physical enjoyments, and imitation, whilst his inconstancy of impression and of feelings are those of the child. Like the child, the negro has no soaring imagination, but he peoples surrounding nature and endows even lifeless things with human and supernatural powers. He makes himself a fetish of a piece of wood, and believes that the ape remains dumb lest he should be compelled to work. The negro resembles the female in his love to children, his family, and his cabin; he resembles the old man in his indolence, apathy, and his obstinacy. Temperate in common things, the negro becomes intemperate if not kept within certain bounds. He knows not steady work, cares little for the future; but his great imitative instinct enables him to become a skilful workman and artistic imitator.'

This is truly German; we have always been told that this superior race are given to speculative theories of the most wild and extravagant nature. No one who knows properly the character of the negro race will read without a smile this exuberant ignorant eloquence of Carl Vogt, which is a borrowed inspiration of the late American slave-state school. When will that happy time come when modern anthropological philosophers, who at present are one-eyed, and totally ignorant of the capacity of the African race, will desist from fabricating in their studies the most egregious calumnies on the race already sufficiently downtrodden?

But we have numerous evidences to prove the fallacy of such statements as those of Carl Vogt. Captain Burton, who is one of the greatest decriers of the negro race, an anthropologist himself, in his evidence in the late Parliamentary Committee was obliged to admit that the *grown-up native* of Sierra Leone is dreaded on the rest of the coast; he can examine a witness in the police-court as well as any lawyer in England. It is certainly impossible for an imbecile to do this. He stated that some of the merchants have considerable fortunes and they are men of ' considerable intellect.' In his work, ' *Wanderings in Western Africa from Liverpool to Fernando Po,*' where he displayed without reserve his hatred for the African race, and where towards that race he is personally abusive, turgidly illustrative, and illogically argumentative, talking of another part of the Coast, he was reluctantly compelled to make a confession from his practical knowledge which throws into shade the wild imagination of the German philosopher : ' There are,' says he, ' about 100 Europeans in the land; amongst these there are many excellent fellows, but *it is an unpleasant confession to make—the others appear to me inferior to the Africans, native as well as mulattoes.* The possibility of such a thing had never yet reached my brain. At last, in colloquy with an old friend upon the Coast, the idea started up, and after due discussion we adopted it. I speak as to *morale.* In *intellect the black race is palpably superior,* and it is, in fact, advancing in the path of civilization.' *   And Colonel Ord, R.M., Governor of Bermuda, in his evidence, states that the high class of natives of Sierra Leone, who are pure negroes, are decidedly intelligent, trustworthy, and highly respectable gentlemen, who have risen entirely by their own exertions. Of the present master of the grammar school, a pure negro, the Rev. Jas. Quaker, Colonel Ord considers him to be ' a native gentleman and a clergyman of the Church of England, *of high character* and *considerable attainments.*'

But Carl Vogt, who, perhaps, has never seen a negro in his life, and who is perfectly ignorant as to the capabilities of the negro

* Vol. ii., p. 75.

race, must needs deceive his pupils in Geneva on subjects that he knows nothing about. He tells them that as the young orangs and chimpanzees are good-natured, amiable, intelligent, very apt to learn and become civilized, so is the young negro ; but that after puberty and the necessary transformation has taken place, as the former becomes an obstinate savage beast, incapable of any improvement, so the intellect of the negro becomes stationary, and he is incapable of any further progress—that, in fact, the supposed sudden metamorphoses (which rest only in his ideas) in puberty, said to have taken place in the negro at this period, is not only intimately connected with physical development, but is a repetition of the phenomena occurring in the anthropoid apes.

If we follow Carl Vogt a little further, we find that, after describing the gorilla as having long arms reaching to the forelegs, a short powerful neck with narrow shoulder, a pendulous belly, a long great toe, and a flat foot, he endeavours to find in his ideal faculty resemblance to the negro corporeal structure. 'The trunk,' he says, 'is smaller in proportion to the extremities, especially to the arm, which in the negro reaches below the middle of the femur. Most negroes can, without stooping, reach with the fingers' end the regions above the knee-cap. The neck is short, the civercal muscles very powerful, but the shoulders are narrower and less strong than in the white. There is a certain resemblance in the form of the neck to that of the gorilla, to which the remarkable development of the cervical muscles, combined with the shortness and curvature of this part, gives something of the aspect of the bull's neck. Surely it is for this reason that the negro always carries his burden on the head, rarely upon the shoulders or back ; and it is for this reason that he, like the ram, uses his hard skull in a fight. The chest is narrow, the auteroposterior is always equal to the transverse diameter, which predominates in the German ; the belly is relaxed and pendulous, and the navel situated nearer the symphises pubes than in the European. Even in muscular negroes the arms are less rotund, the hips narrow, the thighs laterally compressed, the calves lean. The negro rarely stands quite upright, the knees are usually bent, and the legs frequently bandy ; hands and feet are long, narrow, and flat, and they form the least attractive features in the negro figure.

Most of these external characterisitics,' he continues, 'remind us irresistibly of the ape ; *the short neck, the long lean limbs, the projecting pendulous belly ; all this affords a glimmer of the ape beneath the human envelope.*' Thus far, Carl Vogt.

Now, is this not a base prostitution of scientific truth? I have seen more than a hundred thousand negroes, but have not been able to find these characteristic differences which Carl Vogt, who has never seen one, or Prunner Bey, who saw Egyptian negro slaves, essay to describe. Indeed, as amongst every other tribe, white or black, there are to be found some with short necks, and others whose necks are peculiarly long ; but where are to be found negroes with pendulous bellies as the anthropoid apes? not in Africa surely, for from Senegal to the Cameroons the negroes I have met with are peculiar for the perfect flatness of their bellies. But Carl Vogt descends from the absurd to the ridiculous; when, writing on the peculiarities of the human foot as characters differentiating man and ape, he went on to state that ' the foot of the gorilla is more anthropoid than that of any other ape, and the foot of the negro more apelike than that of the white man. The bones of the tarsus in the gorilla exactly resemble those in the negro.' We must only dismiss these absurdities by referring him to M. Aeby's measurements, which led him to the conclusion that individual races are not distinguishable from each other when the proportion of their limbs and these parts are examined ; that the difference between the forearm of the European and the negro amounts to less than one per cent., and even he thinks that this slight difference which he has obtained may, by further and more extended measurement, be greatly reduced. Thus, therefore, there is no material difference in the proportion of the limbs between the European and negro.

CHAPTER V.

SOME ANATOMICAL ACCOUNTS OF NEGRO PHYSIQUE.

But it is in the development of the most important organ of the body,—the brain, and its investing parieties—that much stress has been laid to prove the simian or apelike character of the negro race. The development of its convolutions has been demonstrated by Gratiolet and Wagner to be an important particular in the distinction between man and the anthropoid apes. In the latter, during the development of the embryo, in utero, the convolutions of the spheno-temporal lobe are first developed, and then those of the frontal lobe; but in man the contrary is the case, the frontal convolutions are first developed, and the spheno-temporal last.

If we take for granted the external projecting organ of the brain,—the skul is as regards the sutures intimately connected with the brain; in man, we find that the posterior sutures first close, and the frontal and coronal last, but in the anthropoid ape the contrary is the case. Among the negro race, at least among the thousands that have come under my notice, the posterior sutures first close, then the frontal and coronal, and the contrary has never been observed by me in even a single instance, not even among negro idiots; and yet M. Gratiolet and Carl Vogt, without an opportunity of investigating the subject to any extent, have unhesitatingly propagated the most absurd and erroneous doctrine,— that the closing of the sutures in the negro follows the simious or animal arrangement, differing from that already given as the governing condition in man. ' We know, and Gratiolet has pointed it out, that the negro skull follows, as regards the closing of the sutures, a different law from the skull of the white man; that the frontal and coronal sutures, as in the ape, close earlier than the posterior sutures, whilst the reverse is the case in the white man. Would it then be so very hazardous to assume that the simian development of the skull in the negro extends also to the brain?'

Thus from erroneous data, Carl Vogt wishes to prove that, like the orang-outang, the development of the spheno-temporal convolutions of the cerebrum in the fœtus appears first in the negro, whilst the frontal convolutions appear last; or, that the series of development which in the white man is from Alpha to Omega, is in the Negro and in the orang from Omega to Alpha. Can any doctrine be found based upon a greater prostitution of scientific truth? The supposed specimen of Gratiolet was described from the savage bushman, which Carl Vogt stamped as that of the typical negro.

In Dr. Hunt's *brochure ' On the Negroes' Place in Nature,'* he endeavoured to prove that the negro, being in his opinion intellectually inferior to the European or white race, should occupy a servile position in nature. In his edition of Carl Vogt, ' *Lecture on Man,*' we find the statement that the cranial capacity of the human race in the course of centuries became gradually increased. He states that the skulls of the Parisian population in the twelfth century, when compared with that of the nineteenth century, show a great difference in capacity in favour of the latter period; the civilized modern population has greater increased capacity over the more savage population of the twelfth century. Now by the measurements made by Aitkin Meigs and Morton, it is proved beyond a doubt that the negroes in Africa possess a far larger cranial capacity than the negroes in America. And again, according to Aitkin Meigs, the negroes born in America present a cranial capacity, the volume of which is represented by 1,323·90 cubic centimetres, and according to the same observer, with the same method of measurement, the cranial capacity of negroes born in Africa shows a volume of 1,371·42, exhibiting therefore a difference of 46·52 volumes of cubic centimetres.

Carl Vogt admits that if the tables of Aitkin Meigs and Morton were to be examined with regard to races, they exhibit the remarkable fact that all European nations, without exception, have a cranial capacity of more than 1,400 cubic centimetres, although some have less. He admits, also, that every demoralizing influence on a race tends to diminish the capacity, as mental exercise tends to increase it. The difference between the capacity of the negroes born in Africa and that of the average European cranial capacity, is only about 29·00 cubic centimetres. But the experiments of Aitkin Meigs and Morton were made in America on the dead skulls of negroes, who truly had been transported from their native land in Africa to America, but who for years were subjected to the most depressing influence of slavery, and after years of toil in the field became victims, either of the climate, or some other natural influences, which, of course, must have a damnifying effect on the development of the brain, and, consequently, the cranial capacity, and will at once account for the small difference which is said to exist (deduced from the experiments of the two observers above quoted) between the European and the African negro skull. This confirms the statement of the great German philosopher, Tiedeman, who, by careful measurement, weighing, and other investigations, proved that there exists no material difference between the brain of the white and black races. Besides Tiedeman, Blumenbach, the great German physiologist, has contributed a vast deal of information towards establishing this fact.

Well might Carl Vogt exclaim, 'Is this the effect of that cursed institution which degrades man to the condition of chattel, and deprives him of that liberty which alone can lead to a higher development?' He admits as an indisputable fact that those classes of mankind which in successive generations follow mental occupations, possess a greater development of the skull than the ignorant masses, who are engaged in the meanest occupations. But we must depend upon the direct investigations and experiments among natives of Africa, who have mastered the necessary anatomical and physiological knowledge in European Universities to make these experiments in Africa upon dead and living subjects. This can only be accomplished by a Medical School being established in Africa, and facilities offered for obtaining subjects for dissection and experiments.*

---

* The Author feeling certain of the immense advantage which Africa will derive from so important an establishment, and knowing that for the population to rise they require some tangible stimulus, proposed the following scheme to the Home Government for a Medical School in Sierra Leone, the Central Government of Western Africa, in a letter to the Secretary of State for War (a portion of which is here quoted), dated 13th July, 1861, Dixcove Fort :—
'My Lord and Sirs,—It is an important and universally acknowledged fact,

It is needless to enter here into a discussion on colour, as Prunner Bey himself admits that the negro colouring matter is exactly the same as that found in freckles and the tanned skin of

that the greatest friends of the Africans are the philanthropic sons of Britain; and that the Government under whose sway they obtained liberty, and can consider themselves perfect free-men, and from whom also they have received paramount blessings, both temporal and spiritual, is the English Government. Africa, therefore, has everything to gain whilst Britannia rules the world. By her squadron she keeps a watchful eye on all those nations who would follow that nefarious practice—the slave trade; her adventurous sons, the missionaries, pierce through the very den of barbarism to become pioneers of civilization. The consequence therefore is that the Africans have a natural attachment for the Government that espouses their cause, and also for the philanthropic sons of that Government, who always take advantage of every opportunity to better their condition. Many have been the means which the English Government has used to raise the condition of the African. This is universally known by every nation, and the African also thoroughly knows and feels it.

'The last act which is of great importance to the scientific world, to the rising generation of Africa, and to the whole population of Western Africa, is that which the Government has lately taken, and which was so strongly argued by the late Minister of War, Lord Panmure—viz., of educating young sons of Africa in the medical profession, and placing them in the Army to serve principally in Western Africa. This in the very face of it, carries advantages with it which no other Government has thought of; and we in Africa are certain that when the Government has undertaken a subject of such intrinsic importance, and of so great utility to the country under their Government, they will be the last to stop short when the work is in an embryonic state and with nothing to prevent its germination.

'The system of educating African surgeons for the Army stationed on the Coast of Africa has manifold advantages :—

'1st, As to the Government and its officers on the Coast ; 2nd, As to the country and the people who inhabit it ; 3rd, As to the scientific world.

'Of all the British possessions, the Coast of Africa is rightly considered the most unhealthy and deadly, in consequence of which the best educated professional men are required to take care of those who are sent out to govern and keep order in it. It is a well-known fact, that practical experience and a thorough investigation of certain diseases make a man become acquainted with the different phases which those diseases may take, as well as the best remedies to combat them. The perfection of this truism cannot be accomplished unless some years be spent where the disease is rife, and its pathology and treatment carefully investigated.

'The Coast is so prejudicial to European constitutions, that the Government has been pleased to allow medical officers to remain only one year in it. During that short period it is impossible for them to take any vital interest in the diseases of the Coast, and beyond the ordinary routine of business, the fatigue from the heat of the sun prevents them from a study which some would be only too happy to follow ; and after the lapse of twelve months, their tour of duties being *pro tem.* expired, they are relieved ; or, even before the end of the year, some are invalided home from disease contracted through the baneful influence of the climate.

Europeans. The colour is caused by exposure to the sun, by the effect of malaria, and various affections of the spleen and liver. But I may here remark that European children in the tropics, when

But an African properly educated in Medicine, is in his native soil ; there he remains (not that he is never ill—no—but in the majority of cases it is generally slight); he has the advantage, by his long stay there, of being able to investigate the causes, effects, and pathology of the diseases belonging to the Coast ; he in time becomes acquainted with the different types in which the diseases may present themselves, and therefore is able to combat them, and even prevent them in time, before any injuricus effect is produced in the system ; when, on the other hand, a neophite will be puzzled what to do. This is no mere imagination ; for there have been cases where, by judicious treatment, many valuable lives might have been saved.

'The Government then will be the gainer, as they will have on the Coast of Africa, professional men in their service, who are perfectly acquainted with the diseases of the Coast, and who may lessen the per centage of mortality among the officers and officials employed on the Coast.

'2nd, As to the country and the people who inhabit it.

'The immortal Sir Fowell Buxton has truly affirmed that if Africa is to be civilized and evangelized it must be by her progeny. For reasons before stated—viz., the injurious influence of the climate on European constitutions, as well as the slow and gradual pace with which civilization and improvement find their way amongst a population who are adverse to anything that appears to destroy the customs of their forefathers, and also, the soil not being native to the Europeans, andthat they, therefore, cannot fraternise with the people who are not highly-educated in the same degree as with persons from their own native country—it is impossible for the surgeon employed for such a short and temporary time on the Coast to take any deep interest in examining and developing the scientific resources of the country.

The Government look forward to the improvement of the country, and that improvement can never be properly accomplished, unless by the aid of the educated *native portion* of the *community*. It is the African who can take a deep and vital interest in the rise of the country ; it is he who when placed in a position to raise the standard of his countrymen, will never give up on slight disappointment, but will continue on, till he has accomplished his end. It will, therefore, be of very great importance to the country and to the people, should the Government continue to send to the Coast of Africa, *well-educated natives*, scientific and professional men to serve in it, for the country will be largely benefitted by it.

'3rd, As to the scientific world.

'The scientific resources of Western Africa are entirely in embryo ; and we can literally and truly state that we are perfectly ignorant of them. There are vast treasures in the bowels of this extensive continent, potent medicines in its picturesque field, and objects of great importance to the naturalist, as yet unknown to the scientific world. Here then are subjects which the short stay of a European surgeon on the Coast will not permit him to investigate ; but the African surgeon, stationed in one place at first, say the Gold Coast, and then removed to the other stations—say, Sierra Leone and the Gambia—has ample opportunity of investigating these subjects ; and medicine and science generally, will be greatly benefitted by it.

'In every respect, then, the Government has begun an excellent and delicately and carefully brought up, possess a great delicacy of colour and complexion; but when thrown into the world at a very early age, and subject to the climate and other demoralizing in-

praiseworthy undertaking, and which will make every African invoke blessing on her efforts, as it is one of intrinsic value to the country, the people of Africa, as well as the Government.

' Two out of the three who were first sent to be educated in the medical profession for the Army, have now finished their studies, and are attached to the Army stationed on the Coast ; the other, unfortunately, succumbed to the influence of the cold climate. The testimony, received through the Church Missionary Society by the Government, as to the efficiency and behaviour of the three African students, who were educated through the instrumentality of the Government, from the Dean of the Medical Faculty of King's College, London, the College where they were educated, was of a nature, I believe, to encourage further trial, and to prove that the African, when placed in a proper position, employed his time to the best advantage ; and all the Africans on the Coast, and the friends of African improvement, consider it a misfortune to the country that the wish of the Government and of the Church Missionary Society, that seven more Africans should be sent to receive education in Medicine, has not been carried out.

' It may be asked what would be the best means of effectually carrying out this excellent plan of educating young Africans in the science of Medicine ? Having had ample opportunity of carefully studying all the various bearings of the subject, I hope that the following suggestions will meet with your approbation.

' That a small Government Medical Establishment be made at Sierra Leone, and that certain young men, not above the age of twenty, be selected from those in the Church Missionary College or Schools, who have made some proficiency in Latin, Greek, and Mathematics. [In a subsequent letter the Author proposed that selection should be made from the four Colonies and settlements—viz., Gambia, Sierra Leone, Lagos, and Cape Coast.] That they should be prepared in the preliminaries of Medicine—viz., Anatomy, Physiology, Chemistry, Botany (of Africa), Natural History, Hospital Practice and Pharmacy, for a certain period, from one year and a half to two years. That they should continue during that time their classical studies, limited to those books required by the colleges, in the way the Master of the establishment might think best. That the Master be an African, since, as we have endeavoured to prove, he will take a far greater interest in performing what will tend to elevate his country. That he should have his full power and credentials for selecting young men and managing the establishment from the *Home Government*, and that he should in any case of doubt consult the Church Missionary Society at Sierra Leone. Should it be left to the local power, I am certain that his efforts would be paralysed. That a few wax-works and books be sent for the establishment, according to the application of the Master, who should also keep a laboratory for his chemical class. That the students be allowed a certain amount, according to the discretion of the Government, for their board, clothing, and other expenses, which I am certain would not be too costly.

' For anatomy and dissection, monkeys may be advantageously used, as well as the wax-work. The botany of Western Africa as well as the natural history should be studied, and the Master, therefore, must be acquainted

E

fluences, become exceedingly dark, and show a marked difference in
their form, proportion, and features, the degree commensurating
with the amount of the deprivation to which the young has been
subjected. If this is true among European children born in the
tropics, how much more true is it with those who have been subju-
gated for numberless centuries to the baneful influence of demorali-
zation? Is it not the fact, then, as remarked by Mr. Armistead,
that it is only when the negroes are in possession of privileges and
advantages equivalent to the rest of mankind, that a fair comparison can be drawn between the one and the other. ' The negro,'
said he, ' by nature our equal, made like ourselves, after the image
of the Creator, gifted by the same intelligence, impelled by the
same passions and affections, and redeemed by the same Saviour,
has now become reduced through cupidity and oppression, nearly to
the level of the brute, spoiled of his humanity, plundered of his
rights, and often hurried to a premature grave, the miserable
victim of avarice and heedless tyranny.' How true are the remarks
of the great Clarkson, ' Men have presumptuously dared to wrest
from their fellows the most precious of their rights, to intercept, as

with these subjects. For hospital practice and pharmacy, abundant opportunities are offered at Sierra Leone.
  ' It is a very difficult thing for the student unacquainted with anything in
Medicine to begin in England, and compete with students who generally
have had preliminary education in some of the subjects before they enter the
proper colleges ; and I am certain that by these means the Government
would have their wishes fulfilled, and the country and people be greatly
benefitted.—&c., &c., &c.,

                          JAMES AFRICANUS B. HORTON, M.D.

  The Author received a most favourable reply from the Secretary of State for
War, who said that the subject should have his attention and consideration.
At the same time, communications were forwarded to the principal Medical
Officer and to the Officer Commanding on the Gold Coast, for information
bearing on the subject, so as to know how far the 'intended substitution,
either wholly or in part, of native African for European medical officers, is
likely to be successful.' The subject received a combined and warm
opposition, which nipped it in the bud.
  The Author observing the fearful mortality of European engineers on the
Coast, proposed that natives from the three different Colonies should be
educated for that express purpose also ; but the Home Government has now decided that European officers who have got experience in the diseases of the
Coast, should serve as long as they like in it, with the advantage of each
year counting double for promotion and retirement. But, as yet, no attention has been paid to the subject of native engineers.

far as they can, the bounty and grace of the Almighty, to close the door to their intellectual progress, to shut every avenue to their moral and religious improvement, to stand between them and their Maker,' &c.

On every occasion, modern anthropologists delight to descant on the inferiority of the negro race as regards their intellectual and moral improvement, withholding the fact that they have been for ages exposed to influences not calculated to develop either the moral, or the intellectual faculties, but, on the contrary, to destroy them; such, indeed, as might have reduced them to the condition of wild beasts. ' Treat men like beasts and you will make them such,' is an old but true saying of a philosopher. This treatment had the most degrading and destructive influence on their mental capacity; and ' it might be fairly questioned whether any other people could have endured the privations or the sufferings to which they (the negroes) have been subjected, without becoming still more degraded in the scale of humanity; for nothing has been left undone to cripple their intellect, to darken their minds, to debase their moral nature, and to obliterate all traces of their relationship to mankind; yet how wonderfully have they sustained the mighty load of oppression under which they have been groaning for centuries.'

It is not the negroes alone who, under pernicious influences, become altered, but animals and Europeans also. M. Dupius has conclusively proved this in his report on the effect of long captivity and severe treatment on European Christians among the Arabs. They lost their reason and feelings; their spirits broke and their faculties sank in an indescribable stupor; and when subject to a succession of hardships, they lost all their spirit of exertion and hope; became indifferent, abject, servile, and brutish. If bondage and a depraved life have such damnifying influence on the moral and intellectual condition of man in general, will it here be out of place for me to inquire of the anthropological negro denouncer, ' How men can be elevated while the burdens which oppress are so great? how can they be industrious when the sources of industry are so much crippled? or how can they be expected to discover anything like even a virtuous emulation, while precluded by their circumstances from rising above a condition of slavery the most hopeless and wretched? But let the shackles be loosed from the negro, let him feel the invigorating influence of freedom, let hope enter his bosom, and let him be cheered and animated with the prospect of reward for his exertions, and the foul calumny of his great and inevitable inferiority will soon be refuted in himself.'—*Armistead. 'A Tribute to the Negro.'*

But even Prunner Bey has been more generous in the place he assigns to the negro race, although his commentators have endeavoured to place them among the anthropomorphous apes. He says : 'It results from the examination of the organism of the negro, that it is admirably adapted to the geographical position he occupies. The dark layer on his external integument, and its velvety character, like all blackened and rough bodies, favour the radiation of heat and act as coolers. Experience has proved that black crape protects also the face from the solar reflection in the ascent of snow-covered mountains. The great development of the glandular system of the skin favours the secretions, refreshing the skin, and protecting it by an unctuous secretion. The thickness of the layers of the skin protects the negro from the night frost in his usual condition of nudity. The same considerations apply to the internal integument, the mucous membrane, with its glutinous and abundant secretions, and to all glands, without exception, which, by their really enormous volume, in harmony with the excitation by heat, favour and facilitate the change, and the reproduction of organic matter so rapidly used up in the torrid zone. Do we pass beyond the limits of science, and lose ourselves in the vicious circle of teology, if we venture to suppose that even the infantile form of the brain of the negro may have its relative advantages? What has the noble Hindoo become under an Indian sun, drowned in a sea of spiritualism the most obscure, with his cranium, which by its admirable harmony, its graceful mould, seems exactly to resemble the organic egg which received the divine breath of Brahma? He has, it is true, fulfilled an eminent task, but for many centuries he has been a being severed from terrestrial regions, and of little use to his fellow-beings. Let us finally endeavour to assign to the negro his place in relation to the quadrumana, to which some authors seriously approximate him, and to that of other human races, which either make use of or despise the negro. *As for me, the moment that an organized being uses for standing and motion that admirable pedestal, the narrow base of which supports an enormous weight ; the moment he makes use of the instrument of instruments—the hand—I look upon it as a new order of things.* While recognizing the undoubted value of homologies, which form the bases of zoological science, I cannot but admire the simplicity of the means employed by creative wisdom to separate man from the anthropomorphous ape. The hair on the skin is reduced, a suture is suppressed to draw the teeth closer, and though prognathism is developed, the lips are thickened, the iliac bones are turned aside instead of being adossed to the vertebral column, the muscles of the thumb are strengthened, the great toe is fixed; nature, finally, instead of the temporal lobe, selects the anterior lobe of the brain, there to fashion the instrument of intelligence which reflects her image.'

But it is not only the pure negro that has received so pernicious a handling from the anthropologists of this day; they have been unsparing also to their mixed production—the mulattoes—who are said to be the most immoral people upon the face of the globe. Of them, Captain Burton says, 'The worst class of all is the mulatto, under which I include the quadroon and octaroon. He is everywhere, like wealth—*irritamenta malorum.* The "*bar sinister*," and the uneasy idea that he is despised, naturally fill him with ineffable bile and bitterness. Inferior in point of morale to Europeans, and, as far as regards physique, to Africans, he seeks strength in making the families of his progenitors fall out.' The description of Bosman, in his work on Guinea, published at the end of the seventeenth century, is singled out as the most true and perfect picture of mulattoes as a class. 'Though I have been tedious in this, I hope you will pardon it, for I must own my itch of scribbling is not yet over, and I cannot help giving you an account of a wonderful and extraordinary sort of people—I mean the *Tapœyers* or *mulattoes* —a race begotten by the Europeans upon the *negro* or *mulatto-* woman. This bastard strain is made up of a parcel of profligate villains, neither true to the negroes nor us, nor indeed dare they trust one another, so that you very rarely see them agree together. They assume the name of Christians, but are as great idolators as the negroes themselves. Most of the women are public whores to the Europeans and private ones to the natives, so that I can hardly give them a character so bad as they deserve. I can only tell you whatever is in its own nature worse, in the Europeans and negroes is united in them, so that they are the sink of both. The men, most of whom are soldiers in our service, are clothed as we are, but the women prink up themselves in a particular manner; those of any fashion wear a fine shift, and over that a short jacket of silk or stuff without sleeves, which reaches from under the arms to their hips, fastened only at the shoulders. Upon their heads they wear several caps, one upon the other, the uppermost of which is of silk, plaited before and round at the top to make it fit soft, upon all which they have a sort of fillet, which comes twice or thrice round the head. Thus dressed they make no small show. On the lower part of their body they are clothed as the negro women are; and those who are poor are only distinguishable by their dress, they going naked in the upper part of their body.

'The whole brood when young, are far from handsome; and when old, are only fit to fright children to their beds. If a painter were obliged to paint envy, I could wish him no better original to draw after than an old mulatto woman. In process of time, their bodies become speckled with white, brown, and yellow spots, like the tigers, which they also resemble in their barbarous natures. But I shall here leave them, for fear it may be thought that I am prejudiced by hatred against 'em; but so far from that, there is not a single person who hath anything to do with them, but he must own they are not worth speaking to.'—Bosman. *Soc., cit.* 141. Such, then, is the description which is even now regarded as typical of the mulattoes on the Coast. These people, when properly educated, adorn and enliven society, and are chaste and faithful when properly married. But in the generality of cases we find that whilst the European and the coloured women get married, the mulattoes, especially if not properly educated, are very seldom so, and are therefore placed in a position where they are obliged to live a disreputable life. I have met with several mulatto ladies, who are ladies in every sense of the word, agreeable, amiable, sociable, chaste, and possessing a happy tact of making themselves agreeable with every class; and as regards their broods being frightfully ugly, I emphatically deny this as the general rule.

In an article in the *Saturday Review*, the editor writing on the subject of the negro race, says: 'The Africans are apt to imitate, quick to seize, ambitious to achieve civilization. Whenever brought into contact with Europeans they copy their manners, imbibe their tastes, and endeavour to acquire their arts. The imitative disposition and the imitative faculty, are both in them particularly strong. They are neither unwilling nor unable to learn the lessons, and endure the toils and shackles of civilized existence. In those qualities of acquiring and progressing which distinguish man from the brute, they resemble man. They have now been for three centuries in contact with Europeans, exposed during that period to the most barbarous treatment, and the most destroying and depressing influences, yet not only has nothing occurred to indicate for them the fate of other unhappy races whom European cruelty or European superiority has trodden out, but they have actually advanced under circumstances the most hostile to advancement.'

Carl Vogt would not admit, in *Lecture Seven*, that any influence, whether of locality, food, culture, or progressive civilization, has the least effect of altering the negro; he is now as he was thousands of years ago, ' contemporaneous, probably, with the Biblical Adam;' and yet in *Lecture Fifteen*, he admits that ' many races, though they remain on the same spot, are apt to undergo certain changes, the result of progressive civilization.' ' The same character,' he in another place says, ' which distinguishes carefully the domestic animals from their parent stock, may also be obtained in man by culture.' Why admit this of Europeans and the lower animals, and deny it of the negro race?

To prove that locality, culture, position, and calling, have a most important influence in the formation and development of a race, I must quote Prunner Bey and Quatrefages, on the change of character in the Anglo-Saxon American or Yankees: ' Already, after the second generation, the Yankees present features of the Indian type. At a later period, the glandular system is reduced to the minimum of its normal development. The skin becomes dry like leather, the colour of the cheek lost, and is in the male replaced by a loamy tint, and in the female by a sallow paleness. The head becomes smaller and rounder, and is covered with stiff, dark hair; the neck becomes longer, and there is a greater development of the cheek-bones and the masseters. The temporal fossœ become deeper, the jawbones more massive, the eyes lie in deep approximated sockets. The iris is dark, the glance piercing and wild. The long bones, especially in the superior extremities, are lengthened, so that the gloves manufactured in England and France for American markets are of a particular make, with very long fingers. The female pelvis approaches that of the male.' If only in two generations such changes have taken place, in a climate not far different from that of England and France, through mere local and climatic causes, how much more must such be the case in a race like the negro, who for hundreds of generations have undergone series of metamorphic changes, through climatic and other most depressing influences? Does not this indubitably go to prove the unity of the races of mankind?

But Quatrefages has advanced a step further, and has shown how depressing and degrading influences—the want of proper food and comforts, exposure to the effects of climate, &c.—are capable of materially altering and deforming a race of pure type, both physically and morally: ' On the plantation of Ulster,' he writes, ' and on the successes of the British against the rebels in 1641 and 1689, multitudes of native Irish were driven from Armagh and the south of Down, into the mountainous tract extending from the Barony of the Flews eastwards to the sea. The same race was on the other side of the kingdom driven into Leitrim, Sligo, and Mayo. Ever since that time these people have been exposed to the bad effects of hunger and ignorance, the two great demoralisers of the human race. The descendants of the refugees can still be distinguished from their cognates in Meath and other districts. They have open projecting mouths, with prominent teeth and exposed gums, high cheekbones, depressed nose, and present barbarism on their front. We thus see in Sligo and the north of Mayo, the consequence of two hundred years' misery upon the whole physical structure, an example of deterioration by known causes, which offers some compensation by its importance for the future, in showing the sufferings through which former generations have passed. They are on the average five feet two inches high, big-bellied, bandy-legged, their clothes a bundle of rags—they walk about the spectres of a people once well-grown, able-bodied, and handsome. In other parts of the island, where the people have undergone no such degradation, the same race furnishes the finest models of humanity and strength, both physically and mentally.'

Quatrefages adds to this description the following just remarks: ' Every reader who is in any way acquainted with the distinguishing characters of mankind, will, with the exception of the colour, recognise here the character ascribed to the lowest negroes and the Australian tribes.' The Irishman of Meath keeps the type of the old stock, but that of Flews has undergone a change, and consequently formed a new race quite distinct from the old stock.

All anthropologists admit that a race might become degenerate by certain physical causes, and Carl Vogt also admits of accidental abnormality becoming normal by its permanency; it is also admitted that young infants are the most susceptible to degenerating influences, and to acquire deformities from physical causes through the delicacy of their frame, and the ease with which they can be moulded into different shapes and forms. Might we not trace the peculiarities of the negro race, which have been the occasion of so many learned dissertations to the unwarranted habit of the natives in bringing up their young? The infants are doubled up, twisted, and firmly tied on the back with a cloth, where they remain for hours at a time, their head and face pressed in the concavity of the back, the hands and feet twisted up and properly secured ; and this process is carried out until the infant is grown up. Is this not a system which, when persistently acted on, in the young and delicate frame, must lead to fearful deformity ?

But there is another sort of degradation which still enthralls the population of Western Africa, and under whose debasing influence it is impossible for them at present to raise their head, which is, the employment to a very great extent, of female labour in the field. The young girls thus acquire a rude taste, and a most reckless liberty ; a coarse, loose, and filthy mode of speaking, a rude and uncouth conduct. They lose all refined and polished habits, and are consequently made to hold a degraded position among their more favoured equals—men. Again, in many places we find young girls going about from town to town, and from street to street, hawking thread, and various kinds of cloth and other articles; this is a practice which makes them acquire a wild habit and taste, and which unfits them entirely for that domestic regimen, when they become women, which alone can make home happy and comfortable to their husbands. Thus, there are now complaints and heartburnings in many cases among young married couples, of the unfitness of the girls for domestic duties; it is found that they do not possess those habits of modesty, morality, docility, and domestic usefulness, which are essential to the habits and comforts of a married life. Their loose habits tell not only on their moral character, but greatly on their physical conformation. I have noticed that girls who have been exposed to hard labour in a nation, are generally the most ill-formed; and this acting prejudicially from generation to generation, leads to those abnormal developments for which anthropologists of this age have so much denounced a whole race.

CHAPTER VI.

THE PROGRESSIVE ADVANCEMENT OF THE NEGRO RACE UNDER CIVILIZING INFLUENCE.

It may be asked, what advances in civilization have the negro race exhibited since their free contact with civilized nations untrammelled by the slave trade and slavery, that may tend to prove them not to be behind the most favoured nations in their moral and intellectual qualifications ?

Leaving unnoticed many genuine evidences of civilization to be found now-a-days amongst the coloured inhabitants of Barbadoes and other West Indian islands, and bearing in mind that mankind (in all ages) in different communities, when subject to proper cultivating influences, do not show an equable rate of advance within a given period, I shall endeavour to point out what improvements have taken place amongst the negroes in one of the colonies on the West Coast of Africa only within the last fifty years.

As Sierra Leone is the head-quarters of the British possessions there, I shall select it as the subject of the example, and will commence from the liberated Africans, who were there freed from the fetters of slavery. Prior to their being kidnapped they were governed by kings, or chiefs, who had a complete sway over life and property ; they possessed no written laws, and no proper religion, but worshipped wood, stones, and other material substances ; they were extremely cruel to each other ; polygamy was carried on to a fearful extent ; the lower class were kept in a state of slavery ; warfare was carried on in a most cruel style, and all conquered populations were enslaved ; they lived in huts, made either with mud or cane ; they made only one kind of cloth ; they lived either wholly naked or partially so ; they tilled the ground ; and the Cramantees, from having gold as the medium of commerce, knew weights and measures.

On their arrival at Sierra Leone, landed naked and in a state of abject rudeness and poverty, without the least knowledge of civilization, they are placed under Government supervision for a few months. A portion of land is given them, to cut down the woods and build towns; then commences cultivation; missionary schools are established; gradually they begin to read and write; commerce, by degrees, forms a part of their occupation; they begin slowly to throw off their air of serfdom, which they had imbibed from previous treatment, and become interested in the nature of their Government, so as to require improvement in its administrative and judicial departments. The worship of the living and true God is strictly observed by them, and they manifest great sympathy for the condition of their countrymen. In time they begin to inquire how their children are to be educated, and what are the best means at their disposal for doing so. These, as they grow up (which is the generation at present occupying Sierra Leone), seek after and obtain justice; preach loudly the Christian ethics—viz., mutual charity, forgiveness of one another, fraternity, and equality. Science and literature are taught in some of the schools; the generation feel themselves to possess great liberty, physically and mentally; philanthropic views are extensively circulated amongst them; they build large and expensive dwelling-houses; buy up the former abodes of their European masters; carry on extensive mercantile speculations; seek after the indulgences of civilized life, and travel in foreign countries to seek after wealth. English newspapers are very much circulated amongst them, and are read with eagerness; and they require a voice in their legislative administration. They look out for a better form of governmental administration, and desire to attain it; and they use the best means for arriving at their wish;—the essentials for political progress.

The original condition of the people of Sierra Leone is thus described by Mr. Ferguson, formerly governor of that Colony:—

'The condition of a body of captive slaves on their arrival at Sierra Leone for liberation is the most miserable and wretched that can be conceived—emaciated, squalid, sickly-looking, ill-fed, barbarous, confined in inadequate space, compelled to breathe an atmosphere hardly fit for the sustenance of animal life—is it to be wondered that, in such circumstances, the faculties of the soul should be cramped and benumbed by the cruelties inflicted upon the body? It is nevertheless from among such people and their descendants at Sierra Leone, their minds at length elevated by a sense of personal freedom, and by the temperate administration of just and equable laws, that you are to look for the first practical results of your operations. It is not my intention to trace the progress of the liberated Africans from the depths of the misery alluded to, until we find them, after the lapse of fifteen or twenty years, independent and respectable members of society, but to give you some notion of them as a class, and of the position in society which they occupy at the present day. Of the liberated Africans as a body, it may with great truth be said that there is not a more quiet, inoffensive, and good-humoured population on the face of the earth. Of their religious spirit it is not easy, from the very nature of the subject, to form a decided opinion, but I know that their outward observance of the Sabbath-day is most exemplary. On that day the passion for amusements is altogether laid aside, and the whole body of the people are to be found at one or other of the churches or chapels which abound in the colony.'

But the creoles of Sierra Leone have been stigmatized as the most impertinent rogues in all the coast, even by men who know nothing of them. They will not wait for the truth, the whole truth, and nothing but the truth; no—but they rant upon the platform, seeing who can crow the loudest, or 'forge red-hot sentences at their pens' points;' and when investigation is made as to whether the assertion be true, it is found to be some mere phantom of ignorance and credulity which has been exaggerated in the repetition by those who have had occasion to complain. There is undoubtedly among the low, reckless class, a certain amount of roguery, such as is found among a parallel portion of the population of the whole world; but the stigma is here applied to the whole population; for those who propogate the would-be extraordinary intelligence, magnify the tale to such a degree, that the story in its progress through the fancies and mouths of those who represent it, assumes great magnitude and importance. But we find, nevertheless, that these creoles of Sierra Leone occupy lucrative subordinate positions of trust in both the military and civil service of the Government in the four colonies and settlements on the coast—viz., Sierra Leone, the Gambia, the Gold Coast, and Lagos; which speaks volumes for the indomitable and arduous exertions and perseverance of the missionaries who formed the educational body of the colony. Besides this, they are to be found in every part of the coast sighing after gold in the capacity of merchants, traders, and clerks—in the French colony of Senegal; in the Rivers Gambia, Casamanza, Nunez, Pongas, Sherbroe and Galinas; in the Liberian Republic; on the Gold Coast; in the Kingdom of Dahomey; in Lagos and Abeokuta; in the Niger; at Bonny, Old and New Calabar, the Cameroons, Fernando Po, the Gaboons, and the Islands of St. Helena and Ascension. If they were not an industrious, exploring race, determined to advance their position in life by speculation and other legitimate means, would they not have confined themselves within the limits of the Peninsula of Sierra Leone; and do not their exertions above alluded to, point to a similar trait in the character of Englishmen, who are to be found in every part of the known world where money can be made?

The Obituary* on the death of William O'Connor Pratt, son of the late William Henry Pratt, Esq., merchant, and Marshal of the Vice-Admiralty Court at Sierra Leone (a pure negro of the Eboe tribe), written by one of the European inhabitants of the colony of Sierra Leone, will furnish us with an example of the real worth of Christian and civilizing influence on the native African. He was sent to England at an early age, where he received the rudiments of a sound English education. On his return to the colony, in 1853, he was engaged in mercantile pursuits in his father's house. 'In his career he was at once marked out as a young man who had profited, far more than is usually the case, by the advantages of an English education. He proved himself deserving of the highest trust. He was hard-working, zealous, and attentive; and in the

---

* The *Sierra Leone Weekly Times and West African Record*, Oct. 29, 1862.

year 1859 his father admitted him to a partnership in the firm of W. H. Pratt and Sons.' He had only completed his twenty-sixth year, when he suddenly met his death by the bursting of a blood vessel. 'His death at any time could not have been otherwise than sad, touchingly sad, because his friends and fellow-citizens must always have looked upon him as a bright and living example of the capacity of the African race to accept the civilization of Europe, and of the holy influences of a pure Christianity. But he died, according to human calculation, at an untimely age, before arriving at the meridian of life, when the stronger and more enduring qualities of manhood take the place of the imperfections and waywardness of youth. His countrymen may well mourn for him, and that regret is shared by every European who knew him. We give expression to the unanimous sentiment of the inhabitants of this colony, when we say that the death of so promising a young man, in a rising community that possess so few like him, is a national calamity. He was an African by birth; he loved his country; he disdained not to associate with his less-favoured citizens; but withal he was a gentleman in his bearing and in his language, and in every relation of life he showed the depth and strength of the principles of a refined and gentlemanly culture. Many Africans have received on occasion unqualified praise from the English press, but none ever deserved it more than the young gentleman this colony now mourns. He was far removed from that silly vanity which, doubtful of the reality of equality, attempts to force its acknowledgment by impudence and forwardness. On the contrary, William Pratt was conspicuous for his simplicity and good breeding, and yet he never sacrificed his undoubted and acknowledged position as an educated gentleman. Besides being a partner in the firm of W. H. Pratt and Sons, he held the appointment of lieutenant, paymaster, and quartermaster in the Royal Sierra Leone Militia, and he discharged the duties of those offices to the entire satisfaction and approbation of his Excellency Governor Hill, and the other authorities. During the late Quiah war, he was conspicuous among the native officers for the zeal and attention with which he performed his various duties. At this time it was remarked that his constitution, which was evidently never a robust one, showed signs of a premature decline; yet he bore up manfully, and fought the battle of life for a position of honour and distinction in a manner which proved that a manly and liberal education can bear fruit as strong on an African as on a European soil. We must not omit to mention that for seven years he was the organist of St. George's Cathedral. The emoluments of this office were of little consequence, but it was his wish to make his talents of service to his fellow-townsmen; and his loss will for a long time be felt by the congregation.' The writer thus concludes: 'The supply of such men as William Pratt is sufficiently scarce to make his loss severely felt. The most anxious demand cannot call them forth. His intelligence was far above most of the native young men of the colony, and, in his death, Sierra Leone has lost its highest ornament, and Africa one of her illustrious sons. His premature death cannot be too much deplored, and it is most natural that we should dwell upon his life. The example which he set of a dutiful son is rare enough to call for an expression of public approbation. But we must especially dwell upon the qualities of the heart, which impressed every one who knew him with feelings of respect and regard. The best of us may learn from his example how far good manners and a genial disposition will gain the esteem and goodwill of even comparative strangers. A sphere of great usefulness undoubtedly lay before him; but we must not imagine that he died to leave no trace of his existence. His memory will live after him to encourage others to gain the esteem of their fellow-citizens, and to walk in the paths of duty and usefulness.'

But, unfortunately, in Western Africa there are no prizes held out to ambition; in all well-constituted societies for the progressive development of a community there must be a wholesome stimulus to the aspirants. Invidious distinctions, by which one class of individuals, not because of any superior attainments, but from mere physical configuration, must always take the first place, engender amongst that privileged class pride, arrogance, and a spirit of oppression; whilst at the same time they lead to a spirit of combined opposition to any and everything that appears to be noble and praiseworthy in the less privileged class. Fortunately, within the last few years, in Western Africa there are healthy symptoms of improvement in this order of things; but it will be well that our legislators should remember that, to improve a population, there must be a stimulus to energy and exertion, a motive to industry; and that when a people is kept under mental depression and dejection, indolence, poverty, and stupidity are the inseparable concomitants. 'Give the negro a motive,' says an eminent writer, 'and he is active and industrious enough;' and Dr. Madden has asserted that the negro is not the indolent, slothful being he is everywhere considered to be, which is proved by the progress he is now making in the British colonies; and the same writer is perfectly correct when he adds, 'I am well persuaded, in respect to industry, physical strength, and activity, the Egyptian fellahs, the Maltese labourer, and the Italian peasant, are far inferior to the negro.' Dr. Madden considers that the blessing of education and good government are alone wanting to make the natives of Africa intellectually and morally equal to the people of any nation on the surface of the globe.

But we have seen European nations who in years long passed were themselves as barbarous and unenlightened as the negro Africans are at present, and who have exhibited wonderful improvement within the last century. This should urge the Africans to increased exertions, so that their race may, in course of time, take its proper stand in the world's history. 'The same race,' says Mr. Armistead, 'which in the age of Tacitus dwelt in solitary dens amid morasses, have built St. Petersburg and Moscow; and the posterity of the cannibals now feed on wheaten bread. Little more than a century ago Russia was covered with hordes of barbarians; cheating, drinking, brutal lust, and the most pernicious excesses of rage, were as well known, and as little blamed, among the better classes of the nobles who frequented the Czar's court, as the more polished and mitigated forms of the same vices are at this day in St. Petersburg. Literature had never once appeared amongst its inhabitants in a form to be recognized, and you might travel over tracts of several days' journey without meeting a man, even among the higher classes, whose mind contained the materials of one moment's rational conversation. Although the various circumstances of external improvement will certainly not disguise, even at this day, and among the individuals of the first classes, the *vestigia*

F

ruris, still no one can presume to dispute that the materials of which Russians are made have been greatly and fundamentally ameliorated, that their capacities are rapidly unfolding, and their virtues improving;' and this is mainly produced by the extension of their communication with the more civilized portion of the globe, and by the change of their habits and mode of life. 'A century ago it would have been just as miraculous to read a tolerable Russian composition, as it would be at this day to find the same phenomenon in Haussa or at Timbuctoo ; and speculators who argue about races, and despise the effect of circumstances, would have had the same right to decide upon the fate of all the Russians, from an inspection of the Calmuc skulls, as they imagine they now have to condemn all Africa to everlasting barbarism, from the head, the colour, and the wool of its inhabitants.'

Africa, in ages past, was the nursery of science and literature ; from thence they were taught in Greece and Rome, so that it was said that the ancient Greeks represented their favourite goddess of Wisdom—Minerva—as an African princess. Pilgrimages were made to Africa in search of knowledge by such eminent men as Solon, Plato, Pythagoras ; and several came to listen to the instructions of the African Euclid, who was at the head of the most celebrated mathematical school in the world, and who flourished 300 years before the birth of Christ. The conqueror of the great African Hannibal made his associate and confidant the African poet Terence. 'Being emancipated by his master, he took him to Rome and gave him a good education ; the young African soon acquired reputation for the talent he displayed in his comedies. His dramatic works were much admired by the Romans for their prudential maxims and moral sentences, and, compared with his contemporaries, he was much in advance of them in point of style.'

Origen, Tertullian, Augustin, Clemens Alexandrinus, and Cyril, who were fathers and writers of the Primitive Church, were tawny African bishops of Apostolic renown. Many eminent writers and historians agree that these ancient Ethiopians were negroes, but many deny that this was the case. The accounts given by Herodotus, who travelled in Egypt, and other writers, settle the question that such they were. Herodotus describes them as ' *woolly-haired blacks,* *with projecting lips.'* In describing the people of Colchis, he says that they were Egyptian colonists, who were ' *black in complexion and woolly-haired.'* This description undoubtedly refers to a race of negroes, as neither the Copts, their descendants, nor the mummies which have been preserved, would lead us to believe that their complexion was black. Even the large sphinx, which was excavated by M. Caviglia in Egypt, and which is regarded by all scientific men as a stupendous piece of sculpture, has its face ' of the negro cast,' and is said to be of a mild and even of a sublime expression. 'If it be not admitted that these nations were black, they were undoubtedly of very dark complexion, having much of the negro physiognomy, as depicted in Egyptian sculpture and painting, and from them the negro population, indeed the whole race of Africa, have sprung. Say not, then, I repeat it, that Africa is without her heraldry of science and fame. Its inhabitants are the offshoots— wild and untrained, it is true, but still the offshoots of a stem which was once proudly luxuriant in the fruits of learning and taste ; whilst that from which the Goths, their calumniators, have sprung, remained hard, and knotted, and barren.'* And why should not the same race who governed Egypt,† attacked the most famous and flourishing city—Rome, who had her churches, her universities, and her repositories of learning and science, once more stand on their legs and endeavour to raise their characters in the scale of the civilized world ?

In the examination of the world's history, we are led forcibly to entertain the opinion that human affairs possess a gradual and progressive tendency to deterioration. Nations rise and fall ; the once flourishing and civilized degenerates into a semi-barbarous state ; and those who have lived in utter barbarism, after a lapse of time become the standing nation. Yes, ' how wonderful are the vicissitudes which history exhibits to us in the course of human affairs ; and how little foundation do they afford to our sanguine prospects concerning futurity ! If in those parts of the earth which were formerly inhabited by barbarians, we now see the most splendid

---

* Armistead—A Tribute for the Negro, page 123.

† Down to the time of Herodotus, out of three hundred Egyptian sovereigns, eighteen were Ethiopians. —' *Herod.,*' Lib. ii., cap. 100.

exertions of genius, and the highest forms of civil policy, we behold others, which in ancient times were the seats of science, of cultivation, and of liberty, at present immersed in superstition, and laid waste by despotism. After a short period of civil, of military, and of literary glory, the prospect has changed at once ; the career of degeneracy has begun, and has proceeded till it could advance no further; or some unforeseen calamity has occurred, which has obliterated for a time all memory of former improvements, and has condemned mankind to retrace, step by step, the same path by which their forefathers had risen to greatness. In a word, on such retrospective views of human affairs, man appears to be doomed, by the condition of his nature, to run alternately the career of improvement and of degeneracy ; and to realise the beautiful but melancholy fable of Sisyphus, by an eternal renovation of hope and of disappointment.'*

Such being the tendency of all national greatness, the nations of Western Africa must live in the hope, that in process of time their turn will come, when they will occupy a prominent position in the world's history, and when they will command a voice in the council of nations.

---

* Stewart's 'Elements of the Philosophy of the Human Mind,' Vol. i. chap. 4, § 8.

PART II.

AFRICAN NATIONALITY.

CHAPTER VII.

GENERAL OBSERVATIONS—SELF-GOVERNMENT OF THE GAMBIA.

WE come now to consider the most important subject of African nationality. The desire to give an impetus to this grand development seemed to have pervaded the minds of the members of the late African Committee of the House of Commons. Their third resolution lays it down plainly that the policy of the British Government henceforth in Africa, ' *should be to encourage in the natives the exercise of those qualities which may render it possible for us more and more to transfer to the natives the administration of all the Governments, with a view to our ultimate withdrawal from all, except probably Sierra Leone.*'* This indeed is a grand conception, which if developed into fact, will immortalize the name of Britain as the most generous and enlightened nation that has adorned the face of the globe. It is indeed a glorious idea to contemplate that

* Since placing the above in the hands of the printer, we have been gratified to find that the present Governor-in-Chief, in an address to an influential deputation which waited on him, emphatically declared that education would form an essential element in the government of the Coast. His Excellency remarked : "I am in a position to assure you that Her Majesty's Secretary of State for the Colonies, his Grace the Duke of Buckingham and Chandos, takes a most lively interest in the subject of education throughout the settlements of West Africa, and I am in hopes that ere long all reasonable facilities and encouragement will be afforded for the education of the people, which I regard as one of the *first duties of civilized government. Education*, like all else, is doubtless subject to abuse ; but is, *nevertheless, the broadest, truest, and safest road to honour and prosperity here, and happiness hereafter.*" The italics are ours.

the sun never sets in the vast dominions where the British flag flies, and that the name of England is always associated with liberty, justice, and humanity; but it will be still grander to contemplate that same powerful nation, setting on foot the nationality of a race down-trodden for ages, and giving to those whom she has nurtured and fostered in the principles of government, ' a chance of raising their character in the scale of the civilized world.'*

But we must consider some of the questions put by the late Parliamentary Committee and the reply of witnesses of great experience, before we can fully appreciate the above resolution:—

In the evidence of Sir Benj. Pine, now Governor of St. Kitts, formerly Acting-Governor of Sierra Leone, and Governor of the Gold Coast, we find the following questions and answers :—

Question. I think the sum of your views with regard to the Government of the West Coast of Africa is, that unless we can develop self-government for all the West Coast, we shall never arrive at anything better than establishing very hopeless little Crown Colonies?

Answer. Yes, that is my opinion.

Q. Mr. CHICHESTER FORTESCUE : What do you mean by developing self-government?

A. I mean gradually accustoming the people to manage their own affairs, so that within a given time, it might be half a century, and it might be a century, we should be free to a great extent, and they might then manage their own affairs.

Q, You mean the people directly subject to our Government?

A. The people directly subject to our Government.

Q. In what way would you propose to train them ?

A. I should begin by giving them municipal institutions, by making them drain their towns, and take care of their local affairs. In Sierra Leone they have practically no municipal institutions.

---

* The Committee felt bound to come to some such a decision, because in private as well as public, in the daily press and in written works, when the subject of West African Colonies is under consideration, we find the following questions in one form or other repeatedly asked—Why are we there ? Why not give it up ? It is no country for Europeans ? It is the worst climate in the world ? It is impossible for Europeans to civilize it ? A white man can't live there ? Give it up ! It is a mistaken philanthropy ! &c., &c., &c.

The charter of Sierra Leone provided for that, but it was never acted on.

Q. Lord STANLEY : You spoke of training the natives along the Coast to do without English assistance ; do you look forward to any time within a reasonable space at which you think we can leave them to themselves?

A. It is very hard to say what time, but I should say within half a century, if they go on making the progress that I have seen them make. I do not mean that they could be left entirely to themselves ; we might exercise control over them by sending some officer there.

Q. Do you think that that progress which you spoke of would continue if they were left to themselves ? Do you think that they would be capable of adapting European ideas and habits without the presence of Europeans amongst them to set the example ?

A. I think they would.

Q. But you look forward to a time, not very remote, when we should have made sufficient progress in extending civilization among the African tribes, to be able to leave them to themselves and abandon those settlements ?

A. I think so.

In the evidence of R. Pine, Esq., late Governor on the Gold Coast, we find the following :—

Q. Do you think that this Governorship by the English of certain forts on the Coast is a good system, or do you think we might enable the native chiefs equally well to govern the country by themselves ?

A. I think that the removal of all apparent protection by the British would have a bad effect.

Q. But yet you do not think that even in any process of time, we could enable the chiefs to govern themselves ?

A. Yes, I do think that we might, but not in my time. With one exception, I have not had a difference with one native king or chief in my time of two years and seven months.

In the evidence of Major Blackall, late Governor-General of the West African Colonies and Settlements, are the following :—

Q. But looking to the future, may I ask what your views are presuming that you look to the civilization of Africa, if you are not going to increase the settlements, is it not best to create governments in Africa which may themselves get rid of the slave trade?

A. No doubt that would be the most effectual way of doing it, but it is the cost that is in the way.

Q. It will not cost anything if you have got an African government which is half civilized or, to a certain extent, civilized. Would you consider that the right policy would be to take that and put it under an English governor, or to endeavour, as far as possible, to encourage and to foster a native government, with the assistance of an English consul?

A. If you want to spread English civilization, I would rather take it entirely under the English Government, than have that kind of half government of the natives tribes.

Q. Do you think that this is possible?

A. Not without great expense.

Q. Not of money merely, but of life?

A. It would be attended with loss of life, certainly.

Q. To some extent, civilization having spread, do you think that as much has been effected on the whole from the expenditure of life and money, as you could expect?

A. I was very much pleased to find so much done within the Colony of Sierra Leone itself, and I think I can perceive a very great improvement in the chiefs in the neighbourhood of Sherbro.

But the House of Commons Committee seems to have come to this determination from the great mortality amongst Europeans in the African Colonies. The yearly death-rate is so great, that it could not contemplate the continuance of such slaughter; in fact, tropical Africa must be left eventually for the Africans. In America, in the Polynesian Islands, and in New Zealand and Australia, where civilized nations have settled, the aboriginal inhabitants become quickly exterminated; they die off. They cannot become amalgamated either in social character or in civilized economy; the presence of the one is antagonistic to the presence of the other. The less powerful therefore recedes to a more quiet and undisturbed spot. Exposure, the want of proper food, perpetual fear of the stranger, and periodical outbursts against one another, operate immensely to increase the annihilating effect; until, in course of time, the prior existence in the country of the aboriginal inhabitants is known only as a matter of historical fact. But it is not, and cannot be, so in Africa with the African race. European nations have tried the exterminating effect on a grander and more general scale; they have bereft Africa of millions upon millions of its inhabitants by deportation. To obtain these they encouraged a suicidal exterminating warfare among the different chiefs, by which a tenfold number were destroyed. They employed for centuries the most crushing means to carry out their ends; and yet the race still stands and upholds its head. These means have done much to lessen the population, to degrade them among the nations, to increase the desire for the abominable slave-trade, and to have a most vilifying effect on their political and economical existence as nations; but they have not been and cannot be destroyed or exterminated.

A European race may exist for a short time in any part of Africa, but, ultimately, in tropical Africa, the reverse of what we find in Australia and New Zealand happens to them, and in the course of a very short space of time they die out, leaving their places to be filled up by new emigrants, who also within an incredibly short period share the same fate. Whilst the aboriginal inhabitants increase and multiply, the European race diminish and are ultimately annihilated; their offspring suffer seriously from birth to manhood from internal diseases, the result of miasmatic and climatic influences, and they must either be amalgamated with the white or black race, or they die out in about the second generation. In the tropical countries of Western Africa the idea of a permanent occupation by European settlers, if ever entertained, is impossible of realization; it is a mistake and a delusion. Again, we find that wherever the African race has been carried to, except, perhaps, the East Indies, they increase, no matter under what depressing and burdensome yoke they may suffer; from which it may be safely inferred that the African people is a permanent and enduring people; and the fancies of those who had determined their destruction will go in the same limbo as the now almost defunct American slavery. The English Government is conscious of this; and the House of Commons Committee has now set on foot by resolution (and we hope it will soon be by actual practice) that great principle of establishing independent African nationalities as independent as the present Liberian Government. But simple written resolutions without being carried into practice, are worse than waste paper, because they encourage hopes which may never be realized; and the absence of the necessary means to effect such realization destroys all confidence of belief in several separate nationalities. There is, however, every hope that the contemplated reform will be happily carried into effect. It will, therefore, be well to make a review of the different Colonies, and examine how far they are capable of upholding an independent separate nationality.

1. SELF-GOVERNMENT OF BRITISH GAMBIA.

British Gambia consists of the island of St. Mary, situated on the left bank and at the mouth of the river, on which is Bathurst, the capital of the settlement; beyond this is a large tract of land ceded by the King of Combo, known as British Combo, in which is Cape St. Mary, which latter had, prior to the cession, been obtained by purchase. On the right bank of the river a strip of land, one mile in width, extending from Boonyadoo Creek to Swarra Cundah Creek, beyond Albredah, became, in 1846, British territory by cession, and about 150 miles from the mouth of the river is M'Carthy's Island. These constitute the British possessions in the Gambia.

The principal native inhabitants of the British possessions are the Jollofs and the liberated Africans and their descendants; there are besides a few Serias, Jolahs, Mandingos, and Footah Foolahs. The JOLLOFS are a fine race of people, who originally came from Senegal and Goree and the countries between that and the Gambia, as well as from Goonjour, and are, therefore, intimately connected with families in these two places. The mulatto Jollof at one time had extensive influence in the colony, but it is now gradually decaying; they, or two families (viz., the Lloyd's and Hughes'), are owners of most of the large and substantial dwelling-houses in Bathurst. Among the Jollof nation under French rule, slavery had existed for a considerable time, and has only lately been abolished, and the lower class even in Bathurst still possess that air of serfdom which slavery always engenders. The females especially regard their masters and mistresses with great reverence and fear ; they are incapable, or rather unwilling, to help themselves, but look to them for support. The men and women congregate in one large yard, building small huts in connexion with those of their mistresses.

The young men are excellent traders. At the trading season in November and December, they receive a supply of goods from the European merchants at Bathurst, with which they go up the river. In June or July they return to make up their accounts, when they in most cases receive a large amount of commission. But they are great spendthrifts ; after a few days the whole of the amount is spent, principally on the fair sex, so that at present there is not one native Jollof man who can boast of a large substantial dwelling-house. With the exception of Goree and Senegal Jollofs, the Gambia Jollofs are the best ship carpenters on the whole coast; they build boats and vessels of more than fifty tons; they are good carpenters, and as mechanics they receive better pay than in any other part of the whole western coast. The finest and most elaborately-made country cloths are manufactured by the Jollofs of the Gambia and Senegal, but there is scarcely to be found a wealthy Jollof man of influence and power; they live on the fattest of the land, are very hospitable until the small amount they have accumulated is exhausted, and then they fall into debt. As a nation, the native Jollofs have made but very slight progress in civilization ; the Roman Catholic religion is professed by them, which has a still more depressing effect on an ignorant population. The female inhabitants, whilst aiding in the extravagance of the male, lend not an iota towards assisting in increasing the income. They dress most superbly in expensive native-made clothes, gold trinkets of the purest native manufacture adorn their bodies, and handkerchiefs of the finest French and English importation their heads. They are generally beautifully made and well proportioned ; and most of those met in the Gambia are not a pure race, but are an admixture of Footah Foolahs, Mandingoes, liberated Africans, and Europeans.

Dr. Madden, in his Report to the Committee of 1842, thus comments on the physical character of this tribe. He says : ' The pure, unmixed, and high-spirited Jollofs, who have not been long enough

in our settlements to have been demi-civilized and three-parts
demoralized by European vices, are the finest specimens of the negro
race that I have seen. They differ widely from the Kroomen in
their forms and features. They are far from muscular, and by no
means remarkable for their bodily vigour or robustness; but in that
air of natural nobility in deportment and the stateliness of their
carriage, the Jollofs so far surpass the other natives that strangers
are accustomed to look upon them as the gentlemen of Africa.'
They are warlike and generous in disposition, and, as artisans, are
remarkable for their ingenuity and manual dexterity. The mixture
of Jollof and Footah blood produces a race which, in many cases,
may be regarded as an absolute model of perfection; some of the
young girls, in point of form, appear so perfect that they would
satisfy even the fastidious taste of the classical sculptor—they are
round, firm, and charming.

The next important inhabitants are the liberated Africans. The
two principal tribes are the Yorubas or Akus, and the Egboes or
Eboes, the former in excess of the latter; in addition to these are
traders from Sierra Leone. In former years these people were
despised by the Jollof inhabitants of Bathurst. They had no voice in
their palavers and societies, but they were a people destined to rise.
They are not a spendthrift race; and whilst liberal to a certain
degree, they always manage to balance their income and expenditure
in such a manner as to leave a decided advantage in favour of the
former; and in course of time they aspire to and are now filling up
the positions which had been denied them. They are amongst the
foremost traders in the river Gambia, advancing to a considerable
distance in the interior. The spirit of parsimony exists among
them, and they accumulate wealth, and are now building large and
substantial houses. Some of them are very much respected; their
children are sent to educational establishments at Sierra Leone and
in England. Their female population are hard-working, and make
excellent traders; they also accumulate great wealth, although some
of them enter into reckless speculation. I shall enter more fully
into consideration of these tribes in another place. Some of the
Yorubas are Mohammedans, but the greater part are Christians;
most, if not all, the Eboes are Christians. When first located in

Bathurst they were considered indolent, lazy, and depraved, and Dr. Madden justly remarked that 'if we look to their emancipation alone for their improvement, and locate them where there are no schools for their instruction, no fit soil for their subsistence, and no steps taken for their civilization, we may expect to find them swarming our gaols or skulking about our market-places in idleness and want.' Years have now passed, and the leading merchants at Bathurst speak differently of the liberated African.

The Serias, or Sereres, and Jolahs, who are found in British Gambia, are unimportant races, as their numbers are so few that they occupy no important political position in the colony; the former are the labourers, who are employed for all menial occupations; they are always cheerful in their work, but require to be looked after. There is at present but a very small prospect of their ever rising in the social scale; their earnings are spent in drink, and on moonlight nights they are to be heard making the most fearful noise, at the top of their voices, disturbing the repose of the more quiet inhabitants. The Jolahs are a peculiarly quiet race; generally short, they have curly, flowing hair and well-shaped features, and are very peaceful; their principal occupation is in making palm-wine. They are remarkable for being exceedingly dirty in their habits; neither their bodies nor their clothes undergo that ablution which is necessary for health in the tropics.

MANDINGOES.—The tribe in the immediate neighbourhood of British Gambia is the Mandingo, a tall, athletic, warlike race of men, who are always carrying on war with one another; they are divided into two great classes—viz., *Marabouts* and *Soninkies*. The *Soninkies* are pagans, who do not believe in any religion; the Marabouts, however, are Mohammedans, or followers of the great false prophet. But the *Mandingo Marabouts* are not exclusively called Marabouts, as all Mohammedans receive the same appellation; thus there are Jollof Marabouts and Yorubah Marabouts. The *Soninkies* are strictly the non-Mohammedan portion of the Mandingoes.

The *Soninkies* (as I have described them in another place) were the original inhabitants of the land bordering on the river far into the interior, extending from the mouth to about 600 to 700 miles inland, and in times gone by they exercised so tyrannical a sway over the Marabout inhabitants as to cause a rebellion and a general rise for independence. They employ some of their time in agriculture ; but when compared with the other tribes they are lazy warlike, and troublesome, and are great drinkers of ardent spirits. They live in the commonest cane huts, with grass roofs. They cultivate a little land during the rains, and when the dry season is fully set in, their poor stock being soon exhausted, they remain in a half-starved state until the next season. Those along the sea-coast and the river, by coming in constant relation with civilized nations, become rather hard-working, and are prevented from carrying on those predatory wars which they otherwise make to provide themselves with the necessaries of life. Beyond the reach of European civilization they are excessively lazy, and in times past were in the habit of existing on the Mohammedan population. The females are industrious, clean, and handsome. The *Soninkies* worship the alligator, a piece of iron, large stones, and trees. The Soninkie government now exists in a part of Barra and Saloom (Sahloom) on the north side of the river Gambia where Fort Bullon is built.

The Marabout inhabitants on the river form the most important, influential, and powerful government in close proximity with the British territory. They are a warlike, daring, strategic, crafty, intriguing race, who through their late successes over their neighbours, the Soninkies, have become most impudent and overbearing. When not engaged in any warlike expedition they till the ground extensively, spin yarns, dye clothes with native manufactured indigo, plant large quantities of ground-nuts, Guinea and Indian corn, indigo, cotton, and sweet potato ; they tan leathers and dye them in various colours, afterwards work them into slippers, sandals, pouches, and bags, and into coverings for their charms and various other articles of native importance. They are the principal producers of the commercial wax which forms one of the exports of the river Gambia.

There is another tribe met with along the river who are very hard-working and harmless ; they are great agriculturists and excellent fishermen ; these are the Numinkas. Having examined the different races in and bordering on British Gambia, let

us now consider the practicability of forming a native self-supporting government, capable of existing for a reasonable length of time.

Bathurst is situated on a small piece of land surrounded by water
called St. Mary's Island, which is divided from the mainland,
British Combo, by a narrow channel called Oyster Creek; this creek
is of no great dimensions, and with a plentiful supply of canoes can
easily be crossed by a large number of men within a very short time.
The inhabitants number from eight to ten thousand, composed of
individuals of the different tribes already mentioned, who are not
bound together by any common interest, but, on the contrary, are
very much disunited. British Combo comprises, besides Combo, all
Sabbajee, the territory conquered from the Marabouts. In it are
scattered irregularly the following towns which are occupied by
British subjects—viz., Newcastle, Albert Town, Hamilton Town,
Jassewang, and Coto, besides a few other Mandingo villages.
These British towns are not really now worth the name of towns;
they are merely scattered villages, containing from a hundred to
two hundred inhabitants, the majority of them old and decrepit,
and entirely unfit to hold their ground against a Marabout force of
even one-fourth their number. The property and wealth of the
country is at Bathurst; the young and robust, as soon as they are
capable of distinguishing between *meum* and *tuum*, go off to Bathurst
for occupation.

Bordering on the interior boundary of British Combo are the
Marabouts of Goonjour, composed not only of the original inhabitants of the country, but also of the refugees from Sabbajee—the
Mohammedan population who were expelled after the defeat in the
second engagement under Governor, now Major-General, O'Corner,
and whose territory was confiscated to the British Government.
These people have a deadly hatred against their powerful usurpers;
they would not give up the ownership of the land, but still look
wistfully for the time when they may have an opportunity of reclaiming it. They are perpetually instigating their brethren of the same
faith in Goonjour against the powers that be, and these are ready at
any moment to pour their legions into British Combo. Thus, during
the late battle of Toobabcolong, where the British arms were
successful in a short, decisive, and, in these parts, unparallelled

engagement, the warriors at Goonjour were armed to the teeth, prepared to take advantage of any misfortune that might happen to the British force; they looked eagerly on the rich territory which had been ceded through necessity to the British Crown, and were determined, if the Marabouts of Neomy (Barra) had gained the victory, to advance to British Combo and make themselves masters of it before any assistance could be sent to that quarter; but through the dashing gallantry of Colonel D'Arcy, who led the attacking party, the handful of soldiers gained a complete victory over the Moslem inhabitants, and the would-be invaders were obliged to disarm quietly and send peaceful messages to the Governor, avowing continued friendship.

The other Territory of British Gambia is on the right bank of the river, and not in immediate connection with Bathurst; it is in the neighbourhood partly of Soninkie and partly of Marabout influences. With the Soninkies there is no fear of any disturbance, but with the Marabouts the case is different. There will always be contention between the Moslems and the Christians or Pagans. These Mohammedan inhabitants were at first the subjects of the Soninkie government. When few, they were content to make proselytes by peaceful means, and bow to the decision of existing authorities; but no sooner did they find themselves in great and sufficient numbers than they at once forcibly usurped political power, and began to propagate their religion by fire and sword. They have now completely crippled the Soninkie power, who are in awful fear of them; for, since 1862, they have destroyed numerous Soninkie towns and villages, made captives of many of their inhabitants, massacred a vast number, shaved the heads of the rest, and make them turn their faces to the east at sunrise and sunset in the attitude of prayer. This they did near to the boundary of the British Territory of Barra, on the right bank of the river, in the immediate neighbourhood of Fort Bullon, and would have stepped over it had not his Excellency Colonel D'Arcy, at the risk of his life, on the 24th June, 1863, burned the twelve stockades of the belligerents, securing peace and cultivation to a troubled country for three years. This portion of the territory is not only liable to the incursion of the Marabouts in its immediate vicinity, but has also been exposed to that of the most powerful Marabout chieftain in the River—viz., the late King of Badiboo, Mahba, who secretly aided and abetted all the movements of the Marabout chiefs from Cower to Barra, and who was a most treacherous, usurping, powerful, and dangerous neighbour.

The population of British Gambia is barely fifteen thousand souls ; the Marabouts around number several hundred thousands. The former, with very few exceptions, are weak and effeminate, composed of numerous tribes, who possess no common interest, and who are jealous of one another. If the inhabitants were to be left to govern themselves, there must be either a monarchical or a republican form of government instituted. The latter is unsuited to the taste and feelings of the people. A monarchical government must be chosen, and the king elected by universal suffrage. If once left to himself, without military support for a time, he would find his movements hampered by contending views; his territory, especially British Combo and British Barra, exposed to the inroads of his most powerful enemy. The Marabout chieftains would get sufficient information of all his internal arrangements, and would take the earliest opportunity of trying his strength. In a financial point of view, his revenue would be increased or diminished according to his capacity of affording protection to the merchants and traders. He would find nine-tenths of his population very ignorant and uneducated; that his kingdom lacked good educational seminaries; and that his greatest attention would require to be immediately devoted to political economy and social details. His registrar-general would report to him that the death-rate exceeds the birth by nearly a half; that depopulation to a vast extent is going on every year. On examining into the sanitary condition of his state, he would find it to be truly deplorable ; that there is a large and extensive marsh which stands out as a great barrier to the healthiness of his capital, and which will require a large amount of money to drain, altogether beyond the power of his exchequer to afford. The language of his kingdom is in Babelic confusion, being Jollof, Mandingo, Serere, Foolah, Jolah, and English ; and although four-fifths of the population do not understand English, he would have gradually to develop it among the mass, and make it the spoken and diplomatic

G

language. Having no military at his command, he would find his untrained volunteers unable to stand before the impetuous charge of the Marabouts.

The Marabouts, finding that the king was not powerful, and not supported by any European powers, would make an unprovoked attack on Combo and Sabbajee, and, before a sufficient force could be collected to oppose them, destroy the whole of the towns, and massacre and enslave the inhabitants. And even were the volunteers to meet them in a pitched battle, unless well supported by regular artillery, they would not be able to stand the impetuous attack and cavalry charge of the daring Marabouts; and a victory gained by them would be fatal to the commercial interests of the country. Bathurst will always be protected against any number of the Marabout force, who will find Oyster Creek a good barrier against their onward progress; as fifty volunteers, with good rifles and well officered, could resist the landing of two thousand Marabout warriors from the mainland.

On the right British Barra was always exposed to the attack of the most powerful Marabout chieftain in the River — viz., Mahba of Badiboo. It is only a few months ago that—hearing from Bathurst that the Parliamentary Committee had recommended that the Governors on the Coast were not to interfere with the native Government, and that they were on no account to go to war—Mahfal, the lieutenant of Mahba, who commanded in Marabout Barra or Neomy, became troublesome and overbearing, and afterwards made a desperate attack on British Barra, as will be seen from the following account :—

"A few years ago his Excellency Colonel D'Arcy placed Masambah Kokie in British Neomy or Barra, as a chief of that part of the country, to cultivate the ground and keep peace. At this time the Marabout influence had been growing very strong, and they seemed certain to become very troublesome. Masambah Kokie, being a Soninkie and a British subject, was more peaceful than the Marabout, and all the Foolah flocked about his town—Bantang Killing—with their bullocks, much to the annoyance of the Marabouts in these parts, who, a few months ago, made a night attack against them, and robbed them of all their cattle. Some remonstrances were made to the chief, but nothing decided was done.

They became more restless, and their chief, Mahfal, charged Masambah Kokie with having robbed them of their land, telling him that he was nothing but a stranger, and that the sooner he made his exit the better it would be for him. Masambah Kokie judiciously informed his Excellency the Administrator of what had taken place, and intimated that the attitude of the Marabouts was very warlike. Soon after this they made a desperate attack against his stockade, but he met them resolutely, and after a severe contest they retired, after destroying all his provision and the houses outside the stockade. They taunted him about the confidence he had in the British Government, and told him that they would give him a good thrashing without anything being done to them. The Administrator, on hearing of the fight, went up to Albreda in H.M.S. Mullet, and made himself well acquainted with the state of affairs. Masambah Kokie informed him of the ideas of the Marabouts, and told him that unless he was supported he must either remove to Combo or succumb to the Marabouts. These latter behaved most insolently and insultingly to the Governor, actually defied him to his face, and told him in plain language that they were ready to fight him; and told the Soninkies that the Governor was always peaceful, and that he was afraid to go to war with them. This led to the battle of Toobabcolong, already referred to. If the Marabouts show such determined resistance against a regular force, led by an experienced English officer, how much will they care for an undisciplined volunteer force, without an experienced officer? '

M'Carthy's Island, being the *entrepôt* of the trade in the upper portion of the River Gambia, where the best quality of ground-nuts is obtained, could not be relinquished. It is surrounded by a natural stockade, impassable by the Marabouts—namely, the river; and a handful of troops and a few good field-pieces, with proper management, would be able to prevent any crossing of a hostile force. The inhabitants are ready and willing to defend themselves against their enemy; and although the unhealthiness of the place has led to unparalleled yearly depopulation, yet still those who remain are willing to aid in maintaining it against any attack of the Marabouts; and this is evident from the resolution passed by the people, who were represented by the merchants and principal inhabitants in a council (holden a day after the island was totally abandoned by the British troops) called together by the Commandant. The following were the members present, and the resolutions passed (vide *African Times*, July 23, 1866):—

'President, J. Africanus B. Horton, M.D., Provisional Civil and Military Commandant; Members: James Gray Savage, J.P., Edward Dusseault, John Melbury, John D. Attride, James Dodgin, Joseph I. Owens, George Randell, James Bell, and George Robert.

' The President explained that his intention in calling them together was to deliberate on the best means they should adopt in protecting themselves against any outbreak among their warlike neighbours, as all the soldiers had now been removed, and the island left in a very defenceless state; that any measure now adopted would be only provisional until the Manager who has been appointed takes over the command of the place.

' Resolution 1.—Moved by Mr. John Melbury, seconded by Mr. Jas. Dodgin, and agreed to, " That twelve men be enlisted as volunteers, and kept up until such time as the newly-appointed Manager with his police force should arrive. That the men be armed, and employed in all cases of emergency."

' Resolution 2.—Moved by Mr. James Gray Savage, seconded by Mr. Edward Dusseault, and agreed to, " That of the twelve men, nine should be habited within the barracks, and three enrolled as constables; and that the privates be allowed one shilling and sixpence per diem each for pay and subsistence; the corporal, two shillings; and the sergeant, two shillings and sixpence."

' Resolution 3.—Moved by Dr. Horton, seconded by Mr. John D. Attride, and agreed to, " That special constables be enrolled out of the respectable portion of the inhabitants, and that the subjoined oaths be taken by each."

' Resolution 4.—Moved by Dr. Horton, seconded by Mr. James G. Savage, and agreed to, " That the following gentlemen be sworn in as special constables: Mr. Edward Dusseault, Mr. John Melbury, Mr. J. D. Attride, Mr. James Dodgin, Mr. James Bell, Mr. George Randell, Mr. George Roberts, Mr. Joseph L. Owens, and Mr. Lomanee Fatee."

'Resolution 5.—Moved by Mr. George Randell, seconded by Mr. Joseph L. Owens, and agreed to, " That a notice be given to the inhabitants of the island that after eight o'clock in the evening no tom-toming, firing of arms, or any noise will be allowed without special permission."

'Resolution 6.—Moved by Mr. Edward Dusseault, seconded by Mr. Joseph L. Owens, and agreed to, " That the special constables be furnished with arms and ammunition, to be used only in cases of emergency, and that they be made responsible for them."

'Resolution 7.—Moved by Mr. John Melbury, seconded by Mr. George Roberts, and agreed to, " That the owners of canoes be particularly requested to have their canoes on this side of the river after six o'clock in the evening, and placed under lock and key ; that, after the proposed hour, should any of the canoes be seen on the other side, the Sergeant of Police should give notice to the owners, and should it not be immediately brought over, he should be deprived of its use for three days, or pay a fine of 2s. 6d.

'Resolution 8.—Moved by Mr. George Randell, seconded by Mr. James Bell, and agreed to, " That the head men at Fatoto and Burabah Cundah be instructed not to cross over after six o'clock in the evening more than six men from the mainland to the island."

'Resolution 9.—Moved by Mr. James G. Savage, seconded by Mr. Edward Dusseault, and unanimously agreed to, " That the inhabitants of the island be called upon by voluntary subscription to support the volunteer force, and that the mercantile community undertake to guarantee the payment of their cost, according to the following daily rate: Messrs. Forster and Smith, 5s.; Thomas Brown and Co., 5s.; W. H. Goddard, Esq., 3s.; T. F. Quin, Esq., 2s. 6d.; Mr. John Melbury, 1s. 6d.; Mr. James Dodgin, 1s. 6d.; Mrs. Price, 1s. 6d."

'*Oath administered to each Special Constable:* No. 1. I swear that I will be faithful and bear true allegiance to Her Majesty Queen Victoria, so help me God.

'No. 2. I swear that I will well and faithfully serve our Sovereign Lady the Queen provisionally in the capacity of a special constable in the Settlement of M'Carthy's Island; and that I will not conceal any apparent danger, damage, or harm which may likely or possibly arise, without giving, or causing to be given, speedy notice thereof; and that I will truly, faithfully, and disinterestedly endeavour to use calm and peaceable means to quell any and every disturbance that may arise in any part of the said island, or give immediate notice to the Sergeant of Police, or to any of Her Majesty's Justices of the Peace. So help me God." '

This is an excellent manifestation of a spirit of self-government, *esprit de corps*, and of mutual support against a common enemy—a spirit which, if always encouraged, would lead to most happy results. The whole of the inhabitants went cheerfully and heartily to work in carrying out these resolutions; there was not the least trouble experienced in enlisting the volunteers, and every one threw in his mite towards their support.

From the foregoing it is evident that in the present condition of the Settlement of the Gambia it cannot be left to govern itself. An esteemed Governor remarked, after reading the third resolution of the Parliamentary Committee, that it will take a hundred years before Gambia will be capable of self-government; but I say that if the present system of governing the people be persisted in, it will take more than two hundred years; while if radical reform be made, and if the people be properly trained, it will take less than a quarter of a century to bring the country into such a state of improvement as might enable it to be left with safety in the hands of an enlightened native king, chosen by universal suffrage. How this can be attained, and what are the essential improvements which should commence this new era of West African history, I shall enter upon fully when considering the requirements of British Gambia; and show how by judicious management the native Government can be made strong enough to oppose all the attacks of its Mandingo neighbours, and to insure esteem and admiration throughout the whole of the Mohammedan districts of the Gambia.

CHAPTER VIII.

SELF-GOVERNMENT OF SIERRA LEONE—KINGDOM OF SIERRA LEONE.

' High on a rock, in solitary state,
Sublimely musing, pale Britannia sate ;
Her awful forehead on her spear reclined,
Her robe and tresses streaming with the wind ;
Chill through her frame foreboding tremors crept !
The mother thought upon her sons and wept.

   .   .   .   .   .

' Shame flush'd her noble cheek, her bosom burn'd,
To helpless, hopeless Africa she turn'd ;
She saw her sister in the mourner's face,
And rush'd with tears into her dark embrace.
"Oh hail," exclaim'd the empress of the sea,
"Thy chains are broken—Africa, be free !"'

Thus wrote Montgomery. Africa, through Britannic influence, is free from foreign slavery, and through that same influence has made, and hopes still to make, important progressive improvements in her history. There are several peculiarities characteristic of the physical geography of Sierra Leone, which will enable her to sustain a good and powerful self-government, not threatened by any native tribe of consequence in its neighbourhood, and not easily by any European or foreign nations. Sierra Leone possesses a safe haven where distressed vessels can put in and refit, and the entrance of its harbour is through a narrow channel completely covered by several important elevations and hills. In her claim for independence she ranks with Liberia, her immediate neighbour, having a strong, vigorous, and persevering population, who speak one language. Education of the masses has been going on to a very encouraging extent, and missionary efforts have had most salutary and beneficial results on the population who are holding their ground in various self-supporting systems.

Sierra Leone is, to a certain degree, the best place on the Coast

that the British Government (to carry out their laudable intentions
for Africa) could give up to self-government with hope, of success,
and a due appreciation of the advantages granted thereby. It has a
better and more increasing revenue than any other part of the Coast;
in it are congregated all the blood and sinews of the various tribes
in every part of the Coast; and, according to Kecelle's polyglot
calculation, there are more than a hundred different tribes among
its inhabitants, the principal, both in numbers and influence, being
the Akus and Egboes. In the Blue-book of 1852, Governor
Kennedy, in his report, states that 'the direct monthly communication with England and the whole of the West Coast of Africa, by
means of Her Majesty's mail contract steamers, has already established a new era in the political, social, and commercial condition
of the Colony. Many of the native population and liberated
Africans are doing profitable and safe business, and competing successfully with the European merchants and traders. The improved
habits, the increased comforts, and investment of capital by the
native population, are all highly indicative of prosperity and progress. The absence of serious crime is also very remarkable. In
no part of the world have I seen the Sabbath-day observed with
more decency and decorum. Crime is repressed and order maintained in Freetown (containing a population of 16,000 persons) by
one police magistrate, one police superintendent, and seventy-five
policemen. This latter fact speaks more for the orderly habits and
disposition of the people than any comment I could offer. Encouragement and, above all, good example are all the people require
to enable them to fulfil the high intentions with which this Colony
was established.'

I shall in another place speak more particularly of the characters
and habits of the various tribes in the colony, but in passing I may
here remark that, as a body, the influence exercised by the aged of
the most numerous tribe, produces a most depressing and decrepit
effect on the rising generation of that race. They possess a secret,
freemasonlike influence which checks any exuberance of spirit and of
enterprise in their young, and thus produces an injurious result on the
race. Not independent of such influences, they feel afraid of coming
out openly, fearing a check from some superior influence. If they

enter into speculation on an extensive scale so as to outstrip the aged of the same class; if they follow the bent of their inclination and employ their money in the purchasing of large buildings and extensive estates, they receive a warning voice from some suspicious quarter. This influence is certainly dying away, but much still remains which tells against the body politic of the nation. The next important tribe has offspring who are independent, rather impertinent, and possess but very little of that graceful respect which is due to their superiors in age, influence, &c.; they would take up an unmeaning phrase as insulting, and would make much ado about nothing; and, consequently, there are always disunion and private piques amongst them. But the inhabitants of the Colony have been gradually blending into one race, and a *national* spirit is being developed. The language of the self-government when formed must of necessity be English, and all official and private business must be done in it. It comes readily to all those born in the Colony. There will be no spirit of a native language counteracting, modifying, and balancing it, because it is now the universal language of the Colony.

When Liberia was given up to self-government, the progress previously made as regards the working of state government, was not at all to be compared with what now exists at Sierra Leone; yet still we find that the Liberians have maintained their own ground, have extended their dominions, and are making every year great and rapid progress. Might we not hope that if the latter country were to be placed under somewhat similar circumstances a material progressive advance would take place, which would ultimately lead to a greater consolidation of power, aided and assisted by the fostering mother government?

Of the government of Sierra Leone, the most important town is the city of Freetown, situated at the foot of the hills which run in an easterly direction, of which Leicester Mountain is the highest. It contains a population of more more than twenty thousand inhabitants, which is yearly increasing. The wealth of the Colony is in Freetown; in it are the best educational establishments, the centre of the various missionary establishments, and the seat of government. It possesses many large substantial buildings and a thriving commercial prospect. It extends from Granville Brook to Congo Town Bridge, a distance of nearly two and a-half miles. There is no fertile land about its neighbourhood, so that the people depend on the other parts of the Colony for articles of food, although a small quantity of the garden and surrounding arid land is cultivated. The harbour can receive vessels of any tonnage, being very deep; and from the circumstance of its entrance being completely commanded by hills and elevated lands, it can be easily protected from hostile inroads by good artillery properly arranged and manned. At King Tom there is a dilapidated battery, which, if it were in good condition, would have a telling effect on an enemy's vessels approaching the harbour. But Cape Sierra Leone and Signal Hill are spots where good substantial batteries or fortifications ought to be without delay erected, as they would there completely check the progress of a hostile fleet. In the centre of the town, on a small promontory, is the lower battery, which commands the east side of the river. Freetown, therefore, as a safe haven and as a capital, is well chosen, and would form a nucleus of a very extensive power over the countries north and south of it. The increase of population, the wealth and strength of the city, will ever form a great barrier to its being threatened by the surrounding native tribes, who, I am certain, would never harbour the remotest idea of attacking it.

But we must divide Sierra Leone into several districts, and consider each separately. The districts are the *Mountain, River,* and *Sea.*

Mountain District. — The Mountain District comprises the following towns : Leicester, Gloster, Regent, Wilberforce, Bathurst, and Charlotte. The country, in its present state, is unsuited to the growth of any commercial articles. The heavy rains robbing the soil of its manure leave it gravelly and without strength, and difficult to work ; the inhabitants are therefore principally poor. The only exportable article which formerly was cultivated to a large extent was arrowroot, but the reduction of the marketable value has greatly discouraged the planters. The people are, however, not lazy; they supply Freetown with fruits and vegetables of every kind and other dietetic articles. Sugar-cane and coffee are planted in small quantities. Depopulation is going on in this district to a fearful extent, for the young and robust and healthy seek for employment in the capital, where they ultimately remain. The population grow old, and although some are stricken with extreme poverty, yet still we find them live to a very good age; they do not die off as rapidly as the inhabitants of the lowland. The people are most peaceful. Slight litigation may occasionally exist amongst them, but that is all. This fact is attested by their having no resident magistrate in any of the towns ; one police-constable in each is sufficient to repress all disturbance. They know and care very little for politics. All their children are sent to schools and educated, so that nearly the whole of the present generation can read.

River District.—The River District contains the following towns: Kissy, Wellington, Hastings, and Waterloo ; besides a few small villages, such as Allen Town, Grafts Town, Bengeuma, and Prince Albert Town. Next to Freetown the River District is the most flourishing and well populated. Kissy, by its near approach to the capital and by a peculiar pride of the growing inhabitants for it, is more populated, and is the first in the district. The people are not as simple as those in the mountains; they are in close proximity with the neighbouring tribes, and, consequently, trade largely with them; they are richer and more influential. Most of their children are educated, but education is not so general as in the Mountain District. This district supplies Freetown with some of the most staple articles of food. The people are industrious, and make good agriculturists. They are the principal producers of commercial ginger, which they bring to the market partially clean and exchange for cash or goods. Those in close proximity to the city are more litigious than the others, but they have never taken up arms against each other, except in the infant state of the Colony several years ago, when some tribal difference happened ; but to the Government they have always been submissive. As a general rule, all over the Colony the inhabitants do not keep firearms, differing thus from all other parts of the Coast. At Waterloo and Hastings the people are principally farmers ; they are very quiet, tolerably educated, hardy men, who love their homes. They bring the produce of their labour twice a-week to Freetown, where it is readily sold. The ground is flat, and contains rich alluvium. The young population in the towns nearest Freetown take some interest in politics. One or two magistrates are always stationed in this district, who wield very extensive power. The towns contain a few good and large houses, but frame and quarter-frame buildings prevail. Albert Town is in the lately-acquired territory in Quiah, which is open to and continuous with the territories of the neighbouring tribes.

Sea District.—This is the third district, and comprises Kent, York, and Banana Island. In former years these towns were tolerably large, and contained a good population, but they are rapidly decreasing. There is, to my knowledge, no export whatever from this district. The inhabitants are poor—*i.e.*, they do not possess money in abundance, but they have large tracts of land at their disposal, and are well supplied with the necessaries of life. The palm trees give them abundant supplies of wine, which is sold at a trifling price; when kept for a short time it becomes alcoholic and intoxicating. These people are, as it were, separated from the body politic of the Colony by the high mountains which run through it. They are most of them fishermen, and after drying their fish they send them up to the market of the capital. A resident magistrate is always amongst them, which is necessary, because of the distance from head-quarters. The people do not care at all about politics; they are very simple in their habits, even more than those in the Mountain District; and will bend to whatever form of government is given them, but they love their Queen and reverence her representative.

We must now consider the character of the tribes in the immediate neighbourhood of Sierra Leone, and those countries which are dependent on, and form part of the Colony and its dependencies.

1. *Timneh Tribe.*—These are the nearest neighbours of the Peninsula of Sierra Leone, and to them formerly it belonged. They are somewhat an industrious race, cultivating large tracts of swampy lands with rice, with which they supply the Colony. They are by no means speculative, and their country is overrun by the people of the peninsula, who trade with them to a limited extent, in European goods in exchange for rice, ground-nut, Kola, timber, and beni-seed.

When they land at Freetown they seem to be great cowards ; a little boy ten years of age would frighten and drive away ten men. Here they are peaceful, quiet, dirty in their dress and person, and walk about in Indian file. They are terribly frightened at the people of the Colony within the Colony ; but as soon as they leave it they become cruel and domineering. If they are maltreated by any of the creoles whilst in the Colony, they endure it with patience and take it in good part ; but should he be caught in Timneh land he receives a tenfold reward. He is tied to a tree, receives a good castigation, and is then exposed to great indignities ; and if he has no means at his command to effect his escape, his life in many cases will be in danger. Whilst in their country they are very treacherous, and for the least provocation they would fall on the stores of the trader and pillage them of every article. They are excessively cruel in their treatment to one another. For a most trivial offence a master would tie up his slave and place faggots about him and set them on fire. In war they are great cowards, but extremely cruel ; they almost always employ mercenary soldiers from the Sousou and Korsor tribes. Christianity makes but very little progress among them ; they are hardy and incapable of an advancing, civilizing progression. Their females are, in many cases, handsome, clean, and industrious ; their offspring with Europeans are intelligent and hard-working. The language is Timneh, which is sweet and sonorous, and very few of the people understand, or can speak, English.

2. *Sousou and Korsor Tribes.*—The Sousou and Korsor are allied nations to the Timnehs, but they are very warlike and troublesome; and most of the disturbances which have, from time to time, convulsed the Rivers of Sierra Leone, are, more or less, to be attributed to these tribes. In war their stratagem consists in taking their enemies by surprise. They would not face well-disciplined troops in a pitched battle; but, feeling their weakness, they invariably lie in ambush, and fall upon the troops as they are passing through some narrow path. There are very tall, fine-looking, noble men among them. Domestic slavery prevails to a fearful extent. Attempts at civilizing them have hitherto failed, so that the saying has become proverbial, 'Teach a Korsor man howsoever you like, he

will ultimately return to the bush.' As a race they are very intelligent, apt, and quick to learn, but they are equally as quick to lose the benefit of it. In their social state, they are simple, clean, but very litigious, and hire out themselves to go to war for plunder. They are Pagans. The men are very deceitful, especially to traders. The females are chaste, and the traders are particularly cautious in their dealings with them. As soon as a trader enters a town he is offered a female attendant or a wife. If he accepts her, he pays the parents or guardian a trifling dowry, but if not, he is bound to keep himself continent; for any trespass on his part would lead to the confiscation of nearly all the goods in his store, or a payment of a heavy fine. In some cases snares are set to decoy a trader, by any one who is hard up. If he is in need of tobacco, pipe, rum, or cotton goods, he sends his choice wife to importune the foreigner for that article. If, in pity, he makes her a present of a pipe, a leaf of tobacco, or any other trifle, the husband presently brings up a large box and demands to have it filled with the same article. Should this be refused, a large 'palaver' is brought against him; his store broken open, and his goods stolen, or he is brought before the king, and his trade stopped until he pays a heavy fine. The law of the country strictly forbids any man making presents to another man's wife.

But the Korsors and Sousous are not in the immediate neighbourbourhood of Sierra Leone. They are separated from it by Timneh land, and are placed to the north of the Colony, and opposite Matacong and Is' de Los. They are in close proximity with the Mandingo tribe, and a great many of them are Mohammedans. We have fought against them in the Scarcies and Malagea with varied results; and also in combination with the Timnehs, in the late Quiah War.

But, besides the Timnehs of Sierra Leone, our territory extends, or more properly we own land in Sherbro, which was ceded a few years ago, and in Bulama. The former place is in close proximity with Sierra Leone and can be easily communicated with. The Sherbroes or Shabras are very much like the Timnehs in character, but they are cleaner, braver, and less cruel; progression among them is not very rapid, although they are very acute in some things.

The Sherbroes or Shabras are lighter in colour, and in physique not to be compared with the Sousous. Guerilla warfare is practised by them, but they are, on the whole, peaceful. They trade extensively with European merchants ; make good, large, and heavy country cloth; and are, in fact, a very intelligent race of people. Very few amongst them speak the English—the Sherbro language being chiefly spoken. Bulama is a small island, which is peopled principally by a race of men called Manjagoes, or black Portuguese. The Portuguese still claim the island, but they had no fixed government in it. The men are of middle size, small build, and are very good seamen. They hire themselves to work the small craft belonging to the merchants in the River Gambia, and when they have saved a small sum (independent for a time ! !) they return to their native land and remain idle, after buying a slave or a wife. But Bulama is now extensively peopled by the inhabitants of Sierra Leone, so that there will soon be an intelligent population in it.

We come now to the consideration of the practicability or impracticability of forming a substantial, intelligent government ; and how far it is likely to succeed.

As we have noticed, Sierra Leone is a peninsula, having a population of more than fifty thousand persons ; that the people are almost all educated, especially the creoles of the country ; that it is well protected against any native inroads ; that there are no strong native governments in its immediate neighbourhood capable of giving trouble or great disturbance; that the inhabitants in the city are very commercial, and endeavour to amass wealth, and their wives lend them great assistance in mercantile pursuits ; that the city alone contains more than twenty thousand inhabitants, and its influence is great in the interior, where the extension of commerce and the intercourse of the inhabitants with the educated of the Colony are gradually producing civilization.

The population in the Sea and Mountain Districts are rural in their habits and ideas, and unopposed to any liberal form of government that may be offered them ; they are generally poor ; the government has offered no encouragement for developing commercial articles of mountain growth ; and there being no government agricultural inspector to increase the natural agricultural plant, there is no advance in that direction. From the Mountain and Sea Districts come no article of export at present; but the children of the poorest can read or write. In the River District the people are comparatively advanced—they are good agriculturalists, their soil is excellent, and they are the principal producers of the commercial ginger, and supply the market of Freetown with provisions. They trade extensively with the neighbouring tribes, exchanging European or American imported articles for native produce, which they bring down to the city and exchange for goods and cloth.

The only exposed part of the Colony is the newly-acquired territory of Quiah, with Prince Alfred Town as its chief place. It is in the mainland, exposed to the inroads of its former inhabitants, but it is a garrison town, and the Timneh and Sousou warriors are by no means so desperate as the Marabout Mandingoes of the River Gambia; they received such severe handling during the late war that they would not easily jeopardize the rest of the territory by attempting a war. The rest of the Colony is surrounded by water, and although the Timnehs and Sousous are well supplied with large war canoes, yet still they will not attempt a hostile landing, as they are well aware what kind of reception they will meet with.

Sherbro is being peopled by colonists from Sierra Leone, as is Bulama. The inhabitants speak a distinct language from the Timnehs, and are very peaceful. They may, if they see any weakness, attempt to wage war against the inhabitants of the island; but by good government this can be easily avoided. The natives are good agriculturalists, and Mr. M. P. Horton, a native of Sierra Leone, is endeavouring to teach them, by example, the mode of tilling the ground, and the best means of bringing the produce to market. In Bulama the Portuguese influence might ultimately lead to complications, but the population are quiet and contented.

The language of the British possessions is English, which is universally spoken in the Colony; but the language of the surrounding tribes, on whom we depend for commercial produce, is various and distinct; thus we have, the Timneh, Mandingo, Sousou, Korsor, Sherbro, and then at Bulama, the Manjagoe. The population in the British Territory will be found not less than sixty or seventy thousand inhabitants, scattered in isolated spots from lat. 7° N. to lat.

12° N. These spots are principally islands or peninsulas, which, to
a certain extent, are separated from those influences which always
disturb the mainland. But as it is proposed to teach the people
self-government, to the ultimate withdrawal of British influence or
power, and to leave the natives to govern themselves, there must be
chosen either a monarchical or a republican form of government.
As in the Gambia a republic is unsuited to the taste of the people,
so it is at Sierra Leone. It will never have among the native inhabitants, who have always looked up to their king, the same influence and effect. A national government should be selected, which
should be made so powerful and influential as to create an interest
in its support, extensive and strong enough to counterbalance all
other influences. A monarchical government, then, will be the only
form, and the king should be elected by universal suffrage, supported for some time by the British Government ; he should for a
short period be initiated into the art of governing, by serving the
subordinate position of a governor over the Colony and its Dependencies, whilst the English Governor should act as Governor-
General of all the Coast.

His first policy should be to show himself to be on the popular
side, identifying himself with the growth of the people's liberties, by
which means he will secure an under basis of popular affection,
which will be an important auxiliary in his infant kingdom, where,
at the commencement, conflicting views and opinions are possible.
He should make merit the great high road to public trusts, honours,
and rewards, thus proving to every one that he measures the intellectual worth and dignity of a man, not by the truths which he possesses, or fancies he possesses, but by the sincere and honest pains
which he takes to discover them.   He should be a native-born Sierra
Leonist or a citizen by constitutional adoption.   On his accession
he will find that his treasury is not impoverished, that his people are
intelligent, industrious, and willing to give him every assistance in
establishing and completing the national edifice.   He will have a
population comparatively well advanced and progressing in civilization, who, by the zealous efforts of the missionary societies, have
nearly one-fifth of the whole of the inhabitants at school, which is an
unusually large proportion in any country. By the census of 1860 the

' percentage of the population under education was 22, whereas in Prussia the percentage was 16, and in England 13;' and the effect is manifested in the intellectual, moral, and religious improvements visible in the country.   The schools are supported in some measure by fees and endowments obtained by the exertions of the people. They are good and useful establishments, but open to great improvement.   In Sierra Leone there is a good grammar school, where Latin, Greek, mathematics, and other branches of English education are taught by a native clergyman, which bears most profitable fruit, and is fully self-supporting.   Besides this there is a large Theological College, where the higher branches are taught, under the Church Missionary Society, and which the king could do no better than convert into a university.

One of his principal objects should be to annex the neighbouring territory as an integral part of his kingdom, and to endeavour to give protection and support to the merchants trading in it; this will in every way improve his growing revenue, which it should be his utmost endeavour to increase ; as a good and healthy revenue is indispensable for the support of his authority.   The effect of Sierra Leone in improving the capabilities of the countries in its neighbourhood may be estimated from the report on the subject by a merchant of that Colony, published in the Blue Book of 1856. ' Let any one who knew the Mellicourie and other rivers in our vicinity twenty years ago, visit them to-day, and then let him testify to the almost miraculous change that has taken place in the manners and habits of the people, in their intelligence—in short, in their entire *physique* and *morale ;* this change dates entirely from the time the culture of the ground-nut was introduced among them. Material causes produce the same effect on the African in his country as on the Englishman in his ; the only difference will be in the rapidity with which effect will follow the cause; the change is slower with the savage, but not less certain.

' The natives are, moreover, physically and mentally, inferior to the tribes south of Cape Palmas ; but in spite of all this, the trade has become what it is in the short space of four years. Now, I have a right from this to assume that its growth will be still more rapid amongst those so much more favourably situated. If we wanted additional evidence of this, we have only to look at the marvellous progress of our palm oil trade. It scarcely dates so far back as the present century. In 1808 the quantity imported into England was only 200 tons, in 1851 it had reached to 50,000 tons; and it is only during the last five years of that period that the steamship has come to the aid of the African commerce. . . . No quarter of the world affords such natural facilities for such a trade. The whole country is a network of natural canalization; it commences at Cape St. Paul and extends to the Bonny, running parallel to the coast in its whole length, and extending hundreds of miles into the interior in every direction.'

A constitutional form of government must form the basis of his administration, consisting of a House of Assembly which should be composed of men elected by the people, as it will be difficult for his Government to stand without popular confidence, and the only means by which that can be secured is by giving the people the power of election of one branch of the Legislature; they will be required to direct their attention to the internal government of the State, to sanction the amount of duty to be levied on foreign importation, and regulate the trade with foreign nations, and the imposition of stamp, postal, and other duties. Each member should possess landed property, be over the age of twenty-two, and be properly educated. Besides the House of Assembly, there should be the senate, consisting of men above the age of thirty-five years, and having extensive means, and who may be recognised by all as possessing good practical common sense. The senator should be chosen by the king-elect, and should retain office so long as his character is unimpeachable, either for life or a period not less than ten years, and then be eligible for re-election.

Gold and silver should be made the legal tender for the payment of debts; English money be recognised for a period as the State coin, until such a time as the country will be able to establish a mint. The object of the king-elect should be to discover all those salutary measures which are necessary for the government of his people, and counteract those noxious influences which may sap the healthy progress of the community. He should make himself perfectly acquainted with the internal affairs of each colony, its revenue and expenses, its commerce and agriculture, and with the national character of the inhabitants of each section of the Government; he should endeavour to form a correct judgment of the character of each prominent official in his Government, so that he might be able to select fit instruments for difficult appointments. He should establish good schools in every part of his kingdom, especially in those parts where there are no schools and where the native language is prevalent, and make it compulsory for even a child under the age of fourteen to attend; by this means English, which will be the fundamental language, will be generally taught, and the future generation become well acquainted with it.

The progress and advance of the inhabitants in this kingdom, as attested in the Blue Book report of Colonel Stephen John Hill, C.B., late Governor of the Colony, will prove their capacity for progressive enlightenment and improvement. 'Reflect,' says he, ' on the history of Sierra Leone, and considering the difficulties arising from the peculiarities of its climate, its geological structure, and the habits of its various native tribes, its progress steadily obtaining the philanthropic results intended for it, not only testifies to the benefits following the free exercise of British rule, but encourages also the development of greater efforts for its welfare. For that which has been already attained yields the promise that advantages will accrue to this colony in a ratio such as to excel that even of its past career.

' This seems evident from five principal sources, viz :—

' 1. The stimulus to native improvement and enterprise already abundantly elicited through British protection.

' 2. Commodious anchorage and facilities for river traffic.

' 3. The access of civilized nations competing in commercial activity.

' 4. The abundance of its exportable productions.

' 5. The effective system of its colonial administration.

' It is a proof of civilization, in no small degree established, when a census can be taken of the existing population of this colony, such as I have the honour now to exhibit, for thus it becomes manifest that the inducements to seek a settled habitation have been successful; that the interests of the people, no longer to be considered transient, have been adequately provided for, whether in the encouragement afforded to them by commerce, trade, or manufacture, or the restraints of just, and therefore useful, government.

'This is the more striking when the various elements of the population are considered. Accustomed to separation as factious and jealous tribes, now they seek whatever may be deemed advantageous in combination as a community, acknowledging the shelter of our protecting power, rapidly learning the general customs of civilized society, engaging in commercial transactions with surprising intelligence and avidity, and submitting to the various necessary imposts on the one hand, while on the other gladly reaping the benefits of enlarged communications, and in many instances amassing wealth, enabling them to vie with European enterprise. I would further remark, that in obtaining a criterion of comparing one period of this colony's history with another, and thereby testing its condition, it must be borne in mind that from one of its distinguishing characteristics— the suppression of slavery, and offering a refuge to the liberated African—a retarding element continually infuses itself into the means conducive to advancement. For the civil power the task is to give transition from the degraded habits of barbarism to those of civilization, enlightening and elevating from the fear of the oppressor and dislike of superior power, to respect for just laws and confidence in a Government that has to subdue and regulate while it protects; for the religious teacher, it is to surmount the difficulties of dialects unknown ere he imparts instruction, to overcome deeprooted prejudices, and to convince of idolatry, from which it is nothing less than regeneration to desist; and for the social community, which receives the oft-recurring influx of emancipated slaves, it is to show a sympathy which seems to be retrospective, with but little corresponding impetus to progression; or to regard them as an inferior caste, as those worthy only to render them servitude, forgetful of their own similar origin, their once helpless dependence, and the source of that partial progress which has made them to differ.

'I state these as obstacles to progress, but not insuperable. They only urge to renewed exertion, whether in the adoption of means to meet every such emergency or vigilance to secure the efficiency of those already in operation. It is clear that the mind and disposition of the African race can be cultivated, that the result of patient, determined, and intelligent procedure has been and will be successful; but it is not less certain that if the ends of British rule are to be fulfilled, there must be no relaxation of effort, no diminution of means, because the change of this race is from ruthless oppression to an entire dependence on a liberating power; and if by reason of its fostering care and wise encouragement, however expensive, extraordinary instances of talented enterprise and accumulated wealth have occurred, it will, I trust, appear evident that both for the maintenance of the Colonial Government and the valid realization of its great and indispensable objects, the statistics I have the honour of now submitting should be considered proofs of what is absolutely requisite for the proper management of the population of this Colony. This being secured, I can foresee general progress in morality and integrity, social welfare, and, as a worthy result, grateful acknowledgment of British administration.'

From the foregoing it is evident that there is growing at Sierra Leone an enlightened population, and that under the fostering care of the mother Government the people can, within a short time, be left to govern themselves; that with an enlightened monarch, elected by universal suffrage, and an efficient legislation, the African element, so essential to African civilization, will receive a powerful impetus to intelligent progress, and then will Sierra Leone be able to compete with Liberia in virtuous emulation towards progressive civilization, and in endeavours to raise their much-abused race and country in the scale of civilized nations.

The late Governor - in - Chief, Major Blackall, on the 7th February, 1867, in an address which was received with great applause, remarked on the advancement of the Colony in material prosperity. 'I find,' said he, 'in the town of Freetown good and substantial houses in course of erection, replacing the very inferior class of houses which formerly stood on the same site; in the neighbourhood of Freetown, and more especially in the direction of Kissy, the same improvement may be observed. Land is being cleared and good fences put round it, and everywhere there is a marked improvement in the mode of cultivation. Employment is very general; and lately having occasion to seek for labourers in the neighbourhood of Hastings, for the repair of a bridge, I could obtain none under two shillings per day, as all were busy with their ginger crop. I find the revenue increasing and a diminution in the number of those applying to me for charity, and an evident improvement in the appearance and dress of the inhabitants generally, all which leads me to believe that, notwithstanding individual complaints of the dulness of trade, the material prosperity of the bulk of the population is advancing.'

CHAPTER IX.

SELF-GOVERNMENT OF THE GOLD COAST.

THE Report of the Parliamentary Committee on the summary of their inquiries states the following :—

'Your committee think it would have been better if the actual assumption of Government had in all cases been at first avoided in countries which the English race can never colonize, and where British law is inapplicable to native customs, which have been connived at, but which might have been eradicated by the gradual influence of commerce without such interference.

'The protectorate of tribes about our forts on the Gold Coast assumes an indefinite and unintelligible responsibility on our part, uncompensated by any adequate advantage to the tribes. It is even the opinion of the Colonial Secretary of the Government that it has enervated and disunited the protected chiefs, and that, so far from training the chiefs to a better conduct of their own affairs, it only leads them to lean on the English.

'It rests on no documentary evidence or conditions, excites vague expectations among the chiefs, and practically engages the English Government in maintaining weak tribes against their former sovereigns, and in keeping peace among them all, or even in compensating for losses mutually occasioned by invasion, and generally in administering a territory which we cannot even tax as subjects.

'Even for the object in view, of suppressing the slave-trade, simple commercial treaties with native powers, or the occupation of posts without adjoining territory, might have been a wiser policy.

'But in the sole interests of trade the evidence of merchants is that it is better that their agents should feel the necessity of keeping on good terms with native powers, than that they should be backed by English Governments, or even by consuls, more than is necessary for a reference of disputes to constituted authorities.

' Your committee also deprecate the needless employment of English officers and military on such a shore as costly to this country, not only by actual mortality, but by the numbers invalided in mind and body, and rendered unfit for other active service. The discipline, also, of the naval service in Africa is stated to be most trying and severe.

' The scattering of forces, both naval and military, in such parts of the world is an additional evil, which, in case of general war, would be of serious consideration.

' To govern effectually such settlements would require much larger expenditure than has been made, and more thorough occupation, and undertaking of public works of much larger extent than we are ready to recommend, or Parliament would be likely to consent to.'

In their recommendations to Parliament, they emphatically state that ' the protectorate should only be retained while the chiefs may be as speedily as possible made to do without it. Nothing should be done to encourage them to lean on British help, or trust to British administration of their affairs, whether military or judicial. The Judicial Assessor does not fulfil the first intention of the office—assisting the chiefs in administering justice—but supersedes their authority by decisions according to his own sole judgment. This office, instituted with the best intentions, has been attended by the introduction of needless technicalities and expense, and the employment of attorneys when the natives had better speak for themselves. The chiefs should be rather left to exercise their own jurisdiction, with only an appeal, when necessary, to the English magistracy; Queen's advocates seem wholly unnecessary, and trials by jury inapplicable in many cases.'

The Gold Coast under British influence extends over a coast-line of not more than three hundred miles, comprising Appolonia, Ahanta, Fantee, Winnebah, Accra, and Adangme. The inhabitants are the possessors of the lands they now occupy from time immemorial. The natives are almost all alike in habits and customs, in their mode of living, and almost in that of thinking. The effect of British rule is to moderate in a great measure some of their customs; but domestic slavery, the great drawback to material improvement, runs rampant among them. In the interior, the country is open to the attacks of a powerful and hostile neighbour, the King of Ashantee, who lusts after extending his territory to the water side, and has always interfered with the peaceful government of the country. On the sea-coast, with the exception of a few places—viz., Cape Coast, Anamaboe, and Dix Cove, where there are fortifications more or less strong, and armed with heavy guns, it is exposed in every direction to the attacks of a hostile naval force, which can ride at anchor on the roadstead, and do a great deal of mischief to the towns along the coast, without receiving any check. There is a European Power (the Dutch) whose territories are dovetailed with those under British influence, consisting, with the exception of Elmina, of small, miserable towns, scattered in every direction on the coast, not extending beyond ten miles from the coast, except, perhaps, at Axim, and surrounded in every direction, except seawards, by the British territory; the native inhabitants of its government are Fantees, Ahantees, and Accras; they are closely related to the natives of the same tribes in the English territory.*

As a whole, the inhabitants of the Gold Coast are generally of middle size, kind, good-natured, and hospitable; they are always generous to strangers, but in many instances not particularly so to one another; they are not entirely under British rule, nor are they British subjects; they have their own kings, their own chiefs and caboceers, who exercise indefinite power over them; among those on the sea-coast this power is very limited; the influence of a civilized Government in close proximity to theirs has greatly enlightened the people, and prevented them from receiving any arbitrary treatment from their chiefs. In those who are a little distant from the guns of the forts, their power is more extensive; but they dread being called upon to give an account to the English Governor of their actions, as many of their subjects are always availing themselves of the protecting influence of the English courts.

---

* Exchanges of territory between these and the English took place on the 1st January, 1868, by which the dovetailing is done away with.

Those in the interior, although to some extent they dread the influence of the British rule, yet still exercise extensive and arbitrary power over their subjects. They possess secret means of menacing those who would attempt to divulge the actions of their kings and chiefs, as they and their family are likely to be the greatest sufferers in the long run. In a word, the influence of the kings on the Gold Coast over their subjects, the fear they engender, and the greater consideration which surrounding tribes have for them, are inversely to their close proximity to the British rule on the Coast, directly to the great distance they are from the guns of the forts.

The people on the Gold Coast are by no means an industrious race ; the system of domestic slavery has enervated and almost destroyed the energy of the people ; there are extensive countries rich in gold and other minerals ; a soil exceedingly fertile in many places, especially in the interior ; and yet the mines are not properly worked, and the fertile grounds are left to waste ; a small plot only is cultivated for planting corn, yams, beans, and other cereals, and a few other articles for home consumption. Go into any town, and you will find most of the men sitting down doing nothing but telling tales. They are content with the rudimentary forms of food, consisting of Indian corn, yams, and plantain, with fish and but a trifling quantity of beef. The gold and other mines receive but little attention from their hands, and a country which should be one of the richest in Western Africa is left unexplored and undeveloped from the want of energy in its native element. The female are the most laborious part of the population ; they till the ground, make earthenware pots of great beauty and durability, and supply food to the husband. If a steady and continuous work is required to be done, the female population are the best to be employed, when the work is light enough for them to do. This shows a very low scale of civilization. In the coast towns, such as Cape Coast, Anamaboe, and Accra, there is comparatively a great advance in civilization, although there is vast room for improvement. The principal portion of the inhabitants, who are educated men, are hard-working, pushing, and in many cases thriving ; they possess considerable enlightenment of manner. Agriculture forms no part of their occupation, but they are merchants, traders, and agents for

English firms. They build and live in large houses, which possess
all the air and comforts of civilization; they dress in European
costumes, speak English, some can even speak four or five
European languages; a great many have received sound education
in England and Scotland; and even some of those who are educated
in the old schools of the Coast are not by any means inferior to
them; those who have received a middling education, and could
read and write letters in English, are called among themselves
'scholars.'

But the great bulk of the people are still uncivilized. Their
dress consists of an original or adamic apron, called *shim*, variously
arranged around the middle, and made of cloth of cotton or silk
manufacture; and the rest of the body is covered by a loose cloth of
native or European manufacture, which is sometimes very costly,
being made of silks, satin, and velvet, and is placed around the
shoulders like the Roman toga; but the ordinary inhabitants use
common cotton cloth; they wear no shirts or drawers underneath to
cover their body, so that they are half naked. The uneducated
females cover their bodies with a piece of cloth which extends from
their middle to their feet; unlike the females in the Gambia, they
put on no chemise or short gown to cover the nakedness of the
superior portions of the body, but these are left open and exposed,
and exhibit a very uncivilized appearance, especially to strangers.
The Jollof natives in the Gambia put on four, or even five, of these
cloths at a time, whilst on the Gold Coast they use only one, and
very seldom two; the consequence is that when there is a strong
breeze many parts of the body are exposed. In some part of the
Territory, such as the district of Crobboe, the sight is disgusting,
the females are perfectly naked; girls, of whatever age—eighteen,
twenty, and twenty-four—before they are legally married, although
not in any way incontinent, go about almost in complete nudity.
They use a small, long, narrow piece of cloth, about from four or
five inches broad, which is attached to beads of showy hue around
their waist, hanging down behind to below their knees, giving the
appearance at a great distance of a tail. These girls are known on
the coast as tail girls, and would account for the description of
ancient narrators, who, passing by in ships along the coast, have de-

scribed negroes with long tails. They use no other cloth around any part of the body, and appear in public markets and travel from one town to the other in the same peculiar lack of habit. Among the mulattoes or educated females, principally in the sea-coast towns, the dress is made after European patterns, but not after the fashions of the period; it is set very loosely over the body.

The marriage consists in the male paying a certain dowry to the parents or guardian of the fair sex, ranging from one to four ounces of gold. The damsel then becomes his property; she is bound to do whatever he bids her; to labour to feed him. After a time his affection grows cool, and he may, if he chooses, divorce her by merely telling her parents that she may go to whomsoever she likes; or if in the sea-coast towns, he gives her a *free-book*—*i.e.*, a paper to say that she is no more his wife. On the other hand, if she becomes tired of his embraces, and wishes to free herself of his, it may be, tyrannical rule, or if she is found enamoured with another, her parents are called upon to repay all the dowry and presents he has ever made her, from the time of courting up to the time of her leaving his establishment. Even among the educated natives of the coast, this convenient mode of marriage is preferred; and there are frequent changes in their domestic arrangements. Marriage according to the rites and ceremonies of civilized life, is, unfortunately, but seldom practised; the young gentlemen dislike the restraint which it engenders, and even when it has been entered into, there are frequent misunderstandings from the holy institution not receiving due attention; and separation and divorce are, in many cases, the inevitable consequences. But this mode of living is not sufficiently denounced on the coast; it is a practice which is engendered and fostered by the most disreputable of all institutions, domestic slavery. Polygamy is a law of the country from time immemorial; the chief and wealthy men are the possessors of a great many wives. The love of the mothers for their children is unbounded, and the non-possession of any is almost regarded as a divine curse on the woman. The love of the father is not so deep and lasting. The children love their mother, and their brothers and sisters by the same mother, more than they do their father, or his numerous offspring. In case of death, the property goes to the eldest brother by the same mother, to the sister or to her children; and if not secured by will, or given before death, the children of the deceased are served out. The infants are never tattooed; it is a habit detested by the natives, and every individual who is seen tattooed is regarded as a slave, and called *Donkor*, or slave, whether he be a free man or not.

In some parts of the Gold Coast, as at Cape Coast, there is a very strong feeling against the soldiers of the West Indian Regiments, which has led to outbreaks between them. The existence of a different language from English, Fantee, which the soldiers could not understand, the half-civilized dress of the natives, which gives the appearance of a barbarous condition, induce the soldiers to have but little respect for the common people; and the inhabitants, smarting with the rough treatment they have received from time to time from the soldiers, and the ungenial spirit exhibited by them, are roused to arms at the earliest notice. There is a great deal of antagonism between the soldiers and the civil population here, which is not to be found in any other part of the Coast, and reminds one of the outbreaks in Barbadoes, one of the West Indian Islands. Since the disbandment of the Gold Coast Artillery Corps, and that the West Indian soldiers have garrisoned the forts, many rows have taken place at Cape Coast, which have led to very serious results to both the military and the town; the civilians have been killed, and one of the soldiers was mysteriously lost, and his body, after a few days, found floating down the sea. Reports ran riot as to the cause of his death, but nothing positive was known.

The languages of the Gold Coast are numerous. They are Fantee, Appolonia, Ahanta, Accra, and Adangme. The Fantee is the most extensively spoken, and is almost the current language of the Gold Coast. Its principal seat extends from Secundee to the Seccoom river, a distance of about a hundred and fifty miles, and far into the interior beyond Ashantee under another name. Behind Accra it is spoken in Aquapim, Aquamboo, and Creepee. It is a soft, agreeable language; it is only a dialect, which is called *Otyi*, or *Tyi*, that is spoken in the interior, in Ashantee, and among those tribes in the protected Territory who formerly were politically united with the kingdom of Ashantee, but having separated from it, are now only united by ethnological consanguinity.

These are the Assins, Denkeras, Akims, Aquapims, and Aquambus. The difference between the Fantee and Otyi is, however, not great, as individuals of the two nations can easily converse and understand each other. There is slight difference in the pronunciation of some sounds, the Otyi being more agreeable than the Fantee; there are also discrepancies in the terminations and forms of words. The Fantee language has, as yet, not been reduced to writing, but the Rev. Mr. Rüs, of the Basle Missionaries, has published a small but elaborate and scholastic volume of the grammar and vocabulary of the Otyi, which, unfortunately, is not made the subject of study by the educated natives of the Coast.

The Ahanta and Appolonia languages are harsher and less melodious than the Otyi and Fantee. They are alike to one another, and spring from the Awoween language, which is spoken in the interior of Assin and Appolonia. The dialectic difference between the Ahanta and Awoween is greater than that which exists between the Fantee and Otyi. The Awoween, with slight dialectic difference, is spoken in Dutch and English Ahanta, in Wassaw —especially Western Wassaw—Axim, Appolonia, Asinee, and the extensive country of Awoween, and terminates where it meets with the Krew in the Grain Coast. It has not been reduced into writing. All the people in the British Ahanta understand and speak Fantee, and it is the commercial language.

Accra or *Ga* language is spoken by a very small class of people. It was, no doubt, in years past, a large and influential tribe, which has been crippled and destroyed by the Otyi tribe during their bloody wars for ascendency, by whom they are called "*Enkran.*" It is a harsher language than the Otyi, and very palatal and sonorous. Among the grown-up people the Otyi language is spoken, and in the interior it forms the medium of public intercourse; and the songs of the Gas are in Otyi, probably from the difficulty with which a palatal language can be pronounced in a song. The Rev. Mr. Zimmerman, sen., of the Basle Mission, who had charge of the arrangement of the Ga language, has reduced it into writing, a grammar, and vocabulary. Part of the Old and New Testament, and other scriptural books, have been translated.

The *Adangme* or *Adampe* language is spoken in Adangme and

Crohboe, and is only a dialect of the Awoonah language, which must originally have belonged to the same stock as the *Dahomy*, *Popo*, or *Ewe* language. It is less palatal than the Accra, in which many Ga words have been found to be incorporated. The Awoonah dialect has been reduced to writing by the German missionaries of North Germany, or Bremen Missionaries, a sister mission to the Basle at Accra. West of the Volta the Otyi, and east of it the Ewe (Dahomy), languages are prevalent, each of which is spoken by about four or five millions (?) of people.

Only in the triangle described by the lower Volta, the sea, and the Aquapim mountains, the Accra language is spoken by about 200,000 (?) people. Three colonies of the Accra people have emigrated into the Ewe Country. Among the Otyi and Ewe people on both sides of the middle course of the Volta, a conquered tribe, speaking the Kyerepong or Guang language, but also respectively Otyi or Ewe, are to be found.

Otyi, Accra, and Ewe (as well as Guang) are distinct languages, about as different as German, English, and French, if not more so, and each is again subdivided into different dialects. East of Ewe the Aku or Yoruba language is spoken. Accra, Ewe, and Aku belong to the same, but Otyi to a different, family of languages, though many Otyi words have mixed with Accra and Ewe. ' All these languages are rich and very flexible, and beautifully regular, so that there is not the least doubt or hindrance as to the possibility of their being fixed by writing and printing, or the translation of the whole of the Word of God into them. And any statement of a foreigner or native of their being poor, rough, or unadapted to civilization and regeneration ; or of the necessity or desirability of changing them for a European language (which is pretty nearly the same as cutting one's tongue and driving out his soul), shows only the gross ignorance of such a person. But as the African has a wonderful gift of learning a foreign language, such as is seldom met with in any other part of the globe, it is certainly of the greatest importance to encourage the study of old (classic) and modern languages among the educated and gifted Africans, to make the riches of classic and foreign literature accessible to them, to translate them into the native languages, and by that means make them by-and-bye the property of all, but not as some foolish young gentlemen seem to understand, to forget and despise the mother tongue.'—*Christian Messenger and Examiner.*

The commercial relations of the Gold Coast are extensive, and could be made very productive, but have been of late years reduced in a considerable degree. In the Western District, gold forms the most important and principal article of export. It is obtained principally from the interior countries beyond the Protectorate, especially from Ashantee, but small quantities are brought down from Denkera, Wassaw, Awoween, and Appolonia. It is exported principally in dust ; the natives, being partial to the nuggets, have always kept them. The largest nugget I have seen on this Coast was at Dixcove, in the possession of the late Mr. Essien. It weighed a little over thirteen ounces, but unfortunately when he died it was, with other nuggets, buried with him, such being the custom of this part of the Coast. In the Eastern District, palm-oil in large quantities is brought down through the river Volta and on the heads of carriers into various towns on the sea-coast. The quantity exported is large, and the oil of excellent quality. Besides palm-oil and gold, gum copal, ivory, and, in former years, Indian corn, were largely exported. For these articles the people received cowries, and articles of Manchester, Birmingham, Sheffield, and Glasgow manufacture.

The currency of the country is gold-dust, an *ounce* of which is sold for 3*l.* 12s. The smallest quantity recognised in trade or for general use is a *pessua*, or 1½d., which is regarded by a Fantee man in the same light as we regard a farthing. Thus, when a thing is considered worthless, a Fantee man will say that it is not worth a *pessua*. The sum is equal in weight to a small bead, or the seed of the *Aviculum*, or bird's-eye. The next in value is *Simpoir*, 3d.; and then *Teycoophan*, or *Teycoo*, 6d. A compound is used to denote higher value ; thus, 9d. is called *Simpoir na Teycoophan*, or, *Teycoo na Simpoir*. The most general calculation is one dollar, which in gold is called *Archi*, and equal to 4s. 6d. These conventional names were not originally native, but given probably by the old African Trading Company, so as to produce a uniformity of the currency of the country with the English coin. In the Eastern District, besides a small quantity of gold-dust, *cowries*, a small shell, the *Cypress moneta*, is extensively used in the interior, and is much employed for buying palm-oil. It is a cumbrous circulating medium, and fluctuates greatly in value. One head is supposed to be equal to half-a-dollar, being 50 strings, each string containing 40 cowries. For silver coin, I have known more than 60 strings given for half-a-dollar, or 2s. 3d. Besides cowries and gold-dust, which are purely native currency, English coin, dollars (American, Mexican, and Spanish) are found in large quantity; but for general use the natives prefer the English, from its standing value and convenience; it is very much sought after. The dollars are principally used to buy oil with from the people in the bush. The star, or Mexican dollars, are preferred, as their value is always 4s. 6d., while the others are subject to great fluctuation. The currency value of a dollar is 5s.; but the sterling value, 4s. 6d. This sometimes leads to great confusion among novices; four dollars are always spoken of as a pound, *i. e.*, a pound currency, although its real value is 18s. sterling.

Education.—At present the Gold Coast, as a whole, is fearfully neglected in point of education. The population, according to the latest and lowest estimate, is about 151,000 (1858); but it is in fact more than 450,000. Taking it at the lowest reckoning, there is less than 1 in 300 educated. Among such a large population, there are scarcely 500 persons who can read and write, and not 50 who can boast of a good, sound education. But the educational staff at the Gold Coast is declining every year, so that at present, in some respects, it is a mockery and a delusion. The missionaries belong to the Wesleyan and the Basle Societies.

The Wesleyan missionaries have their stations principally in the Western, and the Basle in the Eastern District. In the interior, the Wesleyans have stations at Dominassie; in the latter district they have stations at Jamestown, Accra, and Aquamboo. In former years, under the superintendence of Mr. Freeman, they had stations in various parts of the interior, where large school-houses were built, and the children educated; but, as a necessary consequence of the extension of the mission-stations, the expenses also increased; the parent committee was displeased with their agent on this account, and he was superseded, which led to their losing a most useful and energetic servant. In former years this body possessed a good institution at Accra, where such men as Timothy Laing, James Soloman, and John Plange, now native ministers, were educated; but as in the Gambia, so here, they are now pursuing a retrogade course, through the want of funds, and all their educational establishment consists of small schools, where the mere rudiments of learning are taught. They have not, as they did in former years at Sierra Leone, and as the Church Missionary Society have and are doing at Sierra Leone and Lagos, sent young men who have made some proficiency in their schools to finish their education in Europe; and even one of the native ministers, the Rev. T. Laing, having written asking to be permitted to finish his education in the Wesleyan Theological College in England, and offering to pay his passage, was refused. This Society, it must be acknowledged, has done well in diffusing useful knowledge and civilizing the natives, but there is great room for improvement in their educational establishment. The chiefs of this Coast feel and confess this want, and have lately sent a most urgent appeal to the Church Missionary Society to extend to them the benefits provided by that Society for Sierra Leone, by providing establishments for a higher education than the schools now in existence; but it appears that, as yet, this appeal has not been complied with.

The Basle Missionary Society is composed of energetic Germans, who have done an immense deal towards cultivating and enlarging the native literature; they have reduced the language of the Eastern District into writing, and taught the people how to communicate with one another in their own tongue; they have large female and male seminaries and schools in the interior, where a sound education is given to the natives in the higher branches, as may be observed from the following report: ' Five pupils came up for final examination lately, at the Theological Seminary of the Basle Mission at Akropong, Gold Coast. They had gone through a course of three years, and were examined in Greek and Hebrew, Church history, logic, exegeses of the Old and New Testaments in the original language, &c. Their answers were prompt, distinct, and clear, in evidence that they had well mastered their work. When these young men have served some years as catechists they will be presented for ordination. It would have been very interesting for the members of the Anthropological Society to be present at the examination—which was conducted for the most part in English—so that they could have judged for themselves whether the negro deserves a place among his *confrères* of the Japhetic and Shemitic races. Four out of the five are of the *purest negro* blood.' May I not suggest to the neighbouring mission, the Wesleyan, the necessity of observing the same principle. What an advantage it would be to the Gold Coast if that body could have presented to the world a similar report!

There is a small school at the head-quarters of the Gold Coast maintained by the British authorities; it is said to be very deficient, and at present scarcely numbers forty scholars; which, when the population of the whole Protectorate is from 151,000 to 450,000, is really a 'bagatelle and a play-house.' In former years, the Government school was the most prosperous and respectable on the Gold Coast. European teachers were sent out for the express purpose of educating the growing population. Sir Charles M'Carthy gave it his entire support. Prizes were offered to deserving students, and this school turned out men like George Blankson, Samuel Brew, Francis Grant, and the late Henry Barnes, and many others; even more recently the Government school turned out well educated young men, such as Samuel Davies, Mark Hausen, and Joseph Adams; but for many years a process of degeneracy has been gradually going on, until it has arrived at its present low condition.

An excellent lady, Mrs. Moseley, wife of a late energetic and much esteemed Chief Justice of the Gold Coast, has been endeavouring to raise up a fund for establishing a female school on the Gold Coast; her heart burned with Christian and English generosity for the neglected children whom she saw, when she first arrived on the Coast; and she has now collected a sum with which she expects to commence a school. But it behoves the people of the Gold Coast to help themselves also, and imitate the examples of the other colonies. They have recently read what improvements are going on in Lagos, and that the educated native merchants there, who are composed principally of young men from Sierra Leone, have established an academy, called the *Lagos Academy*, which is an institution for the promotion of literature, arts, and science; it was opened to sub-

scribers, and presided over by the Bishop of the Niger, the Rev.
Dr. Crowther. Let them put their shoulders to the wheel, and
carry out material reforms in their own country; they have the
means; why not use them in the proper way?

One of the greatest drawbacks to the civilization and improvement of the Gold Coast is *Domestic Slavery*. This institution, wherever it exists, produces the most deplorable effects on the moral and
physical condition of the population; it enervates and deteriorates
their strength, destroys the doctrine of man's equality, demoralizes
their social condition, places a deterrent effect on the energies of
the missionaries, vitiates the mind and principles, and has a most
damnifying effect on the body politic of a nation. Civilization
and domestic slavery are antagonistic terms; where the one exists,
it is impossible for the other to thrive; and where civilization pro-
gresses, this slavery must be abolished.

Our rule in this unfortunate Coast has been that of an undefined,
undetermined, unmeasured power; extensive under one ruler, very
much confined under another. The coast line is so considerable, and
the interior so extensive, that it is almost impossible for the Governor, with the limited means at his command, to localize certain
measures that are essential to the improvement of the Coast; and
these obnoxious institutions, which have shaped the customs of the
native community from time immemorial, and which are diametrically
opposed to the British Constitution, cannot be properly handled. If
the Governor of the Gold Coast should proclaim that, by the power
in him vested, he abolishes domestic slavery on this Coast, as being
an illegal institution, his proclamation would be a dead letter, as the
area of his government occupies several thousand miles, with a population ranging from 151,000 to 450,000, of which three-fourths are
slaves or descendants of slaves. He could not see that his proclamation was carried out; he might liberate a few who presented themselves to him, but the country would still suffer from slavery, and the
treatment by the masters, especially of those in the interior, would
even become worse. The land is very large, and the people too
much scattered about; so that a concentrated action, with the
minimum force and empty exchequer at his disposal, is impossible.

Domestic slavery is the great cause of that lazy habit and immorality which are traceable on the Gold Coast. A man has a lot of domestic slaves. He invariably does nothing. A few of the slaves work for three or four hours of the day, and sleep away the rest of it. They are fed by their masters, who give them a piece of canky and fish in the morning and evening. They possess no energy; there is no life in anything they do; no intellectual vigour; no effort such as springs from the rights, duties, responsibilities, and cares of property. They know that they are slaves, and that slaves they must always be; that though they might improve the property by their exertion, their sound judgment, and persevering labour, none of the results would be, in any way, their own; and, consequently, they only look to the treatment of their masters for an incentive to work, which generally vacillates with their strength. If the statement of Professor Fawcett is true about hired labour, how much more true it is of domestic slave labour! ' The condition of a man who can enjoy the entire fruit of his own labour,' says the Professor, ' is in every respect superior to the condition of one who is simply a hired labourer, and who, consequently, has no direct interest in the work upon which he is employed. The faculties of the latter are never fully stimulated; his hopes are not excited by success; his energies are not called forth to contend with the difficulties and disorders to which every employer is liable. His life is, in fact, one of dull routine. It may be said, that he is spared many anxieties, with which the labourer, who is his own master, has to contend. But it is almost a truism to assert that these cares and anxieties are the most valuable instruments of education, and that without them the human faculties can never be adequately developed.' It is this slavery that effeminates the Gold Coast, and leads to such a deplorable lack of enterprising spirits. The land is rich to overflowing. Extensive gold mines are waiting; but the people, satisfied with the costless articles of food, remain in miserable huts, when they should be ploughing the mountain sides and changing the courses of the rivers in which these precious metals are to be found. This is not a time for mincing matters, and my friends on the Gold Coast must understand that I speak of the natives at large; and although a few, comparatively very few, hard-working men may be found in the Coast towns, yet still, by their keeping domestic slaves, they are supporting an institution which has a most deplorable effect on the rise of their country. Instead of the population flourishing, and the people becoming great men (advancing with the world's advancing civilization), they are degenerating; and when the few men who now occupy important posts in the country, such as Blankson, Grant, and Brew, shall have passed away, Cape Coast will not have men to point out as evidences of its importance. Who among the rising generation, so far as we can now judge, is there to fill up the places of a Bannerman, a Hansen, a Richter, and a Barnes of olden time? and so long as the educated population support domestic slavery, so long will Cape Coast —the oldest establishment of the English on the Coast—occupy an inferior position as regards progressive civilization.

Domestic slavery also engenders and fosters great immorality and polygamy. This is essentially the case on the Gold Coast. In the interior towns I have noticed most of the female slaves become wives or concubines of their masters, whose offspring are, in some cases, particularly despised by the children of the free women. In a yard or family, many of these slave women are the mothers of pretty daughters, who all become the property of the master, or pass to the indiscriminate use and indulgence of their sons; and thus boys commence such matters very early in life, before the age of puberty, and, in many cases, come to early maturity, and are puny and short-lived.

One circumstance which produces a positive injury on the energies of domestic slaves is that after their death their property goes to their master or mistress, as the case may be, and their children are set adrift or still kept in slavery. The system of domestic slavery, therefore, is rotten and vile in every respect.

Foreign Neighbours.—There are only two foreign nations in close proximity with the Protected Territory of the Gold Coast, which might occasion some trouble to the head of a native self-government—viz., the Dutch and Ashantee. The Dutch Territory is in the neighbourhood of Cape Coast Castle; its greatest extent of country is in Ashanta; and the chief town is St. George d'Elmina a well-fortified place, about seven and a-half miles from the Castle at Cape Coast. The Dutch possess few native troops, and in case of hostilities could not, if backed with their native force, withstand the combined action of the natives in the Western District of the English Territory. But should there be a disturbance between them and the native government, and this be unprotected by any European Government, they would at once bombard the sea-coast towns with a man of war. The Dutch power will give much trouble and constant annoyance to a native government, if the latter be entirely unsupported by the English.

The *Ashantee Neighbour* is the most powerful and most dreaded. The Kingdom of Ashantee* skirts the interior of all the Protected tribes. The Ashantee men I have seen are a short, thin, filthy, bony race, of a nervine (neurine) temperament, who are immersed in gross ignorance and superstition; they are sharp, active, and very warlike; and possess a remarkable power of combination. Their military organization is very creditable for a savage race; implicit obedience is forced by military laws. In time of war, to the Ashantee life is of no consideration, but the pleasure of the king is everything. The least display of cowardice, or any questionable strategic movement which may lead to the supposition of fear, is immediately punished with death. Victory or death is generally their war-cry at the commencement of an engagement; and, consequently, the nation has founded a large empire. The king resides at Coomasi (Kumasi), his capital, and extends his despotic sway not only over several kindred tribes of common descent and language, but also over 'Mohammedan tribes of different speech, who, in the more remote interior, are said to furrow with their ploughs and feed their herds of cattle on grass-grown plains dividing the Kong Mountains from that woody and mountainous district in which the Asante themselves and their consanguineous tribes have their abode. They even, during the first part of the present cen-

---

* The spelling *Ashantee* is wrong, and is not according to the native pronunciation. The word *Asante*, says the linguist Mr. Rüss, has been spelt erroneously *Ashante*, and still more erroneously *Ashantee*, putting the accent on the ultimate—it is to be accented on the penultimate; *Asänte*, and the *s* is not *sh*, but is distinguished from the common English *s* only by having a more palatal aspiration.

tury, went so far as to assail the English settlements on the Gold Coast; and by carrying on a bloody war with the Protectorate, made themselves formidable for a time to the settlers, and the name of Asante generally known to Europeans.' They are the great supporters of the merchants in the Western District. When at peace with the Protectorate, trade flourishes, and wealth accumulates; but when there is misunderstanding, trade diminishes, and general bankruptcy is the result. They are of the greatest importance to the Coast towns. They buy up a large quantity of the imported goods, with which they carry on extensive commerce with tribes interior to their countries, and bring down many thousand ounces of gold-dust in exchange; they also bring down for sale monkey-skins and ivory. They are a formidable enemy, and ought always to be much conciliated and tolerated.

Each of the different countries within the Protectorate Territory has its own king, its own caboceers, or head men, and is governed by its own laws. They are distinct, separate from, and independent of one another, connected only by tribal ties. They respect each other according to the number of their subjects, their reputed fame, and the distance they are from the guns of the fort. There is not one of the kings who can be said to have a commanding influence over the whole country. The British Governor possesses authority over the whole Territory according to his mode of dealing with them. If he is kind, affable, and friendly to them, respects their authority, but entirely prevents their carrying out any barbarous customs, he is respected, and beloved; his influence and power is extensive; and the kings readily obey his authority and do anything for him. Thus, during the government of Mr. Richard Pine, when the country had been for several years suffering from misgovernment and the authority of the governors was not respected in the interior, through his urbanity of manners and magnanimous disposition, he exercised considerable influence over the kings in the interior of the Protectorate; his orders received obedience; his word was law; his summons met with quick reply; he respected the kings, and they, in turn, reverenced him; he grappled with difficulties which his predecessors dared not meddle with. But he was unfortunate. The Ashantee war broke out as he was in the zenith of his popularity; the kings and their people crowded to his standard, and went willingly to the field; but there was no engagement with the enemy, and a great many of the population died from the effects of bush life. A second expedition was organized, which shared the same fate. The natives did not go to the field this time, but a large body of the troops penetrated far into the interior. The climate proved deadly to a great many of the European officers and the West Indian soldiers; and the whole affair was fatal to the interests of the country and to Pine's administration.

As it is now under contemplation to give up the Gold Coast to native rule, the first point for consideration is to establish one or more kings who should exercise great influence over the others during the period that the British rule still exists. How this can be done I shall consider in another place.

Before entering more fully on the subject of self-government in the Gold Coast, I shall say a few words on the feelings of the military officers serving in the Gold Coast command. In the present condition of the country, the feeling is that of disgust. I remember the time when officers were glad to come to the Gold Coast service; when they preferred it to even Sierra Leone or the Gambia; but this is not the case now. The Gold Coast, in point of healthiness, is not behind the other two places; in fact, so long as bush work is prevented, it is superior to those places in point of healthiness; it is not subject to those periodic epidemics of yellow fever which devastate those two colonies. Its exposure to the influence of the strong south-west wind places a veto on its development. Unhealthiness is not therefore the cause, as a great improvement has lately been made in its sanitary state. In former years there were a great many jolly merchants, European and natives, on the Gold Coast, who were constantly giving dinner parties, picnics, and fêtes, and, consequently, there was much life and activity in the place; but at present everything is almost at a standstill; the merchants are in a state of semi-bankruptcy, most of the jolly fellows are either dead or reduced to poverty, and the Gold Coast service is that of a dull, monotonous routine; whilst at Sierra Leone and the Gambia, but especially the latter, there are always social parties for the officers and pleasant gatherings, which diminish that dull routine of service which is so disagreeable. In former years the military officers on the Gold Coast command held several colonial appointments, which brought them a yearly income of from 100*l.* to 400*l.* pounds, and seemed to occupy most of their time, and improved and enlivened the service. These were that of commandant of Dixcove (150*l.*), Anamaboe (150*l.*), Winnebah (125*l.*), Prampram (200*l.*), and Quillah (150*l.*); the appointment of Collector of Customs (300*l.*), and Acting Queen's Advocate (200*l.*), being a total of 1,275*l.* These appointments have either been abolished according to the new arrangement, or are otherwise filled up.

As, according to the decision of the Home Government, the Protectorate of the Territory is to be retained, whilst the ' chiefs may be, as speedily as possible, made to do without it,' and that they are on no account to lean on British help, or trust to British administration of their affairs, let us consider what would be the most judicious and most fitting self-administration of such an extensive Coast. The British Gold Coast must be divided into two parts, each governed separately, called respectively *Fantee* and *Accra*. The form of government best suited to Fantee is monarchical; and that to Accra, a republic. I shall, therefore, consider these two separately, under the heads of *the Kingdom of Fantee;* and *the Republic of Accra*.

CHAPTER X.

SELF-GOVERNMENT OF THE GOLD COAST.—KINGDOM OF FANTEE.

I HAVE in the last chapter detailed the extent of territory comprised within the term, *Protectorate Territory of the Gold Coast*, and stated that it is formed of separate kingdoms ruled by separate and independent kings ; but the people regard the Governor of the Forts as supreme head. The country extends from Apollonia to the River Volta. The Dutch Government owned lands in this extent of coast line which were inconveniently placed between the English towns.

The first point on the Gold Coast to be taken into consideration, whilst endeavouring to prepare the people for self-government, was either to buy the Dutch out of the Coast entirely, or to separate the country into two distinct halves, one under the sole government of the Dutch, and the other under the English ; and both have the same Customs regulations. This latter method has lately been arranged by treaty with the Dutch Government, and its provisoes place British Ahanta, Apollonia, and Wassaw under the Dutch ; and Dutch Accra, and a few miserable Dutch towns to windward of it, under the English. In this arrangement the Dutch are the gainers ; they thus acquire a large extent of compact and rich country, about 300 per cent. larger than the territory exchanged, the population containing about 100,000 at least, whilst the exchanged land contains less than 15,000 inhabitants ; but the measure is of intrinsic political advantage to the British portion of the Coast. Our Government will therefore exercise sole authority over the countries from the Sweet River, near Elmina, to the River Volta. This should be divided into two separate independent self-governments—viz., *the Kingdom of Fantee*, extending from the Sweet River to the borders of Winnebah; and the *Republic of Accra*, extending from Winnebah to the River Volta; the former to comprise the kingdoms of Denkera, Abrah, or Abacrampah, Assin, Western Akim, and Goomoor; the latter Eastern Akim, Winnebah, Accra, Aquapim, Adangme, and Crobboe.

The next point to be considered is the political union of the various kings in the kingdom of Fantee under one political head. A man should be chosen, either by universal suffrage, or appointed by the Governor, and sanctioned and received by all the kings and chiefs, and crowned as King of Fantee. He should be a man of great sagacity, good common sense, not easily influenced by party spirit, of a kind and generous disposition, a man of good education, and who has done good service to the Coast Government. He should be crowned before all the kings and caboceers within the kingdom of Fantee; the kings should regard him as their chief; his authority should be recognised and supported by the Governor of the Coast, who should refer to him matters of domestic importance relative to the other native kings, advise him as to the course he should pursue, and see that his decisions be immediately carried out.

He should be assisted by a number of councillors, who, for the time, should swear allegiance to the British Government, until such time as the country is considered fit for delivery over to self-government. They should consist not only of men of education and good, sound common sense, residing in the Coast towns, but also of responsible chiefs, as representatives of the various kings within the kingdom.

One most important consideration is the yearly vote of a round sum out of the revenue as stipend to the king elect whilst under this probationary course, such as would allow him to keep up a certain amount of State dignity, and would enable him to carry out his authority over the kings and chiefs. Each State should be made to contribute towards the support of the temporary Government; a native volunteer corps should be attached to the Government, officered by natives of intelligence, who should be thoroughly drilled by paid officers and sergeants, supplied from West Indian regiments stationed on the Coast. The English language should be made the diplomatic language with foreign nations; but Fantee should be made the medium of internal communication, and therefore ought at once to be reduced to writing.

The territory of the kingdom of Ashantee is larger than that of the Protected Territory of the Gold Coast, but we find the reigning king possesses absolute power over the different tribes composing it. True enough, the edifice was constructed on the blood of several nationalities, which gives it greater strength; but the kingdom of Fantee must be erected on a peaceable footing, supported, for a time at least, by a civilized Government, with a prince at the head who is versed in native diplomacy, and well known and respected by the various kings; such a man as the Hon. George Blankson, whose experience and deserved fame would make his appointment meet with universal support; a prince who would be able, like the potentate of Ashantee, to concentrate a large force at a very short notice, at any given point, when menaced by their powerful neighbours.

The appointment is absolutely necessary, since King John Aggery, of Cape Coast, has been dethroned by the local government, and this has been sanctioned by Her Majesty's Government. The proclamation is definite, and runs thus: 'Be it therefore known and proclaimed that the said John Aggery is for ever deprived of his stool and dignity, and that the office and title of King of Cape Coast no longer exists, and is abolished from this day forth' (the 21st March, 1867). The Home Government have distinctly told the kings that they will have to defend themselves against any hostile tribe, without ever expecting to receive support from the British Government, except when the few sea-coast towns are attacked. The condition of the interior kingdoms is therefore in a most precarious state. Since the last disastrous expedition against the King of Ashantee, where several lives were lost through encampment during the rains in the fields, and a large waste of money resulted without the least advantage, the Home Government have turned their faces against all such expeditions, as ' costly to England,' not only by actual mortality of English officers and military, ' but by the number invalided in mind and body, and rendered unfit for other active service.' They (the Parliamentary Committee) therefore recommend to the Home Go-

vernment, and this to that of the Coast, that the chiefs are to be
' *as speedily as possible made to do without the British protectorate ;*
they were on no account to encourage them to lean on British help, or
trust to British administration of their affairs, whether military or
judicial.' The aim, therefore, should be to form a strong, compact
native Government, which would command the obedience of all the
native kings and chiefs, and which would immediately undertake the
quelling of all disturbances in the interior, and command the native
force if attacked.

But the present disunited condition of the kings of the Protectorate is woful in the extreme. If a war should break out with
Ashantee, they have got no superior authority to look to, except
the Governor, whose instruction is not to give them support in the
interior. He will supply them with a few guns and ammunition,
but each king will have to take care of his own fireside, with a number of men so small as to be insufficient to withstand a detachment
of the Army of Ashantee. The stratagem of the Ashantee generals
has always been to fight each king in detail ; and having completely
mastered one, they proceed to another ; and thus always come off in
these wars victorious against the various kings. The Ashantee Army
numbers from forty to fifty thousand men. Should the attack be
first made against the kingdom of Denkera, with a detachment
which could muster from five to ten thousand fighting men, the
terror of the very name of Ashantee alone will make them take to
their heels to the sea-coast towns, and leave the country in their
hands. Exactly the same would be the result if the kingdoms of
Assin and Akim, frontier countries, were to be attacked. The consequence would be that the people would always feel themselves perfectly insecure, life and property within the Protectorate unsafe,
and their condition worse than if they were under the despotic rule
of Ashantee.

Let them, therefore, have a ruler in whom they have confidence,
and generals experienced in bush fighting ; let them be united, offensive and defensive, to one another, under one head, whose
authority is paramount ; let good, large, open roads be made con-
necting the kingdoms with one another, which would lead to the
easy movement of a large body of men ; let the strength of every

kingdom be known by the head centre, who could call out at any time what number of men he might require; let him have a good magazine and a large supply of useful rifles, and the people be taught the use of them, and I guarantee that a compact, powerful, and independent Government will be formed, which would defy Ashantee and give confidence to the whole country.

We must now briefly consider those countries or districts which should combine to form the Kingdom of Fantee; and taking for granted that Wassaw, British Ahanta, and Apollonia are transferred to Dutch rule (which, from their distances and disconnexion with the towns in Fantee Proper, would be a source of great weakness and perplexity rather than of strength), we have DENKERA, ASSIN, FANTEE PROPER, WESTERN AKIM, and GOOMOOR. These kingdoms occupy a coast line of nearly a hundred miles, taking into account the various indentations; but they are extensive in the interior, where they are interrupted by and bordering on the Kingdom of Ashantee.

Denkera.—This is the most western district, and is bounded on the east by Assin, west by Wassaw and Ashantee, north by Ashantee, and south by Fantee and a part of Wassaw. It is a hilly country, and surrounded by large forests. The inhabitants were formerly under the Ashantee rule; but, through the despotic and arbitrary treatment which they received from that potentate, they claimed and received protection from the British authorities on the Coast. The capital is called Denkera; but the present king, Quakey Frame, from the late disturbances with Ashantee, fearing that he might be secretly caught in a place so near to his powerful enemy, made another large town—viz., Adjuquah—his royal residence. The population of Denkera is large, being nearly fifty thousand. The towns are small, containing from a few hundred to four or five thousand inhabitants, who are in a perfect state of barbarism. Civilization has made no progress whatever among them; the women labour in the fields; cultivation is limited, and only for home consumption, and consists principally of corn and yams. The king exercises an absolute rule over the people, assisted by his councillors, who are generally old men. Each town is governed by a chief or a deputy from the king. The king has absolute power over life and property ; any one who disobeys his orders is secretly killed. This is known to all the population, but none dare make it known to the British Governor. They are secretly menaced by the Fetish man, whom they dread; and should any one attempt to give information, his life and those of his entire relatives will atone for it through secret poisoning by unknown hands.

Denkera is celebrated for being rich in extensive gold-fields. Through it run two branches of the Boosom-Prah River—viz., the Ofin and the Prah—and by their banks the inhabitants collect a large quantity of surface gold; but the people are lazy, and imbued with superstitious and absurd ideas. Thus it is against the Fetish of the country that the people should dig very deep for gold, as they believe that that would lead to its escape ; it is also against the orders of the Fetish that any man in European dress or who can read and write (scholars), should go to the diggings, for similar reasons. The result is, that the extensive gold-fields of that country are still undeveloped. My comrade, Dr. Davies, whilst at Acroful Denkera, during the late Ashantee expedition (1864), by examining the subsoil of some of the districts, pointed out to some of the women who were washing for gold, certain places where gold was to be found. They tried them, and after washing, found a large quantity of gold-dust. The abundant gold-fields of Denkera require to be developed.

Assin.—Assin is situated on the east of Denkera, and was formerly a powerful province of Ashantee ; it is bounded on the north by Ashantee, south by Fantee, west by Denkera, and east by Akim. There are two political heads or kings in Assin—viz., the King of Assin, who resides in Assin Yancoomassie; and the King of Mansue. The former is the superior king, and a young man who has but recently ascended the throne. The office of a king in these parts consists in sitting down all day on a large stool, surrounded by his chiefs and head men, who sing or speak words of praise to his ears and drink his rum ; he settles palaver, fines the people heavily, and runs away when his territory is attacked by a powerful enemy. Not long ago the King of Mansue, who commands the district of the Prah, attempted to declare his independence and to have nothing

K

to do with the young king at Yancoomassie. His people advised him to buy plenty of rum, and treat his chiefs, and thus show that he was equally as great a chief as the other. He did so, and afterwards disobeyed the orders of the lawfully-constituted king, who could not enforce them. The question was, however, referred to the Governor of the Coast for settlement, and the King of Mansue again became a vassal.

Assin is by no means a well populated country. It consists of towns on the highway to Ashantee, with a few scattered hamlets from the main road. The country is covered by thick impenetrable forest; there are a few low hills here and there, but no mountains; the soil in most parts is very fertile, and could grow any quantity of ground-nut, Indian corn, arrowroot, &c., but it is only partially worked. A small quantity of gold exists in Assin, but there are, to my knowledge, no gold mines, except, perhaps, towards the borders of Denkera. The people are generally poor, their habitations consisting of low, miserable mud-walled huts, which cost but a trifle in building. The women make a large quantity of *croupie* or *Touloocoona* oil, principally for home consumption; a small quantity is brought down to the markets on the Coast for sale.

The inhabitants are in utter barbarism and uneducated. In former years there was a school at Mansue, and a large one at Tabiesamang, which is a little village near Mansue in a divergent line from the road to Essicoomah and Ajimacoo. When I visited these places in 1864 (25th January) the school-house was still standing, but it was now the residence of the king. It was an oblong building, raised a few feet from the ground and floored, containing four large bedrooms and two parlours; the ceiling was also floored and painted green; this useful establishment in Assin, as well as many others, were long ago abandoned, and the people left in gross ignorance and idolatry. The inhabitants respect the British rule, in so far as it gives them protection.

Fantee.—Under this designation I shall include all those countries extending from Elmina, or the Sweet River, to Mumford, including Cape Coast, Anamaboe, Abrah or Abahcrampah, Dunquah, Dominassie, Mankasin and Ajimacoo, all which, and many other towns, are governed by separate kings and chiefs. This is the most confused part of the Gold Coast as regards political existence; the close proximity to the guns of the forts, and the keener eyes with which the domestic affairs of these states are watched by the Protecting Government, enable any man who can plant a village, make a stool, and sit himself on it, to call himself a king, without his claim being called in question by the surrounding kings, or even disputed. In every small croom or village there is a king, although his territory does not extend beyond a mile round his capital; this is absurd in the extreme, but the habit exists, and will remain so, unless a radical change is made in the administrative department, or a powerful neighbouring chief, such as Ashantee, overruns the country and puts it down. But Fantee is the most civilized portion of the western district of the Gold Coast. Here the labours of the Wesleyan missionaries are bearing fruit; at Cape Coast are the head-quarters of the mission, and they have sub-central stations in Anamaboe and Dominassie. The children under instruction receive rudimentary education in the day-schools, but they possess no colleges or large central educational establishment. At Cape Coast and Anamaboe there are a few substantial buildings, some of which are built of mud called *swish*, and others of native-made bricks or stones. But these towns are all devoid of properly laid streets; the small huts are actually jumbled up together in a very confused manner; most, especially at Cape Coast, are without roofing, excepting a plaster of mud, presenting a barbarous and unfinished appearance, especially to strangers. In Fantee about one out of every one hundred inhabitants could read and write. Some of the natives dress in European costume, especially those who are educated and those in a high state of social existence, but ninety-nine in a hundred wear their native dress. The kings and chiefs, with the exception of John Aggery, late king of Cape Coast, dress in the same fashion.

Gold is found in small quantities below the surface soil, which is washed by the women; the men consider it *infra dig.* to be thus occupied, although a large number are to be seen during the whole of the day sitting lazily about under the cool shade of a tree. Domestic slavery exists in all its various forms, even within fifty yards of the fortifications; men, women, and children are sold within a few yards of the Governor's residence. The women are most laborious; they till the ground, and bring to the market their produce, which they exchange either for gold or silver. Yams, plantains, cassada, Indian corn, and a large quantity of vegetables are grown, principally in towns a few miles from the sea-coast. There is nothing of native growth exported from this fertile and extensive country. Any quantity of Indian corn might be grown in the interior, but the system of domestic slavery and plurality of wives enervates the energies of the male inhabitants; and, instead of thousands of bushels produced yearly for exportation, there is scarcely sufficient for home consumption.

The currency of Fantee is principally gold-dust and silver; but in the towns leeward of Cape Coast, where a small quantity of palm-oil is produced, cowry shells are also current. Gold, palm-oil, monkey skins, and ivory, are the only articles of export from this district. Gold and ivory are brought down from Ashantee; monkey skins from the interior towns, such as Assin and Akim; and palm-oil from the countries below Anamaboe—viz., Salt Pond, Assafa, Ahkrah, Mumford, &c., and the towns in their immediate interior. There are only a very few educated natives employed in the various branches of the Government; the supply is generally from Sierra Leone, and, consequently, there is a great want of political life amongst them. An encouragement in this direction is very necessary. The religion of a vast majority of the people is rank Fetishism; among the lower class it is much feared, as its priests go clandestinely to work to injure those who dare to disregard its orders. Mankasin in former years was a famous Fetish town for all the Fantees, and exercised considerable control over the government of the country; but, through the exertions of the Government, aided by the educated inhabitants, it has now no influence.

Western Akim.—This is a woody forest country, situated on the north-eastern borders of Ashantee and east of Assin; the inhabitants were, till lately, under the King of Ashantee. Their late King, Ajeman by name, was a brave old man, resolute and powerful, but governed with moderation and good judgment, and was much liked by his people. Western Akim is separated from Ashantee by the Quaho Mountains, which look down upon his capital, Ojedam, which is large and surrounded by a thick forest. The king formerly swore allegiance to the Danish Government, and, when their Territory was sold to the English, he also took the oath of allegiance to the British rule. Ajeman always regarded Accra as his head-quarters, but as his Territory is one of the high roads of Ashantee to the kingdom of Fantee, and within its prescribed limit, it must be incorporated with it.

Ajeman did not favour missionary operations in his dominions, so that his people are very ignorant. No export is obtained from the country. The people are few, but very brave.

Goomoor.—Situated on the east of Fantee and south of Akim is the large district of Goomoor, which has a very large population. The towns are all surrounded by dense impenetrable forest, except the seaport towns, the chief of which are Mumford and Tantum, or Tantumquady. The people still maintain their barbarous practices, and are uneducated. They plant a large quantity of Indian corn and plantains, which form their principal articles of food.

Having examined the political state of the countries in the Western District of the Protectorate, let us now consider the practicability or impracticability of forming a powerful native self-supporting government.

The Western District of the Gold Coast is composed of several distinct kingdoms, not united by any common bond. They regard the Governor of the Coast as a supreme head and as a referee in all their external and internal quarrels. They are within easy reach of a most powerful and hostile nation, the Ashantee, which has constantly taken advantage of their disunited and uncombined condition to overrun the country and cut them up in detail. In former years they looked to British help, and received it in time of need, and the Ashantees were very much afraid of British power and influence; but now the Governors are on no account to order troops to the interior, but are only to defend the coast towns if attacked; and the kings and chiefs are not to be encouraged to lean on British help. The sending of troops in dense forests where no enemy is to be found has proved not only fatal to life, but expensive in the extreme to the Home Government, without any advantage being derived from it; the kings, therefore, have been told to fight their own battles. In the present political state of the country no king is safe in his capital. Should Assin be the point of attack, the King of Ashantee (such have always been his tactics) will send a large corps of observation on the borders of Akim and Denkera. Assin would be overrun, and neither the Kings of Denkera, Fantee, Akim, or Goomoor would stir from their kingdoms to assist the Assins, if not impelled to it by the British Government; and even then the people, especially those on the frontiers, not being under any military organization, would remain to defend their own firesides; and before the people at Cape Coast, Anamaboe, and Fantee could move to the interior, the Ashantees would have done their work in Assin.

But the Assins, on the mere report of an Ashantee invasion, would not remain for a second in their towns or croons, but would fall back on the sea-coast towns for support. After invading Assin the corps of observation over Akim would descend to Akim and join the Assin division, and they would clear everything before them; for the whole of the interior countries would fall on the sea-coast towns, and the Ashantees would become masters of the important interior towns. There are no roads between any of the various kingdoms, so that on an attack the people have to move in Indian file, and, consequently, are unable to withstand a body of men well disciplined and accustomed to bush fighting. The result of this is that every invasion made by the King of Ashantee on the Fantee or Protected Territories, has always produced and always will produce a general panic all over the country.

Cape Coast Town is well guarded against any attacks of a native tribe, being well commanded and protected by excellent forts, which look down on all the hills, valleys, and avenues to the town; and no Ashantee army, however numerous, will ever attempt to measure the effects of their brass, lead, and iron slugs, their pebbles from the rivers, fired from rusty, unserviceable Dane guns, with the rockets, shells, canister, round balls, and lead bullets of a well-disciplined European troop. The Ashantees will therefore always keep on the interior, and will carry on a guerilla warfare against their traditionary enemy.

The Fantees, or the Western portion of the Protected Territory, have no chief to look upon as their head, none whom they can regard and obey as their superior chief; they have therefore no organization and no discipline, and can never, in their present confused state, withstand the active bravery of their powerful neighbours; and if left exactly as they are to fight their own battles, it would be almost better—or, at all events, it would lead to great saving of life and property—were they to become at once vassals to the King of Ashantee. Ninety-nine in a hundred of the population are still in a barbarous condition, without education or the means of educating their children. There are in the countries large gold mines which are not developed and worked; and no article of commercial importance is grown and exported, except a small quantity of palm-oil. The languge, which is Fantee, with the prevalence of the Otyi dialect, is unwritten, and the people do not communicate with one another in it.

From the foregoing, it is evident that from the unsatisfactory political state of the Western District of the Gold Coast, it cannot, at present, be left to govern itself; that radical reforms are imperatively necessary before this can be done with safety to the population; that no sooner would the British Government be withdrawn, than intestine warfare would spring up, resulting in fearful and barbaric massacre and bloodshed, and every man's hand would be against his neighbour. Before the country should be given up to self-government, a responsible king, of education and experience, must be crowned, assisted, acknowledged and supported by the British authority, both on the Coast and in Downing-street; and a British Consular Agency should be formed, and the Consul appointed be a man who would aid and advise the native Government, and guarantee it against European invasion.

CHAPTER XI.

SELF-GOVERNMENT OF THE GOLD COAST.—REPUBLIC OF
ACCRA.

THE territory to be included within this Republic should extend
from Winnebah to the River Volta. Awoonah, at present, should
be no part of it, as it would only be a point of weakness to the
young Republic. The constitution of the several states in it, the
feelings of the inhabitants, the physical geography of the country,
as well as the peculiar habits and customs of the people, lead me to
believe that no form of government would be so suited to their
wants and requirements as the republican form. Within this territory,
which extends over a coast line of about a hundred miles, and to a
very great distance into the interior, are included EASTERN AKIM,
WINNEBAH, ACCRA PROPER, ADANGME, AQUAPIM, CROBBOE,
AQUAMBOO, CREEPEE, ARGOTIME, containing a population of at
least 200,000 souls. The capital of all these places, or, more properly,
the principal sea-port town, is James Town, commonly called English
Accra; it is the picnic spot of Western Africa. The educated
population are always jolly; life is made a source of perpetual enjoyment. In no part of the Coast is the caste distinction of colour
so trampled under foot as at this place. Many of the natives are
properly educated, and would countenance no tampering with their
privileges ' as a man and a brother.' Some attempts were recently made to originate here that party Americanized feeling
which existed on other parts of the Coast; but the originators were
scouted and almost ' cut ' by every one; and in a place like Accra,
this is not a trifle, as it destroys their social well-being. The old
European inhabitants are identical with the educated natives in interest and social habits, and are ready to fight their battles against
any invidious attacks which new comers in their superior wisdom
(rather ignorance) might think fit to make. There is always a

happy union and agreement between the Europeans and natives—
the counsel of the latter is sought after in important matters. There
is not that display of empty boasted dignity which is only inherited
whilst on the West Coast of Africa; nor the existence of private
pique, which in other parts disorganizes the social happiness of every
class of the population. In time of pleasure all enter into it with
heart and soul, expense being of no consideration; but when time of
business commences it is all work and no play.

James Town, Dutch Accra, and Christiansborg are within an
area of two and a-half miles, but they are governed by separate
kings. The towns contain a few large houses, but the majority of
the native huts are so completely jumbled up together that they present a confused mass. There are no properly laid-out streets, but the
towns are intersected with crooked lanes. The men are generally
of middling size, not hard-working as a rule, except, perhaps, the
upper class. Domestic slavery exists in all its forms, and morality
is at a very low ebb. The lower class of the population is very
litigious.

If this place must ultimately be left to govern itself, a republican
form of government should be chosen. An educated native gentleman, of high character and good common sense, who has the welfare
of his country at heart (such, for example, as Libercht Hesse, Esq.,
of Christiansborg), should be selected by the Government as a candidate for the presidency, and offered for the votes of the populace
in the various districts; and, when once elected, he must be regarded
as supreme in everything, and the natural referee in all their
quarrels and differences. He should be assisted by counsellors
chosen by the people as their representatives. The term of office
of the president should not be less than eight years, and he should
be eligible for re-election.

The absurd custom of having kings in every petty town should
be, as speedily as possible, abolished. They should be called by
other names than that of kings, and in case of their death the
'stool' should be done away with. The president for the time
being should be the recognized constitutional king. A good strong
government would thus be formed, which would receive the assistance of the European residents. If a proper custom-house is esta-

blished a large revenue will be collected. There should be one at
Prampram and another at Addah, and every effort should be made
to develop the vast resources of the country.

Let us now consider, *seriatim*, the various countries which should
enter into the formation of the Republic of Accra, viz.:—

Eastern Akim.—Like the Western Akim with the Danes during their
occupation, the Eastern swore allegiance to the Danish Government,
ever since its escape from the despotic rule of the King of Ashantee.
It has always regarded Accra as its head-quarters. It is bounded
on the east by Aquapim, west by Western Akim, south by Goomoor,
and north by Ashantee. Under the Danish sway, the King of Akim
ruled with absolute despotism and did exactly as he pleased. De-
capitation and confiscation of the property of the wealthy were
very frequent, and for very slight misdemeanours; even now the
same practices are carried on by the king, although not so publicly as before. Life and property are unsafe in the rapacious hands
of the kings and chiefs. Under the most ludicrous pretences heavy
fines are inflicted, for trivial offences, amounting only to indiscretion
on the part of the offender ; and in such cases, sometimes influential
men have been beheaded, and their property confiscated for the
benefit of the kings and chiefs.

The inhabitants of Eastern Akim are very brave ; they are the
most warlike people in the whole Protectorate, and single-handed
they have fought successfully against the Ashantee power when it
was in its greatest strength and glory. The country is surrounded
by thick, impenetrable forest ; agriculture forms but a very small
portion of their labour ; their principal occupation is gold-digging.
They, however, plant a small quantity of articles for provision for
home consumption, but their chief supply is from Goomoor. Akim
contains one of the largest and most extensive gold districts in all
the Gold Coast ; the mines are generally dug to the depth of
from eighteen to twenty feet in a horizontal direction, and, from a
superstitious notion entertained by the diggers, they do not make
horizontal shafts. The soil is loose, sandy, and deficient in tenacity,
so that 'it falls down as soon as they cut under it in that manner,
without support ; ' and they believe that the Fetish, who is regarded
here as the guardian spirit of the gold, is the prime cause of this

accident, which he causes in order to put a limit to human avarice, impelled by the *auri sacra fames*. Thus the gold mines are imperfectly worked, and immense wealth lies buried in the earth.

The people are wholly uneducated; they speak the Otyi dialect of the Fantee language; some of them understand the Ga or Accra language. The king is very wealthy, which, together with his despotism, inspires fear and implicit obedience. The currency of the country is gold-dust; any large nugget found is absolutely and indefeasibly the property of the king; this rule holds good in every part of the Gold Coast.

Winnebah.—The district of Winnebah has a coast line of nearly forty miles, extending from long. 25 to 52 west; it comprises an extent of country rich and fertile, which, in its general features, is flat and very much cultivated. The principal town is Winnebah, which is situated near the river Iyensu. The inhabitants are great agriculturists; industrious and hard-working, and cultivate plantations of ground-nut, palm-oil, plantain, banana, and various other articles. They are remarkable for supplying the Coast with a large quantity of native-made canoes; even the inhabitants of the Bight of Benin are always in quest of them. They trade in palm-oil, maize, and gold-dust.

The inhabitants are partially educated. The Wesleyans have established schools in some of the towns, where English is taught; but the native language is disregarded. Political life is in a very low state; the people acknowledge a king, who resides within a stonesthrow of the Civil Commandant. He is a man of education, of good common sense, and, unlike the host of other kings in this Protectorate, not only respects the Sabbath, but also makes his people respect it. He is civilized in manners and habits, and his residence is got up in European style. But King Henry Aquah's influence is very limited, and does not extend to all the districts of Winnebah, which, following the patriarchal mode of government, has kings in every petty town.

The forest of Winnebah contains large durable and valuable woods, which would turn out excellent timber. Among the number may be mentioned the Doom or Edoom, the Duntah, the mahogany, and the African cedar. In the interior the district is rich, extensive, and fairly populated; being surrounded by friendly tribes, the inhabitants are generally free from those political panics which have from time to time convulsed the various towns and districts in other parts of the Protectorate. They are, for the most part, peaceable in their habits and respectful to strangers. Winnebah is about forty miles from James Town, Accra. The language is Fantee, but a vast majority of the population also speak the Accra or *Ga* language.

Aquapim.—This is a mountainous country, situated on the north and north-west of Accra, and contains a small, but active, warlike, and industrious people. The principal town is Acropong, where exists a large establishment of the German missionaries. The young generation are educated both in English and in their native tongue; they are also taught the art of agriculture. Politically, they dread their king, but this despotic influence is greatly modified by the peaceable and happy teaching of the missionaries. Palm-oil, gold-dust, and coffee form the principal exports from Aquapim. The country is partially sheltered from the inroads of the Ashantee potentate by the powerful kingdom of Akim. The inhabitants are all farmers. The language is Otyi, but Ga is also spoken.

Accra Proper.—This is the metropolis of the eastern district of the Gold Coast, and comprises James Town, or English Accra; Dutch Accra; and Danish Accra, or Christiansborg. The first two are united to one another, forming one town; the latter is situated about a mile and a-half to leeward of these. Each town has its own king, Cudjoe in the first place, Taccie in the second, and Dawoonah in the third; but the King of Dutch Town is considered the head from the circumstance that the head Fetish man resides in it, and from the extensive influence of the late king. With a very few exceptions, the people are by no means an industrious, hard-working population. A few of the merchants have large coffee plantations at some distance from the town, but the majority of the men lounge lazily about all day in the town, doing nothing. Education in the English town is favourably progressing. The Wesleyans in James Town and the Basle missionaries in Christiansborg are doing good service to the rising generation. Some of the inhabitants have a very superior education, with a fair knowledge of law and government. Accra extends a short distance into the interior, but is limited by the Aquapim mountains. The country is flat and dry, and towards the interior is dotted with a few plantations of coffee and other articles of domestic importance. Its capability is very limited so far as it has been developed; in fact, there is nothing exported from the district of Accra Proper, but all its exportable articles are derived from the interior. The spoken language is Ga.

Adangme.—This district is situated on the east of Accra, and extends from it to the River Volta. The country is generally flat, but contains several abrupt hills, such as the Shai Mountains, Ningo Grand, and other small hills. The inhabitants are closely related to the Awoonahs, who are from the same national stock, speak the same language, and resemble each other in manners and customs. They are generally tall, fine, athletic men, who trade considerably in palm-oil, which they buy from the interior. The soil is admirably adapted for planting yams and ground-nut. The finest specimen of yams which I have met with on the whole Coast was in Adangme ; it weighed thirty pounds, but the country had produced larger specimens. The people are still in a most degraded and savage state, and imbued with superstitious Fetishism. The principal towns are Prampram, Ningo, and Addah, in which mercantile factories are established for buying oil. In the last place there is an old dilapidated fort which was built by the Danes when slavery was being carried on in this Coast, but it is now in complete˙ ruins. The inhabitants are no agriculturists ; the women plant a small quantity of articles for domestic consumption, the men occupy their time principally in trading. There are no missionary establishments among them, as the general working of the Basle Society has not as yet been extended to them. Politically they would accept any liberal government given them, and even now they consider themselves under the government of Accra. They speak the Adangme dialect of the Awoonah language, but they understand and speak Ga equally as well.

Crobboe.—Crobboe is the richest district of this portion of the Protected Territory of the Gold Coast, and is the place from which the largest quantity of palm-oil is obtained. It is about forty miles from the sea-coast, and consists of an extensive plain covered with palm-trees. It is the largest palm plantation I have seen, and for several miles one could walk in the shady groves of these, queens of the forest. The inhabitants are very industrious, and labour hard in the manufacture of the oil. The rising generation are more or less educated. The Basle missionaries have laboured amongst them for some time, and have taught them not only to read and write, but also agricultural pursuits. The people are governed by two kings—viz., Ologo Patoo and Odonko Assu. The latter is well-disposed, supports the missionaries, and receives them as his counsellors; the former is very treacherous, and not to be relied upon. The currency of the country is cowry-shells; they are used for buying oil. A rich man has a house full of them, which are generally buried in the earth. The inhabitants are not very warlike; but when attacked they ascend a natural fortress—the Crobboe Mountain— (which is an abrupt volcanic hill) and defy the approach of even a regular army. It has been well designated the African Gibraltar. The dress of the men partakes of the character of those in the Gold Coast generally; but the females go about in all but perfect nudity. The Crobboe girls are known for their nakedness, but they are generally well formed. The commercial port of Crobboe is Kpong, which is on the banks of the river Volta, and was once a Government station. They speak the Adangme and Ga languages.

Aquamboo.—A small country situated beyond the range of hills known as the Aquamboo Mountains is the district of the same name. The inhabitants are few, but very brave. They are now not regarded as within the Protectorate, having a few years ago disobeyed the commands of the British Government, At present they are in league with the enemies of the Coast towns, and even seek an opportunity of combining against them. They speak Ga and Adangme.

Argotime.—This is a small trans-Volta tribe, who are considered brave and energetic by the tribes around. The country has some resemblance to that of Crobboe. The towns and villages are partly concealed by cocoa-nut trees. These people are Ga colonists, who emigrated from the neighbourhood of Ningo, Shai, and Addah, and settled there some 80 or 100 years ago. Through Mlamfi they have intercourse with the Coast towns, especially Ningo. They possess no political connexion with the people of Little Popo and

Saigodshi, who years ago migrated from the Shai and Ga. 'A curious feature of their towns are the town-halls, if we may so call them, which are common shady street trees, whose limbs are propped up by wood, and drawn like vines to form a spacious shed in the midst of the market-places.' The people are said to be very industrious and respectable. The country is well supplied with water. There are good houses, and much industry is observable. In every yard there are cotton spinners, weavers, and dyers. The language is Adangme; but being so much blended in manners, customs, and intermarriage with their neighbours of the Ewe language, that language is becoming more predominant among the younger generation. Argotime is situated between Creepee and Awoonah, on the left bank of the River Volta.

Creepee.—This is a large, well-cultivated, and extensive country on the banks of the Volta and interior of Argotime. The Basle missionaries have stations here. It supplies the large quantity of cotton shipped from Accra and Awoonah. The inhabitants are amongst the most hardworking people on the Gold Coast. The country is in close proximity with Dahomy on the one hand, and Ashantee on the other. The Ewe language is spoken.

The countries composing the Eastern District, which can with profit be included within the Republic of Accra, are much more united than those in the Western; they have always regarded Accra as their head-quarters, and would gladly form with it any combination. Their only enemies are the Ashantees, who being at a great distance from them would think twice before they attempted to over-run the country; in fact, since the engagement in the plains of Dooduah, when Major Chisholm commanded the combined forces of Fantee and Accra, and through the use of the Congreve rockets, the Ashantees were thoroughly defeated and driven from the field, they (the Ashantees) have always regarded the Accras as a brave, dashing, impetuous, and energetic people, who are not to be trifled with; consequently their policy has always been to keep them as friends, so that they would not form any hostile combination with the Fantees against them. But since the late war between Awoonah and Accra—where a few hundred of the former routed, drove, and pursued nearly ten thousand of the latter, who skeddadled helter-skelter from the battle-field, disgracefully throwing into the bush their guns, ammunition, and cloth, leaving the heavy artillery lent to them by the British Government in the field, until their king, Cudjoe, after fruitlessly endeavouring to rally them, sat on the howitzer, and proclaimed his willingness to allow himself to be captured by the enemy unless his followers removed the British gun—the Ashantees have become daring, and saw their mistake as to the prowess of the Accras. They are now endeavouring to effect a political combination with Awoonah, offensive and defensive. But the Awoonahs know that they are on the sea side, leeward of the Volta, and within very easy reach. They also know that in such an alliance they have everything to lose and nothing whatever to gain; they therefore most prudently but politely declined the offer.

The only points open to an enemy on the borders of the Republic of Accra are Akim, Aquapim, and Aquamboo. In the two former places the Ashantees know that they would meet with powerful resistance in the mountain fastnesses of Akim and Aquapim, and they will hesitate to make the attempt. The Aquamboos are already in alliance offensive and defensive with them, and they can easily pour hosts of their ill-clad army through the Aquamboo mountain passes; but as soon as they enter the plains of the Republic they will first be met by a powerful tribe, the Crobboes; and being in an open plain, a strong force can easily be sent against them, and a second Dooduah would inevitably be the result. It is, therefore, almost without a shadow of doubt that the young Republic will exist without an external enemy capable of giving her much trouble.

The Basle missionaries have completely renovated the aspect of the country, and the extreme savage and barbarous habits of the people, wherever they have laboured; they have established the literature of the language, and make the rising generation to feel the beauty and pathos of their mother tongue when reduced to writing; they have introduced the cultivation of new plants in the country, and taught the people how to prepare them, some of which are now becoming staple articles of commerce, such as coffee, cocoa, Virginian and Kentucky tobacco; they labour continually in the country, and many of them marry lawfully with the native ladies, which increases their influence and power over the native population; they make good, open roads into the interior, dig deep and expensive wells (94 feet cost £600) in their stations where water is scarce, and supply good wholesome water for their own use and those of the inhabitants of the towns, who, consequently, highly appreciate their efforts for their welfare; they introduced European horses, which, unfortunately, could not withstand the climate of the country. Besides teaching the people the value of agricultural pursuits, and affording them every opportunity of realizing the value of their produce, they teach them mechanical arts; they send out shoemakers, tailors, wheelwrights, carpenters, and coopers, to teach the people these useful employments, so that vast improvements are being made by the natives; and yet I have heard the labours of these pioneers of civilization scoffed at, and these laborious men disrespectfully spoken of. In my opinion—and I think this is shared by all men of sound judgment—they ought to be held up and encouraged, not only by the European and native population of the country, but also by the Government, who should support and recognise their efforts by giving employment to the best students of the establishment. At one time the Government of Sierra Leone was in the habit of sending to the Church and Wesleyan missionaries' schools for young men when there was a vacancy in some of the Government departments; if such a system were now carried out here, it would be a boon to the country.

The Republic of Accra can be made to be one of the richest provinces in Western Africa; its resources are vast and extensive, and require only to be developed. It presents a varied number of exportable plants not easily found in other parts of the coast; the soil is peculiarly fertile and rich, and could grow any articles planted in it, rapidly and luxuriantly. It has a large river which runs into its very interior, and which might be made use of for bringing down the accumulated riches of the interior countries. The principal articles of export are gold-dust, palm-oil, monkey skins, gum copal, and cotton.

Gold-dust.—There is only a small quantity of this valuable article exported from Accra, which is obtained from Akim, Aquapim, and Ashantee. Most of the tribes in the interior and

L

on the sea-coast regard gold as Fetish property, which if they keep would kill them ; they therefore would not on any account keep gold-dust or even any gold coin, or touch it ; if they unwittingly do, they immediately wipe their hands. They receive all gold coin on pieces of paper or handkerchiefs ; this is observed in Adangme and Crobboe.

Monkey Skins.—At one time this was a very important importable article on the Gold Coast. Mr. William Bruce, of Jamestown, was the first who commenced the trade, and he realized a very handsome amount for shipments made to England. In 1856 the black monkey skins were exceedingly abundant and cheap, twenty to twenty-five were sold for a dollar (4s. 6d.) After the trade had commenced the price rose abruptly, so that in June, 1859, the merchants were eagerly buying them at a shilling a-piece. In 1860 the price rose still higher, and a good skin could not be obtained for less than a dollar. The black monkeys which furnish the skins are abundant in the forest at Akim, the interior of Accra, and at Crobboe. The natives hunt them in the months of May, June, July, and August, when they are within range of musket-shot. During the dry season they pass their time in the tops of lofty trees, where they cannot be killed ; but in the rains they descend to shelter themselves among the trees and bushes from the rain. There is scarcely any business doing now in monkey skins; the demand in England has ceased.

Palm-oil.—This is the most important article of traffic in the eastern district. A small quantity is made in Winnebah and Aquapim, but the largest supply is from Crobboe.

Gum Copal.—In the fields interior of the sea-coast towns of Accra, in Aquapim, and in many other parts of this district, gum copal, which is used in making varnish, is obtained in large quantities. Mr. William Addo was the first to commence the trade, but at present that which is exported does not produce a sufficient remuneration to encourage the trade. Not long ago a large quantity was exported to England, which laid in store for nearly a year, and, when sold, the amount realized scarcely covered the expenses. The trade has greatly fallen off.

Cotton.—This important article is now being abundantly shipped from this part of the Coast. The merchants have given the impetus to the people, who are certain that, whatever quantity they may bring into the market, it will meet with a buyer. A large district—Creepee—situated on the banks of the River Volta, beyond Argotime, and between Ashantee and Dahomy, is fully under cultivation with cotton. The merchants have established factories there, and have cotton-gins at work. The trade has only lately been opened, and shiploads of cotton have been exported from the country, and there is every hope of its further increase.

Besides these articles, others of not less importance are gradually making a show in the exportable list. Coffee was first introduced by the Basle missionaries, who planted a large quantity in their station at Accrapong. At present they have in their plantation 60,000 trees, 30,000 of which are yielding fruit. Not only this, the Christian and heathen population about their stations are following their examples, and have their own plantations of coffee. The native merchants have also taken the initiative ; Mr. Freeman has about 30,000 trees; Messrs. Leutrot, Hesse, Briandt, Bruce, and Dodo have all coffee plantations more or less large.

The same missionaries have commenced the planting of Virginian and Kentucky tobacco ; they thus supply all that is required for their own use. Already they have sent specimens to Bremen, where it was considered good, but required improvement in the preparation. Besides this they are endeavouring to naturalise the Mexican cocoa or chocolate plant in this part of the Coast. They have a few trees growing at Accrapong which have borne very large fruit, and hopes are entertained that it will be a complete success. The natural advancement of this country is therefore being vastly increased by these Basle missionaries, who call themselves *Germano-Africans.*

India-rubber and gutta-percha trees exist in the interior of this district ; the inhabitants (women) use it principally for repairing earthenware pots. A small quantity was shipped to Bremen by Mr. Hillginbergh, clerk to Mr. Julius Ungar, who is connected with the German missionaries. It was in great request and remunerative, but the mode adopted for collecting it by the natives is very extravagant and destructive. They cut down the tree, burn one end, and allow the gum to exude from the other ; the tree is therefore destroyed. The mode to be adopted should be to make fissures on the thick bark of the trunk of the tree. and the gum would easily flow out; when collected and exposed to the air, it gradually coagulates.

The *Indigo plant* is abundant in the fields of the Eastern District, and the natives use it for dying their native-made clothes. Ebony is also found in the woods of the interior, especially in a place called Pallimah, or Adapalmah, where the trees are said to grow in large numbers. A few sticks have been obtained on the Coast from individuals in this district.

From considering and examining the geological structure of this district, I am under the impression that there are extensive *coal-fields* in the interior of the country and in the kingdom of Dahomy, and this view has been confirmed by circumstantial evidence. When the rainy season is very severe, and the streams of the Volta swell up and become very rapid, large masses of coal have been known to be brought down from the interior and left on its banks. The last seen was at a place called Kpong, in Crobboe.

Seven years ago, whilst examining the conchology (shells) of this part of the Coast, I was forcibly struck with their resemblance and identity with those on the coast of Brazils. From the above description of the plants, and also if reference be made to my *flora* of the West Coast of Africa, it will be seen that there is great resemblance in the botany of the two countries. The geological structure of the two countries is almost identical. These facts led me to the belief that when the resources of the country are much more developed, *diamonds* will be found, not only in the Eastern District, but also in the rivers and lagoons of Awoonah and Dahomy. I made fruitless researches myself whilst stationed at Quitah and Addah, but it is my firm belief that in years to come, all things being equal, and development progressive, the diamond will ultimately be one of the exportable articles.

The planting of ground-nut should now be encouraged, as the soil of Accra district is in a great many places very much adapted for it. It will bring a very large revenue to the Government, and much cash into the country, to replace the cowry-shells, which everyone proclaims a great nuisance. Its leaves will serve as excellent fodder for horses, and strengthen them infinitely better than the common grass, which they now use.

One great circumstance which enthrals the population of this part of the Coast is the implicit belief they have in the Fetish. We have seen that in the Western District the people have little or no belief in Fetish, but it is exactly the contrary here, where it is feared and dreaded by the whole bulk of the population. They build houses for it, sacrifice sheep and oxen to it, consult it in all their affairs; they dare not go to war without receiving its benediction and undergoing certain forms and ceremonies; and therefore the mental freedom of the population is completely cowed down. Not that the educated, nor even some of the illiterate and barbarous, believe that a lump of clay, a feather, or a few beads, is really and truly their god, and worship it as such; but the first doctrine of their natural religion is that there is one god, who is most high, and everyone believes this; but the Fetish is a plurality of inferior gods, and is regarded as the creator of man and all things in the world. It is believed to be capable of at once killing and making alive, and to human beings it communicates through the Fetish priest. But the great terror felt by the followers of Fetishism is not for the ' unknown god,' but for the secret influence which the Fetish priest has over the minds of the people. Any disobedience to his command is almost always followed by death through secret poisoning, which is proclaimed as the act of the Fetish; consequently, the ignorant, and even those who know better, are terrified. An example of this will not be out of place here. In 1866, when the war broke out between Awoonah and Accra, the young King of Aquapim was solicited to take part in it. He consulted with the Fetish and was told not to go. He, notwithstanding, went with his followers; he proved himself to be the bravest king in the whole campaign, and saved the Accras from total destruction. He returned to his kingdom in perfect health, with all the laurels of war; three days afterwards he was a corpse, of course secretly poisoned; and the priest gave it out that ' the Fetish god had killed him because he disobeyed his command.'

The Eastern District of the Gold Coast is composed of numerous separate kingdoms, which are more or less united in habits, interest,

and nationality.   Each king regards the principal Coast town as his
headquarters, any orders from which receive immediate obedience.
The Coast towns are not within easy reach of their powerful neighbours, the Ashantees, who have, since the battle of Doodooah, regarded the Accras with a certain degree of fear, and would hesitate
to fight in plains with well-disciplined troops.   Besides, situated in
the neighbourhood of the frontier towns are powerful tribes, who
have, years ago, fought single-handed with them with decided advantage.   The mountain passes and defiles prevent a large body
of troops being marched into the country without their being cut off
in detail with the loss of many of their men.   They therefore have
no great risk or fear of any molestation from an enemy in the interior.

Superior education is making gradual but certain progress in the
various districts of Accra; the language is in writing, and many of
the people could communicate in it.   There are industrial establishments, a great many carpenters, bricklayers, and other mechanics ;
agricultural pursuits have taken a great hold on the minds of the
population, and new commercial plants are being introduced.   In a
word, this district has vast resources, and, the country being level,
if these are developed, with a very small outlay, a railway can be
made from Christiansborg to Crobboe.   A small steamer, having a
small draught of water, launched in the Volta and plying to beyond
Creepee, would certainly develop and bring down the ivory, cotton,
and other products of the country.

Domestic slavery exists here, as in other parts of the Coast, with
all the enervating influence which it engenders ; but one of the
greatest drawbacks to any improvement is the presence of petty
kings in every small town, within a stonesthrow of each other.
This should be done away with ; after the death of the king the
title should be abolished and a headman appointed.

Before the place should be given up to self-government (say two
or three years before) the different kings and headmen should be
assembled at Accra, and a treaty drawn up, binding them, offensive
and defensive, with one another.   The Government should introduce to them one of the natives, whom it may consider to be of good
practical common sense, educated, and possessed of influence in the
country, as their nominee for the post of head centre, or President

of the Republic of Accra—such a man, for instance, as Libercht Hesse, of Christiansborg. They should give in their votes, and, when elected, he should be inaugurated in their presence, and considered as their chief. As soon as this is done, he should be made to regulate the internal government of the country, under the supervision of the Governor. A yearly grant out of the revenue should be voted him; schools and educational seminaries should be established in every town. A militia force should be enrolled, and drilled by paid officers and sergeants of West Indian regiments. In all such efforts I am certain that he would receive the assistance, not only of the educated natives of the place, but also of the Europeans of long residence in the country, who would lend him the weight of their influence, as well as assist in developing the resources of the country.

It is, therefore, evident from the foregoing that there are more advantages in the Eastern District than the Western for forming a good, useful, native self-government, which would ultimately be profitable to the British Government and the native population; but that there are vast rooms for improvement in the various branches. That if the kings be left as they are to govern themselves, the base being rotten, the whole fabric will, within a very short time, tumble to the ground. Confusion, massacre, and bloodshed would be the inevitable result. That before the people be given up to govern themselves a new order of things must be established, and an entirely new government formed, under the auspices of the British Government, supported by all the kings of the districts; and the British Consul of the Gold Coast should always be ready to advise them in political matters, and preserve the country from foreign invasion.

CHAPTER XII.

SELF-GOVERNMENT OF LAGOS AND ITS INTERIOR COUNTRIES. KINGDOM OF THE AKUS.

THE Committee of the House of Commons, in their report, state that ' the annexation of Lagos was a strong measure, of which not only the wisdom may be questioned, but the alleged justification also—viz., the incapacity and faithlessness of a king, who was first set up by the English against a very doubtful usurper, and whose powerlessness over his subjects was much caused by their interference. The wisdom of the act may be tested by the consideration that, had we refrained from assuming the government, we need not have been complicated in the Egba Wars, nor in the perplexity of having to recognise at the same time that we prohibit, slavery within our own territory.'

Among the questions put to witnesses examined, and their answers, we find the following :—

To William Wylde, Esq., Superintendent of the Slave-trade Department of the Foreign-office, referring to the annexation of Lagos, we find the following reply :—

Answer. The annexation was because we found that, notwithstanding all the influence we possessed there by having a Consul, the traffic in slaves, although it was watched closely around Lagos, was carried on up and down the lagoon just the same as it was before. Wars were going on, depopulating the country, and where there had been valuable trade, it was at a standstill; and we sent our ships with a view to put a stop entirely to the slave-trade all through the lagoons, for the purpose of using our influence on the surrounding countries, and compelling them, if possible, to keep the peace, so as thereby very considerably to augment legitimate trade there. If you suppress the slave-trade, you must supply its place by encouraging legitimate trade, or they will take up the first opportunity they can of reverting again to the slave-trade. We find that where we put a stop to the slave-trade, and a legitimate trade is developed, the slave-trade will not break out again, because there are so many parties that get interested in the legitimate trade, that if they find the chiefs or any parties in the neighbourhood are encouraging the slave-trade they tell of it.

Q. But there is a paper laid on the table of the House of Commons—a paper from the Secretary of State in the Queen's name: ' You will carefully explain to Docemo the motives which have induced Her Majesty's Government to take this step. You will inform him that Her Majesty's Government are not actuated by any dissatisfaction with his conduct, but that, on the contrary, they have every wish to deal with him in a liberal and friendly spirit, and that their object in taking this step is to secure for ever the free population of Lagos from the slave-traders and kidnappers who formerly oppressed them ; to protect and develop the important trade of which that town is a seat; and to exercise an influence on the surrounding tribes, which may, it is hoped, be permanently beneficial to the African race.' Now, does Lord John Russell there in the slightest degree charge King Docemo with having connived at the slave-trade?

A. No ; and he never did. I am not aware that there had been any charge against him.

Q. Other witnesses before the Committee have made statements that Docemo had broken the treaty. Are the Committee to understand your opinion to be that these statements of Lord John Russell's contained the real reasons, and that Docemo had never broken the treaty ?

A. He most certainly had never broken the treaty, but he had not the power of preventing his subjects and people living in Lagos from doing so. They were as much engaged in the slave-trade as before, though indirectly. Slaves were even taken out of Lagos and sent up the lagoons and sold at Whydah.

David Chinery, Esq., Managing Director of the London and African Trading Company, gave the following evidence.

Referring to the bombardment of Porto Novo, he was asked :—

Q. Was it your brother's opinion, and is it your opinion, that there was the same injustice in what was done by the English there as in the assumption of Docemo's Government?

A. I think it was a most glaring piece of injustice and cruelty.

Q. What was the ground on which it was justified?

A. It was upon a point of etiquette only. Mr. Consul Foote went up in the gunboat, accompanied by the troops, and after lowering his anchor, he sent to the King to say that he had come for the purpose of getting him to sign a treaty, and that he must go off to him on board the steamer. The King received his messenger very politely, but told him that he feared that the Consul had forgotten himself, and that the King of Porto Novo was a man of as much importance in Porto Novo as the Queen of England was in England, and demanded a corresponding amount of respect; and he thought that if the Consul required him to sign a treaty, that he should take the treaty to his house. To that the Consul replied that he thought that the dignity of his position there demanded that he should not stoop so low to the King of Porto Novo, but that the King should go off and sign the treaty on board the steamer; and, taking that view of the case, he gave him a given hour to consider it, and if he failed by that hour, the town would be blown up at all hazards. The King did not do so, and the town was at once fired on without further to-do; some 600 or 700 human beings were sacrificed by our gunboats. The town was burnt down, and the trade was destroyed for an immense time; all upon a point which I consider absurd and ridiculous, and a lasting disgrace to us.

Q. Has the nature of your imports changed of late, on account of a more civilized demand there for cloth and other things, so as to lead you to suppose that the civilization of the interior was improving?

A. Yes. The last advice from my brother as to our taking Badagry, writing from January, 1864, says, as to Okeodam, which is a very important place, that he had just returned from there, and that trade bids fair to increase in all the towns, not even excepting Abeokuta. He says: 'I have taken a large piece of ground to build stores on, and to begin to trade, and it is to be hoped that there will be no Government official sent there to imperil our interest.'

Q. Are you aware that in 1860, Consul Brand, writing to Lord

John Russell, described the state of things in Lagos in this way: 'Lagos at present may be said to have no government; there is no effective protection to property, and no mode of enforcing the payment of debts.' He goes on to say that the small vessel, the 'Brune,' was their only protection; that whatever government did exist was carried on by the British Consul; that King Docemo was a mere puppet, who was quite unable to preserve law and order. Do you differ from that statement?

A. I should, myself, certainly differ from that statement, from my own experience; things must have been vastly changed since I was there with Consul Campbell, not two years previously.

Q. Mr. CHICHESTER FORTESCUE: I find in 1861 that Lord John Russell wrote to Consul Foote in these words: ' Her Majesty's Government would be most unwilling that the establishment of British sovereignty at Lagos should be attended with any injustice to Docemo, the present chief of the island; but they conceive that as his tenure of the island, in point of fact, depends entirely upon the continuance of the protection which has been afforded to him and his predecessor by the British naval authorities, since the expulsion of Kosoko, no injustice will be inflicted upon him by changing his anomalous protectorate into an avowed occupation, provided his material interests are secured.' Do you state to the Committee that you take an entirely different view of Docemo's position from that?

A. I do.

Q. You think that he was *bonâ-fide* governor of the country, and able to maintain himself against the wars of his neighbours without our protection?

A. From my experience, I must say yes, decidedly; from all the information I have ever had from my brother and on the spot, and very recently too. I think the safety of Lagos, or its inhabitants, or the trade, would be as good under Docemo, with an English consul, as it is now.

Q. You think that if we were to withdraw to-morrow, Docemo would be able to make Lagos a safe place for trade?

A. I think that if we continued our consulship at Lagos, it would be so; and for my part, I should prefer my interests in the trade to be subject to a consular agent rather than a colonial government.

On the subject of the decline of trade by native wars, he replied:—

Q. At all events you would admit the native wars to be in a great degree the cause ?

A. Certainly. When Consul Taylor went to Abeokuta he was told by the king himself that the English people first sent a consul to Lagos, and then, after the consul had been there a little time, they came and took the place away from them; and he said ' We cannot let a consul come here, because if he does you will do so again.' The consequence was that he was sent home without being allowed to be treated with common courtesy, or being received for even a day.

Q. I understood you to say that you thought that the presence of the Government officials was an obstruction to the trade at Lagos?

A. Yes.

Q. I ask whether that might be avoided by a different conduct on the part of the authorities ?

A. Partially so. If it had remained a consulate we should not have had that misunderstanding.

Q. You say that the Government has not had anything to do with the Abeokutas ; with what tribes have we had misunderstanding since 1860, which has hindered trade ?

A. I do not know with what other tribes we have had a misunderstanding, but I can speak for Badagry, Palma, and Porto Novo ; *it is a fact that our having taken Lagos at once depressed trade to a great extent, and it caused a general ill-feeling at all of these places, a feeling of distrust and almost revolt.*

In the evidence of James Aspinall Tobin, Esq., Director of the Company of African Merchants, we find the following :—

Q. Do you think a British merchant would rather have a consul than a government to deal with.

A. I think so; but I have not had experience of Lagos. If it were asked me whether I would at those places where there are not English settlements at this moment rather have commercial treaties, with a consul to visit them from time to time, than an English settlement, I should say I would rather have commercial treaties with a consul. At a settlement custom dues must be heavier, and that must drive trade to the nearest free port.

Q. Mr. CHICHESTER FORTESCUE : Are you speaking with reference to the oil rivers ?

A. The oil rivers and other places.

Q. CHAIRMAN: Take Bonny ; do you think that King Pepel is more likely to maintain peace there and to promote commerce than an English governor placed there ?

A. I should be very sorry to see any English governor placed there.

In the evidence of Captain R. F. Burton, late British Consul in the Bight of Biafra, we find the following :—

Q. Do you think that, with our present purpose in view—namely, the suppression of the slave-trade, it is necessary for us to hold the four posts of Badagry, Lagos, Palma, and Leckie ?

A. I believe that a consul there with the crusiers would do, at Lagos, for instance, as much as our present settlement.

Q. In saying that you think a consul would be sufficient, do you imply that the Government establishment might be dispensed with, both civil and military ?

A. Yes.

Q. Do you think, then, that we might dispense with all the civil and military establishments on that Coast ?

A. At Lagos I am of opinion that you might.

Upon the above and other evidence, the Committee in, their recommendations, states that ' Lagos will require an English commandant until the native rule can be re-established, when he would resume the office of consul, or rather, confine himself to that office, which he now incongruously holds with the Government of Lagos, as Consul of Benin.

' That Houssa police should suffice for all military purposes.

' Nothing but the most necessary establishments should be retained or put in order on the island itself, trusting to the squadron preventing any slave export reviving from the shore.

' The assumption of territory round Lagos, while domestic slavery continues under our legal prohibition but practical recognition, seems most undesirable ; nor is it possible at once to abolish slavery.

Possibly English commerce, with less of Governmental interference, may gradually effectually eradicate the custom.'

From the foregoing evidence it will be supposed by the casual reader that the existence of British rule was a curse to this part of the Coast; that the country was infinitely superior, commerce much more advanced, and life and property safer in the hands of the superseded native government than under the sovereignty of Britain. But viewing the growing civilization of Lagos and its suburbs, the immense and progressive improvement going on, the march of intellectual development among the mass of the population, the increase of commerce both in imports and exports, the sanitary improvements everywhere observed, and the imitation of the civilized mode of government among surrounding potentates, we must unhesitatingly state that it was the greatest blessing that could have happened to Lagos and the whole of the Yoruba or Aku tribe, that such a responsible, civilized, and powerful government should have at that opportune moment commenced her regeneration.

I do not at all by this intend to justify the means adopted, but, looking to the results achieved, we must forget the past and hail what has been so instrumental for the country's good. Lagos is, therefore, a star from which must radiate the refulgent rays of civilization into the interior of the Yoruba or Aku Country, and every effort must be made, especially by the native inhabitants, to support the hands of the Government in their work of regeneration. It should have been expected that the assumption of the territory would have, at first, led to internal rows and distrust on the part of the interior population, who knew nothing of British arms and power, and after this storm which might have led to destruction of trade, and even to open hostility, with all its concomitant woes, there would be a happy lull, and things would take an entirely opposite turn. It was on this account that we applaud the manly and determined actions of Governor Glover, who succeeded to the government of Lagos soon after it became a British colony. It was necessary that the savage tribes around should be made to acknowledge the supremacy of British power ; it was necessary that they should look to the new authority as one which cannot be cowed down by any native king, that they should feel that any trespass on

British property will be met with peremptory and severe rewards from the Government of the island; in a word, it was necessary, for the Government of Lagos to be carried on successfully, that the surrounding tribes should respect it and otherwise regard it with fear. Governor Glover knew this, and his whole policy turned on this point, and as each sign of disrespect met with severe punishment, and as complication in the interior war was unavoidable, he soon made the interior tribes taste the power of the new Government. Trade, as a necessary effect, was temporarily stopped; he was traduced by some of the merchants and traders, and no diatribe was found sufficient to characterise his rule, but time wore away, and trade again began to be healthy, and now produce is flocking abundantly into the port of Lagos from all sides, and there is more certain hope of a long and continuous peace.

But Lagos is only an isolated and important seaport town in the kingdom of the Akus. From want of a more specific name and from the whole of the tribes being once subjected to the king of Yoruba, the Church Missionary Society has designated it the 'Yoruba Country,' but as most of the tribes, such as the Egbas and Egbadoes, have objected to their being called Yorubas, and as there is no national name by which all the tribes speaking the same language but differently governed is known, I have employed the name which is given to the whole nation at Sierra Leone, and which is generally adopted in every part of the Coast—viz., the *Akus.* The kingdom is bounded on the north by the right or Quora branch of the River Niger, on the south by the Atlantic, on the east by Benin, Kakanda, and part of Igara, and on the west by the kingdom of Dahomy.

The kingdom is divided into various tribes, who are governed by their own chiefs and by their own laws, but who are extremely jealous of one another. The principal tribes are the Egbadoes, which include 'Otta and Lagos, near the sea-coast, forming a belt of country on the banks of the Lagoon in the forest, to Ketu, on the border of Dahomy. * The next tribe occupy Ketu and Shabe, on

---

* According to Captain Burton the Egbadoes are distinctly negroid, without showing the characteristics of the full-blooded negro. The skin is of a dark,

the border of Dahomy on the west, then comes Ijebu on the east, on the border of Benin, then the Egbas of the forest, now known by the name of Egbas of Abeokuta; then comes Yoruba Proper north-ward of the plain. Ife, Ijesha, Iyamo, Efou, Oudo, Ideko, Igbomna, and Ado, near the banks of the Niger, from which the creek or stream a little below Iddah is called Do or Ido.' Years ago all these tribes were politically united under one head as tributaries to the King of Yoruba, amongst whom were included Benin on the east and Dahomy on the west. A large portion of Yoruba Proper is governed by a Mussulman king, who is subject to the Sultan of Sokoto, on the other side of the Niger; the principal town and seat of government is Ilorin.

Properly speaking there are seven independent provinces in the kingdom of the Akus. Captain Burton * thus gives a summary of them :—

1. *Iketu*, in our maps Ketu, with a capital of the same name, is a small country lying between Agbome and the River Ogun, south of Yoruba Proper, and shut out from the sea. It has hitherto with-stood the power of Dahomy, and as the soil is poor, whilst timber and water are far from abundant, it is not much coveted by its neighbour. Population, 100,000.

2. *Ekko*, or Lagos (Portuguese). The chief town is Aoni, or Awini—*i.e.*, descended from Ini or Bini-Benin. The limits are Egba-land to the north, the sea to the south, the Ijebu Country on the east of Badagry, now its dependency, on the west. Population, 80,000.

3. *Egba* is a small kingdom lying on both sides of the Ogun River, but principally on the left bank. It is bounded on the north by Yoruba Proper, south by Ekko, east by Ijebu, and west by Iketu. It includes the kingdom of Otta. This is the head-quarters of the Aku nation; its capital is Abeokuta. Population, 200,000.

delicate copper, sometimes black, whilst several of the chiefs are almost light coloured. The lips are not thick, but the gums are blue, and the teeth not improved by chewing. The diet is poor, their climate poorer; calesthenics un-known; they are industrious. In the country pottery is abundant, nets are hung everywhere, canoes numerous; the men skid their little creeks with fish traps and the women ply the paddle.

* 'Abeokuta and the Cameroon Mountains '—page 244.

4. *Ijebu*, or Jaboo, is situated between Egba-land and Benin; it is bounded northwards by Yoruba Proper and Kakanda, southwards by the sea, or more properly by the Lagoon, called the Ikoradu or Cradoo Waters. It is divided into two parts, the Ijebu Ode to the east, and westward the Ijebu Remo. The Awajali, or great king, however, resides at Ode. The Ijebus are warlike, and are the most deadly enemies of the Egbas. Population, 200,000.

5. *Ijesha*, capital Ijesha, lies between Yoruba and Kakanda. Very little is known of it. Population, 200,000.

6. *Kakanda*, more properly called Effong or Effon, extends from Yoruba Proper to the Niger and the Kwara Rivers. The people are celebrated for working copper.

7. *Ilori*, a province and city of the same name, inhabited by Moslem, Fulas, and Gambari, a tribe of Hausa men, together with a few Pagan Yorubas. The king is a Fula, and the chiefs mostly Gambari and Kaniki. It is one of the great marts of Central Africa.

The tribes included within this territorial definition, although they differ from one another in interest and religion, form one nation, speaking the same language, having identical customs and usages. They have suffered more than any other nation in Western Africa from the depredations of the slave-trade.* Before Lagos fell under the power of the British, it formed, with Badagry and Whydah, the principal slave-port towns on the seaboard of Western Intertropical Africa. The number of Akus emancipated as slaves in

---

* 'According to Mr. T. B. Freeman, one of the earliest visitors to Abeokuta, a war had lasted nearly a century between the Kings of Dahomy and of Great Benin. The lands lying between the two rivals had suffered greatly ; and even in the present day, the line of country between Badagry and Abeokuta, which is 100 miles long, does not contain more than 500 souls. In those days the Egbas dwelt to the eastward of their present homes, but were driven out by their neighbours the Ijebus, who had sided with Benin. Under their chief, Ladmodi, the Egbas made head against the violence of the enemy, but he was at last slain, and the tribe dispersed.

' Without attempting to decide which account is true, it is evident that during the first quarter of the present century there was a general dispersion of the Egbas. We know that about 1820-22 there was a great influx of Aku captives into Sierra Leone, and that they found their way east and west, to the United States, Gambia, Fernando Po, Hausa, Borneo, Central Africa, the Fezzan, Egypt, and even to Stamboul. It was a race worsted and spoiled, not, as is commonly asserted, by Europeans, but by its own folly and want of proper despotism.'— ' Abeokuta and the Cameroon Mountains '—page 236.

M

Sierra Leone, the West Indies, and America is almost double that from any other part; and even until this day the country is a prey to the rapacious slave-hunting expeditions of the King of Dahomy, who makes nightly attacks on small and unprotected towns, carrying away their inhabitants captives to Abomy, disposing of some by supplying the slave market at Whydah, and sacrificing others in his inhuman annual 'custom.' But the country has ever and anon been largely supplying the slavedealers on the Coast, who gave them the impetus; and the Mohammedan chieftains beyond the Niger carry on wars of destruction and depredation wholesale, to swell the slave markets of Yoruba. Hausa and other interior tribes are brought down from Central Africa; most of the men sold as slaves, and the women and girls, especially if they have any pretensions to beauty, become wives of the native slavedealers. Through the continual drain from the land, and the destructive wars which were generally waged among themselves, the nation has entirely lost its purity, and may be rightly considered as Hausa, Kakanda, Nufi, and other interior tribes.

The Akus, as a race, are amongst the most industrious, persevering, and hard-working people on the West Coast of Africa. They are, as a rule, parsimonious in the extreme, and are consequently very wealthy. They make excellent traders, are very speculative, but saving. The men are generally hardy, strong, and cunning in their dealings with one another; when their interests are concerned they (the uneducated especially) are very obedient, and would undergo any degree of insult without manifesting any great displeasure; they are particularly jealous of one another, and hate to be opposed by any of their own tribe. The heathen portion especially deal greatly in poisonous medicine, which some employ for secretly depriving individuals of their lives, or otherwise producing in them some bodily distemper. At Sierra Leone and other parts of the Coast the Akus are very much feared; not so much by people of different nationality, but by those of the same tribe.* Various kinds

---

* Describing the appearance of the King of Abeokuta, Captain Burton said : 'The chiefs were bareheaded, naked to the waist, wholly unornamented, except with a few cheap beads, and clothed with a common native loin wrap, or a bit of unbleached domestics. *To retain wealth in such lands*

of poisonous drugs—'agoomoos'—are exported from Lagos, and are employed for different purposes. They believe that, by the aid of medicine, riches, honour, education, and worldly favour can be secured, so that their medicine-men are generally sought after.*

The Akus have a strong power of combination; they obey implicitly, and put great confidence in the advice and orders of the old men, around whose banner they will rally; this is done not out of pure love of combination, as it is well known that their headmen have a secret way of making their orders obeyed, and when it forms a case of life and death this obedience is not to be wondered at. Cases are on record, or report makes cases, where very wealthy men have disobeyed these councillors; they were threatened at the time, and within a very few weeks or months they were carried to their long home.

requires care and caution ; and an ostentatious man, however rich, will die'— page 138. 'The Alake is waxing old, his legs are weary of him ; there is a report that he has made too much money, and signs appear that his subjects will send him a quiet message to "go to sleep"'—page 144. 'When present at Abeokuta they were celebrating the obsequies of the Akpena, or messenger of Igemna, a high officer who had lately died, not without strong suspicions of poison. He had been engaged in a quarrel with his superiors, the Ibashorum of his town. The people found business at a standstill ; they therefore sent to the less useful personage—the messenger—their compliments and a humble request that he would "go to sleep ;" so to sleep he went'—page 157. It is not an unfrequent habit to tell one to go and eat grass; the individual, although previously perfectly sane, gets in the course of a short time a regular lunatic.

* The Akus or Yorubas are eminently clannish; 'they have strong virtues and vices, and by dwelling upon one side, to the neglect of the rest of the moral development, it would be easy to make them the best or the worst of men. They are kind and courteous, hospitable, and not eminently dishonest ; on the other hand, they are covetous, cruel, and wholly deficient in what the civilized man calls conscience. With considerable shrewdness in business, they are simple in some points as children. They are somewhat litigious, and there is a numerous judiciary, whilst private disputes are settled by a kind of *consiglia di famiglia.* Their cruelty is shown rather in their religion than in their laws. Murder, treason, and arson, sometimes adultery and theft, are punished by death, the offender being beheaded or garrotted with a rope. In Ibore the neck is broken with an iron mace ; minor offences are visited with the whip, fine, or imprisonment. Men amongst the Egboes are farmers, tillers of ground, blacksmiths, woodcutters, carpenters, weavers, tailors, and barbers. Women do the housework and sell at markets ; between whiles they spin, wash, cook, draw water, dye cloth, and make soap and pottery. They rise early, and after a bath repair to their farms, their meals consisting of vegetables, farinaceous food, and meat.'

The women make excellent traders; within a very short time they would double, treble, and even quadruple a very small amount. Their diet and living are generally simple and inexpensive; they are very litigious; some of them are very good looking, nicely shaped and formed, although marked; others are hideously tattooed.* With the old Akus, as a general rule, it is difficult to know when you have offended them. They take offence quietly, and maybe an apology is made, which apparently is accepted; but the insult or offence is still harboured, and at some future day it will be satisfactorily revenged.

The educated Akus are making great advances in civilization, especially when untrammelled by any secret influences; some of them are most liberal and patriotic, and would spend a great deal towards developing the resources of their country. In the Colony of Sierra Leone they are numerous, and rising in wealth and influence, offshoots of whom are now at Lagos, who form the educated and thriving population of that infant Colony. Of the Akus in general it must be admitted without a question that there are no people on the Coast who are so hard-working and so long-suffering in proportion

---

* Captain Burton well describes these marks : 'There was a vast variety of tattooes and ornaments. . . . The skin patterns were of every variety, from the diminutive prick, to the great gash and the large boil-like lumps. They affect various figures—tortoise, alligator, and the favourite lizard, stars, concentric circles, lozenges, right lines, welts, gouts of gore, marble or button-like knobs of flesh, and elevated scars resembling scalds, which are opened for the introduction of Fetish medicines, and to expel evil influences. In this country every tribe, sub-tribe, and even family, has its blazon, whose infinite diversifications may be compared with the lines and ordinances of European heraldry ; a volume would not suffice to explain all the marks in detail. The chief are as follows : The distinguishing mark of the Egbas is a gridiron of three cuts, or a multiplication of three upon each cheek. Free-born women have one, two, or three raised lines, thread-like scars from the wrist up to the back of the arm, and down the dorsal regions, like long necklaces. They call this " entice my husband." The Yorubas draw perpendicular marks from the temples to the level of the chin, with slight lateral incisions, hardly perceptible, because allowed soon to heal. The Effons of Kakanda wear a blue patch, sometimes highly developed, from the cheek bones to the ear. The Takpas of Nupe make one long cut from the upper wheel of the nostril, sweeping towards the ear. At Ijesha, a country lying east of Yoruba Proper, the tattoo is a long parallelogram of seven perpendicular and five transverse lines. The areola in the female was not unfrequently a dull dark blue, the colouring matter being native antimony, found in Yoruba and on the Niger, and levigated with pepper and nitron upon a stone.'

to what they expect in return as they; they are generally passive, supine, inaccessible to curiosity, or love of pleasure, and not easily moved by political vicissitude.

The language of the district under consideration is the Aku or Yoruba Division of the great Ewe, or Dahomean, family. The Aku, Dahomy, Popo, Awoonah, and Accra or Ga, are cognate languages, which are spoken in the extensive tract of country lying between the River Volta and the Niger. Through the labours of the Church Missionary Society, the Aku or Yoruba dialect has been reduced to writing; the Bible, Prayer-book, Bible stories, and other religious books have been translated into it. The mass of the population has for some time been taught to write and communicate with one another in their own language; a great many of the inhabitants, especially those in the interior countries, can read and write the manuscript Arabic. Unfortunately no scientific work has as yet been translated into Yoruba; the mysteries and beauties of the arts and sciences, of modern and ancient history, and of geography, have not yet been brought, through the medium of their own language, within the comprehension of the natives, but advances are being made which we hope will ultimately lead to that very desirable result.

The religion of the Yoruba or Aku Kingdom is Mohammedanism and heathenism; the former has made great progress in the northern portion of the country—*i.e.*, in Yoruba proper; from the principal town of Ilorin, the Mohammedans travel into various parts, making proselytes of the heathen population, whilst at the same time carrying on active commerce in slaves. Intellectually and morally they are superior to the heathen population, who, on their part, assert a still greater superiority over them after their conversion from heathenism to Christianity. Their idolatrous worship is similar throughout the country. 'There is an established religion connected with the government, which is the worship of the dead, or their deceased ancestors, the secret of which every male is acquainted with, and is bound to keep the female ignorant of, on pain of death on its being revealed to the weaker sex. Thus it has become a sacred law to be observed by all the male population throughout the land; notwithstanding the national enmity against each other, yet this law is observed to be unviolated, even during those times of bitter rancour and revenge, when slave wars depopulated the country. The people are very superstitious ; besides the worship of their deceased ancestors, they worship the gods of thunder and lightning, the devil, snakes, rivers, some particular trees, the white-ant hills, and rocks with caves, in which they suppose the spirits of the gods to dwell. To these objects of worship, sacrifices of bullocks, goats and sheep, fowls and pigeons are made, and sometimes human beings also.'

The country is governed by separate kings, whose right is hereditary, but only in the male issue of the king's daughter ; his power is, in many instances, absolute ; his person and those of the royal family, sacred. He is assisted in making laws and settling palavers by the elders in the kingdom, who are designated in Yoruba, *Iweffa*.

The capabilities of the kingdom of the Akus are very great and extensive ; populated, as it is, by a hard-working, persevering people, with a rich, well-watered country. This territory, when fully developed and explored, bids fair to become one of the richest in Western Africa. The conversion of Lagos into a Colony, with a display of all the improvements, power, and civilization of a European nation, is a work of vast importance to those regions. The country is intersected by small streams, which swell considerably during the rainy season ; they are only navigable for boats and canoes, or vessels of very small tonnage. The principal streams are the Opara, which divides the kingdom of Aku from Dahomy, running between Ketu and the latter country ; the Ogun, which runs through the centre of the kingdom at the back of Lagos through Abeokuta ; the Iyewa, which empties its waters into the Lagoon a few miles from Badagry ; and the Palma, which runs through Gebee, east of Lagos.

Lagos is one of the richest Colonies in Western Africa, and the kingdom of the Akus is abundantly supplied with a vast number of marketable articles. The chief exports are palm-oil, palm-kernel oil, shea butter, cotton, and ivory. Ever since Lagos has become a British Colony, although intestine warfare has interfered with the general trade of the country, every circumstance points out that, within a very short time, the trade will be more than double its present extension, and this is the natural effect of the healthy influence of legitimate trade over that inhuman traffic, the slave-trade; and so long as the naturally vigorous natives are kept away from kidnapping and selling each other, so long will their energies be turned towards the developement of the rich resources of the country. The most recent contributions on the subject of this extensive kingdom give the following interesting details : ' Yoruba is a valuable and an unexplored field. Its products are cereals (maize and millet), vegetables (peas, beans, cassava, yams, koko, onions, and sweet potatoes), sugar-cane, ginger in small quantities, and lately introduced cubahs, and various oil seeds, bene or sesamun, talfaria, castor plant, ground-nuts, cocoa-nuts, and physic-nuts. Coffee has been grown, but it has been allowed to die out. Copper abounds in places. Indigo and coarse tobacco would flourish anywhere, and the minerals have not been explored.' Thus there is an extensive room for the adventurer. The spirit of self-government seems to be taking a healthy hold on the inhabitants of the metropolis of Aku—viz., Abeokuta ; the savage old native government is now undergoing a very decided change for the better, and it is modelled according to civilized constitutions, which shows the happy influence which British civilization has upon minds otherwise disposed to improvement. It is true that in Abeokuta, liberated slaves (and their descendants) of the country, who had been instructed and educated at school at Sierra Leone, had returned and made it their permanent abode and rendered the existing native government great service ; but it was not until there was established in Lagos a European Christian power that we saw the march of improvement rapidly advancing. At present, there is established at Abeokuta a board of management for the express purpose of directing the native government, of forwarding civilization, and promoting the spread of Christianity, as well as of protecting the property of European merchants and British subjects. The Secretary and Director of this Board, which is styled the Egba United Board of Management, is an educated native of Sierra Leone.* The first

---

* Since placing the manuscript in the hands of the printers, a most lamentable outburst of indignation amongst the heathen population has taken place in Abeokuta against Christianity, which led to the pillage and destruction of the churches and missionary establishment. The ostensible cause of it is the

ordinance enacted relates to the imposing of custom duties, which
is necessary for the development of the Government. Such duties
are imposed on exports, which must have an injurious effect on
trade. The conditions of the ordinance are :—

1. That it shall be lawful for any person or persons (without
exception) to have free access in Abeokuta for the purposes of
trade, and to export therefrom any goods or produce, passing from
Abeokuta to Lagos by the River Ogun, or elsewhere, subject to the
regulations hereinafter mentioned.

2. That on all goods exported from Abeokuta to Lagos, by the
River Ogun, or elsewhere, there shall be paid the following duty in
cowries or produce, at the time of such exportation—viz., ivory
and shea butter, three strings of cowries on every pound ; palm and
nut-oil, one string on every gallon ; cotton, twenty cowries on every
pound.

3. That all other goods not named shall be charged or charge-
able with a duty of three per cent. on the marketable value of such
goods and produce at Abeokuta at the time of such exportation.

4. That such duty shall be payable and paid at the Custom-
house of Abeokuta, on all such goods and produce as shall be intended to be exported by the River Ogun, and that on such payment
a permit for the export thereof shall be granted by the collector,
deputy collector, or such other person or persons as shall be sent
with and accompany such goods or produce on their exportation,
and shall be produced, if required, by any person or persons in charge

---

supposed encroachment of the British Government of Lagos on Abeokutan Territory, and consequently the dread that such aggrandizement might lead to the
ultimate absorption of the whole Abeokutan Territory. There has been correspondence between the two Governments which throws but a faint light on the
cause of attack upon that most unoffending and harmless body, the missionaries. The Bashorum Secretary has received his share of blame, but it
must be remembered that Abeokuta was never in such organized social condition and progress as it was before the outbreak—that a secretary in a
heathen court, however good might be his intentions, however sane his advice, however civilized his state, can never without national force stop the
infuriate zeal of a dozen obdurate heathen chieftains. Whilst disapproving *in
toto* the late barbarous and savage actions of the heathen Abeokutans, I hope
Christianity will soon be triumphant in that land, and that a progressive and
civilized form of government will be carried out upon a better and more aus-
picious footing.

of such goods or produce, and that the payment of the duty on goods and produce exported will and shall be payable at such place as shall be from time to time appointed.

5. That any goods or produce being exported from Abeokuta by the River Ogun or elsewhere, for which a permit shall not on demand be produced to any person appointed for the examination of such permits, shall and may be seized, and on proof before the Board of Management, or any four justices of the peace appointed for that purpose, and the non-production of such permit, the goods or produce shall be declared forfeited; and on sale, the produce of such sale shall, after deducting the necessary expenses, be paid as follows : viz., one-third thereof to the seizer and collector, and the balance to the Treasurer of the Board of Management for the use of the Egba Government.

6. That this ordinance shall take effect immediately on publication thereof.

Passed in the Board of Management, this 11th day of October, in the year of our Lord One Thousand Eight Hundred and Sixty-five, and confirmed on the 23rd day of March, 1867.

By command,

SHOMOYA, Bashorum, President-General.

GEORGE W. JOHNSON, Secretary and Director.

The most powerful and troublesome neighbour to Aku or Yoruba Land is the kingdom of Dahomy, which has for a long time been looking eagerly for the destruction of Abeokuta; twice has the Dahomean potentate attempted to destroy that town, and twice has he received a signal thrashing, with the loss of several thousands of his warriors; the last was so terrific, that it is certain that Abeokuta will never again be made a point of attack. It will still continue to harass the small towns on the frontier, until such time as a combined action of all the petty kingdoms is made against the common enemy, and Dahomy receives a final check in the slave-hunting exploits eastward of its dominion.

The natural capital of the Aku or Yoruba Territory is Abeokuta, and its best seaport town—or Liverpool—is Lagos. As yet the country and people are unprepared to be thrown on their own resources, it still requires more nursing. There are no roads in the interior, the water communications are not yet properly opened, and no regular native police or soldiery is paid by the native government. Things are only just germinating, and it would be an unwise step in the British Government were it to withdraw at once from the place.   Abeokuta is by no means strong enough to withstand the several native growing powers.   Ibadan, for example, will not receive any dictation from it, and it is not in a position to make it do so; should, therefore, the country be given up, anarchy and disorder will run riot throughout all the territory, and the slave-trade in its worse possible form will devastate the healthy growth of the kingdom of the Akus.

CHAPTER XIII.

EMPIRE OF THE EBOES (IBOES, IGBOES, EGBOES).

SITUATED between the Rivers Niger and Old Calabar, and bounded on the north by the left or Binnue branch of the first river, on the south by the Atlantic, on the east by Old Calabar and the Dwalla Countries, and on the west by the River Niger, Benin, and Igara, is the extensive and well-watered tract of territory included in the Empire of the Egboes.* According to Dr. Baikie, Egboe extends east and west from the Old Calabar River to the banks of the Niger, or Kwora, and possesses also some territory at Abo, in the westward of the stream ; on the north it borders on Igara and Akpoto, and is separated from the sea only by petty tribes, all of which trace their origin from the great race.

It is divided into several districts or counties, each speaking different dialects, although derived from one root. The principal counties are Isuama, Elugu, Isielu, Isiago, Abaga, Mitshie, and Djuku, all of which are situated on the north; in the middle are Abo, Abazim, Aro, and Amazunie ; and in the south are Brass, Nimbe, Okrika, Ebane or Bonny, and Adony. Very little is known of these districts ; their histories are shrouded in impenetrable darkness; expeditions have been made through the great water course into the interior; but no cross expedition, starting from the eastern banks of the Niger to the Old Calabar River, has as yet been attempted.

---

* *Egbo, Igbo, Ebo,* and *Ibo* are the various spellings met with in books describing the race inhabiting this part of the Coast. Among the soft *Isuama* and *Elugu,* the soft *Ebo* and *Ibo* is used ; but among the inhabitants on the coast, such as Bonny and Okrika, the harsher name Egbo is prevalent. In the interior north of the Territory, the nations are called *Igbo,* which approaches more to the original name of the inhabitants.

In the south the districts are intersected by numerous streams and rivulets, which enter to form the delta of the Niger; mangrove swamps are abundant in various places; except between Bonny and Old Calabar, the soil is rich and fertile. Further up, the country is more open and elevated, and numerously populated. In Isuama most of the towns are built on rising grounds, dry, and well selected; so that Isuama, Elugu, and Isiago, are far healthier and dryer than the sea-coast towns. But there are yet several large and important countries in the interior of Egboe of which nothing is known, as the country has not received that attention among civilized settlers that other parts of the Coast have. After the great failure of the expedition of 1841, no adequate attempt was made to open the River Niger until 1854, when a new impetus was given by the complete success of that year, but which, unfortunately, has been followed by tardy operations. The country is governed by independent kings and chiefs, whose extent of dominion varies greatly; some exercise authority over large and extensive districts; others rule over a town or village; and amongst these latter, such as in Oru or Jamen, the inhabitants are found to be wild, rude, savage, and treacherous. The title of king, unlike in the countries west of the Niger to as far as Senegambia, is hereditary in the male line. After the death of the father, the son is proclaimed king; in default, the brother. This may be seen in the coronation of the Kings of Bonny. So far back as could be remembered, Papa reigned for a certain period, and was succeeded at his death by his son Zhedie, who was also succeeded by his son Peppel I., who was succeeded by his son Peppel II., then by his son Opubu, who was succeeded by his son Peppel III. Bribo, his cousin, then succeeded him, or Peppel IV., and on his death, Dappa, the son of Peppel III., ascended the throne, and was succeeded by George, his son, the now reigning king.

In some of the districts the people endeavour to assume the elective power; thus, after the death of King Obi, of Abo, two parties sprung up, one supporting the claims of the king's sons, whilst the other advanced an influential person named Orisa as a candidate for the vacant crown; these two sections were known respectively as king's people, and the Oshiodapara party. Whilst the rights of the parties were still in dispute, law and justice were administered by a neutral party, having no connexion whatever with either side. The kings exercise very extensive powers over their subjects, but they are not absolute monarchs, as any excessive use of power may lead to their dethronement; they are assisted in making laws and transacting public business by councillors, who in Isuama are generally four principal persons; here the king is called *Obi*, and is addressed by his subjects kneeling, by the title of *Igue*, or supreme head; in Abo the king is called *Ese*. The king very seldom goes out beyond the precincts of his premises, especially in the interior countries, because, before publicly showing himself in the town, a human sacrifice must be made to propitiate the gods. His revenue consists of a portion of the fines inflicted for misdemeanour, and a portion of the game obtained in hunting. His throne ' is a raised bank of mud in the verandah, about four feet long, two wide, and two feet high from the level of the floor;' on this is spread a mat and a white piece of calico over it, which cloth is also spread on the walls against the king's back, extending from the top of the wall to that spread on the floor of the throne. ' This is a sign of royalty and the prerogative of the king, which no one in the country is to imitate.' No stranger is allowed in the king's palace a seat of any kind before his majesty, whether mat or stool, excepting the loose red earth, as the king took an oath to that effect.

Among the Egboes, women hold a very superior rank in the social scale; they are not regarded, as among other heathen tribes, as an inferior creation and doomed to perpetual degradation, but occupy their ' rightful status in society.' Nothing would, however, induce them to place a woman on the throne as their ruler; this they consider as subverting nature itself. In colloquy with the King of Nsube, Mr. Taylor was asked what was the name of his king. On being told that he had no king, but a queen, the king drew back with astonishment and said, ' *What! Can woman rule over man?* ' This, he afterwards said, accounts for the greatness of England, as there is no partiality among her people.

The language of the whole of the district is Egboe, but there are strong dialectic differences as we recede from the interior to the Coast towns. In Isuama, or by contraction Isu, the purest and

softest Egboe is spoken, and from it more or less differences occur
as we enter different districts; even the language spoken in Old
Calabar and Dwalla is derived from the great family of Egboe, only
far removed. Oru, Brass, Bonny, Okrika, and Andoney bear
dialectic affinity to Isuama Egboe, and are derived from the same
root, as may be noticed in the following collections made by the late
Dr. Baikie :—

English	Isuama. Egboe	Bonny	Nimbe	Oru.
Water	*minyi*	*mingi*	*mindi* or *migi*	*megi.*
Fire	*oko*	*fene*	*fendi*	*fini.*
Firewood	*unyi*		*fingia*	*fendia.*
God	*Orisa*	*Tamono*	*Orisa*	*Orisa.*
Idol	*dju-dju*	*dju-dju*	*owu*	*owu.*
House	*ulo*	*wari*	*wale*	*wale.*
Mat	*ute*	*bile*	*ute*	*ute.*

The language of the Egboes differs entirely from that of the
Yoruba or Ewe, westward of the Niger; after crossing that great
river we are brought at once among an entirely new and distinct
tribe, who are allied in tongue to the Lichuana, the Gala on the
north, the Tumali, and the Kaffir, which ethnologically forms the
South African Alteral family; this relation of the Egboe to the
Kaffir tongue has been also pronounced by the great ethnologist,
Dr. Latham.

The population of Egboe is unknown. Unlike the countries between the River Volta and the Niger, where at this present moment
external slavery is being carried on, and Dahomy making yearly
devastation among peaceful populations, Egboe, since 1835, has
been freed from these internal convulsions.* There is no large, independent, warlike power in its neighbourhood, as in Ashantee and
Dahomy; but the population, since the limitation of the external
slave-trade has been known to be wonderfully increased; and, judg-
ing from the extent and population of the known towns along the
banks of the river and on the sea-coast, it will not be far short of

---

* 'Throughout Egboe,' writes Dr. Baikie, 'great wars are now seldom
heard of, but petty quarrels often occur. The last time Abo was at war
was about 1851, with Dasaba, when one Abo man and ten or twelve of
Dasaba's party were killed. The usual style of disputes generally ends in
the capture of a canoe, or the confiscation of a cargo.'—*Exploring Voyage*,
page 317.

the mark if we state the whole at from 10,000,000 to 12,000,000, all of whom speak one language, with slight dialectic differences.

In stature the Egboes differ very considerably according to the region whence they are taken. In Isuama and the north central districts the inhabitants are tall and majestic looking, some well formed and shaped; they carry themselves very erect and consequentially. In other parts they are of a middling size, averaging five feet two. In the deltas of the rivers the inhabitants are short, stout, bull-necked, and very strong; specimens of them are even now to be found in Sierra Leone or the Gambia; they are scarcely above four and a-half feet, having very broad shoulders, and are stoutly built.

The Egboes are considered the most imitative and emulative people in the whole of Western Africa; place them where you will, or introduce to them any manners and customs, you will find that they very easily adapt themselves to them. Stout-hearted, or, to use the more common phraseology, big-hearted, they always possess a desire of superiority, and make attempts to attain it, or excel in what is praiseworthy, without a desire of depressing others. To them we may well apply the language of Dryden—

A noble emulation beats their breasts.

Place an Egboe man in a comfortable position, and he will never rest satisfied until he sees others occupying the same or a similar position. Of this emulative power, the Right Rev. Bishop Crowther, scarcely a year after the establishment of the Church Missionary station at Onitsha, in Isuama Egbo, thus wrote: ' From all I could gather by observation, the Iboes are very emulative. As in other things, so it will be in book learning. Other towns will not rest satisfied until they have also learned the mystery of reading and writing, by which their neighbours might surpass them and put them in the shade.'

Again, when the Expedition of 1854 ascended the Niger, the Commissioner, on visiting the son of the late king, Tshukumia by name, found him attired in the following style, ready to receive him. He had on a ' woollen nightcap, a white shirt, and home-built pantaloons of native manufacture, shaped after an extreme Dutch design.' The younger brother, who was received on board, appeared

' dressed in home-made scarlet cloth trousers, a scarlet uniform coat, a pink beaver hat, under which, apparently to make it fit, was a red worsted nightcap, no shoes, beads round the neck, and in his hand a Niger Expedition sword.' Now these men have never been on the seacoast, and have no connexion or communication direct or even indirectly with civilized men, so as to learn their habits, so that their imitative faculty must have been excited by the Expedition of 1841, which made but a few hours' stay in their town, and yet they persevere and imitate what then struck them.

But this quality is essential to civilization and advancement; it is the second passion belonging to society. 'This passion' writes Burke, 'arises from much the same cause as sympathy. This forms our manners, our opinions, our lives. It is one of the strongest links of society.' This is proved in the fact, as says the Rev. Alex. Crummel, 'that all civilization is carried down from generation to generation, or handed over from the superior to the inferior, by means of the principles of imitation, based on sympathy. A people devoid of this passion are incapable of improvement, and not only must stand still, unimpressive, but, by another law of nature, which makes progress a condition of vitality, must go down and perish; for stagnation necessitates decay and ruin. Thus through this stolidity and rigid self-consciousness, has followed the inevitable failure of the American Indian. On the other hand, the negro, with his pliable and plastic nature, with a greed of absorption, which, in fact, is the principle of receptibility, seizes upon and makes over to himself, by imitation, the qualities of others. First of all observe that, by a spontaneous native assimilation, he repudiates himself by becoming the like of the people to whom he is subject. He is always characteristically the negro; but among Frenchmen, he becomes the lively and sardonic Frenchman; among Americans, the keen, enterprising, progressive American; among Spaniards, the stately, solemn Spaniard; among Englishmen, the phlegmatic and solid Englishman.' *

The Egboes divide society into various social ranks; the higher

---

* A Sermon by the Rev. Alex. Crummell, B.A., Theological Tutor of the College at Monrovia, Liberia.—*African Times.*

grades are only obtained after a heavy sacrifice. Before merging from one rank to another of a superior position, a large sum must be paid, as each rank carries its own influence, consideration, and estimation in society. On the day of admission or initiation into such there is great merriment; this may be exemplified by the account of the Rev. J. C. Taylor, of the Onitsha Mission, who was an eyewitness to the honour of *Jasere* being conferred on Orikabue. He said: 'as I approached nearer our abode, I saw the people were in high glee, marking their faces with stripes of red ochre, or *ure*, and white clay. The deafening sounds of musketry, the play of swords and spears, the decoration of Orikabue's house with pieces of hand-kerchiefs, young men and women, old men and children, all vigorously employed in giggling, clapping their hands, and uniting in boisterous mirth, each in their turn dropping into a circle.'

The highest nobility, called *Ndidzi-boriba*, which rank is obtained by paying a very large sum, carry bells attached to their bags or borne before them wherever they go, producing a continuous jingling sound. The number of this rank, even in towns containing from 15,000 to 20,000 inhabitants, is comparatively small; at Onitsha there are only six. Bishop Crowther, in his observation of the dignitaries, says: 'The bell they carry about them is called *Mboriba*. Upon their entering a room, everyone must stoop and address each of them by the title he bears; thus, if an *Onown*, he is addressed *Onown, Onown, Onown*, ever so many times; if *Ogene*, or *Adze*, in like manner. It is a great insult to salute these gentlemen with the common salutation, except by the title they bear. Each one must occupy a separate seat; and a bench may be twelve feet long, but as soon as Onown or Adze has made towards it, it must be quitted by all its previous occupiers, in honour of him. On this account each one carries his sheepskin or goatskin about him, and sometimes his stool.' Even this destinction is observed in the churches, so that small stools are made expressly to accommodate them when they do attend service, in order that people of inferior rank on the benches may not be disturbed by giving room to them. It is no wonder to find that they are not a little proud of their greatness.

Another rank in the social scale, inferior to the above, is that

N

known among a class of gentry called *Ndi Nze*, or *Ndo Nze*. Now, to obtain this rank a smaller sum than that required for the rank of nobility is paid. This sum, when compared with the impoverished state of the country, must be regarded as considerable, and yet we find a vast number of the population vie with each other to obtain it. It consists of 15 large Egboe goats, 200 fowls, 100,000 cowries, a large quantity of yams, from one to two tons, and an immense supply of the country beverage, *palm wine*. As insignia of this rank, each individual is allowed to carry a horn made of ivory, with a hole made in it to blow into. Its sound is shrill and discordant ; when heard, he in whose hand the ivory horn, or *odan*, is seen, is recognized as a great man or Nze—one of the gentry who has purchased his rank.

An individual, however rich, cannot assume any title unless by purchase, or conferred by the king, which last seldom occurs ; a man of property is called *Ogan-ranyan*. In Isuama a hideous practice is observed ; it consists in entirely destroying the natural skin of the forehead, as if with a hot iron, of the sons of the wealthy, among whom it is confined. It is regarded by the inhabitants as very becoming, and entitles them to respect ; the people so tattooed are called *Mbritshi*, or *Itshi*. We have a very early account of them in the description of Captain John Adams (pages 133 and 134): ' A class of Heeboes (the Ibo or Eboe, whose chief town is Abo, at the head of the Negretian Delta) called Breeche, and whom many have very erroneously considered to be a distinct nation, masters of slave ships have always had a strong aversion to purchase, because the impression made on their minds by their degraded situation was rendered more galling and permanent from the exalted rank which they occupied in their own country, and which was thought to have a very unfavourable influence on their shipmates and countymen in misfortune. Breeche, in the Heebo language, signifies gentleman, or the eldest son of one, one who is not allowed to perform in his own country any menial office. He inherits, at his father's death, all his slaves, and has the absolute control over his wives and children which he has left behind him. Before attaining the age of manhood his forehead is scarified, and the skin brought down from the hair to the eyebrows, so as to form a line of indurated skin from one temple to the other. This peculiar mark is distinctive of his rank, the ordinary mark of the Heebo being formed by numerous perpendicular incisions in each temple, as if the operation of cupping had been often performed.'

One distinguishing rank among the Egboes is the *Odogo*, or captain of war, of which there are several grades; the title is distinguished by the individual carrying on his cap a long feather, which signifies that the wearer has killed in war a person of rank. These feathers are either white or red. The highest rank of captain, equal to a general, wears six, and the field-marshal is entitled to display seven. To perpetuate their valour in war, not having any written chronicle to leave their name to posterity, they plant a young bombax whenever they kill an enemy of consequence. As regards the management of warfare, they have peculiar laws. Bishop Crowther gives the following : ' It is a peculiar law among the Ibos, that when the inhabitants of one town are at war with another, and one part or division of the town will not join in the war, they can, without molestation, visit their relatives in the town which is at war with a division of their own, whether men or women, no person touching them.' Strangers living in the country might visit the belligerent towns freely, without apprehension, because they are said not to have a hand in their quarrels. ' Should there be an intermediate town between the two contending towns, neither the one nor the other can step over the intermediate one to attack his enemies without a due notice and permission from the intermediate one, unless they beat their way in a roundabout direction to effect their purpose. When they do come to an open fight in the plain it is said they are fierce. They do not capture to make slaves, but they kill everyone they lay hold of, and take their heads as trophies to their homes, to prevent their dead bodies being taken away by their enemies. Women follow them to their battles, and are employed in removing the dead and wounded out of the way, so that the men do not lose time in doing this, but continue to force their enemies.'

The doctor, or *libia*, is by no means an inferior personage; he is also a priest, and carries himself with great pretensions; is much feared, and exercises a great sway over the people. He pretends

N 2

to foretell things to come, to drive out evil spirits, and discover secrets, and, consequently, is much respected. Dr. Baikie fell in with the shop of one of these learned gentlemen in Angiama. 'It is a small round room,' writes he, 'wonderfully clean and painted, the sides being striped with blue, black, red, and white, and the back checked with the same colours. Two pots of herbs in steep were placed on a tripod, composed of three branches springing from a common origin. Two divining rods and many long-pointed sticks (one cut like a crocodile's head, another carved to resemble a tortoise, and a third painted rudely to represent a man,) were in different corners, while hanging around the walls were numerous strings of cowries and other charms.'

The doctor's service is much required in time of war; he has to administer the oath of allegiance and faithfulness to the Crown and to fight valiantly. He first takes a wooden bowl and fills it with pebbles and stones; with this he walks round three times, the assembled warriors standing, and everyone cries unanimously, '*According to this oath so would we have it.*' Before the troops a black stone is placed on a green leaf. The troops standing, the doctor or one of the captains, taking up the stone with the leaf, says, 'Young men or troops, be on your guard, and fight for your rights; none must be a coward, but be bold and manly. Remember this *izi* (oath-stone); it has been done so in byegone days by our fore-fathers. They were stout-hearted, and never shrunk back in anything they had determined to perform.'

The introduction of the new yam is, as among many other Coast tribes, an occasion for the performance of several rites and cere-monies. Here the doctor figures conspicuously. This Fetish cus-tom is called Waje, or the eating of the new yam. It is not, as in other parts, participated in by the general public, but is performed by a certain class of people who carry a long trumpet tusk about them. Mr. Taylor gives the following as the manner in which the custom is performed: Each head-man brings out six yams, besides some kola nuts and fish, and cuts down young branches of palm leaves, and places them before his gate; three of the yams are roasted, after which the *libia*, or doctor, takes and scrapes them into a meal, and then divides it in two. He then takes one piece and places it on the lip of the person who is going to eat the new yam. The eater blows out the steam from the hot yam, and afterwards pokes the whole into his mouth and says, 'I thank God for being permitted to eat the new yam.' He then begins to chew it heartily, with fish. The doctor receives as a fee for performing the ceremony the three remaining yams.

In their salutation, individuals of an inferior position, on meeting their superiors, place one knee on the ground and then bow with great reverence. Among equals they shake hands, which is performed first in the regular manner, but before separating the hands, they partly take loose hold of the fingers of each other, and then sharply slipping them so as to make at the same instant a snapping sound; this process is assisted by the thumb.

In Yoruba, Nufi, and many other parts of the Coast, the mothers carry their children about on their backs, but not so in Egboe; there they are carried chiefly in their arms. The children are very seldom punished, consequently are found to be self-willed and have their own way; 'yet they are docile and imitative, and with very little trouble will soon be made intelligent scholars.' *Life* for *life* is a law throughout the country; whether taken accidentally or not, one life must go for the other; this is imperative. If the murderer himself manage to escape, some one of his family must be killed in his stead. If the murderer or homicide be inferior in rank to the murdered man, some one of equal rank in the family must be delivered in his stead. Neither the king nor any individual member of a family has any right to alienate land; and before any sale or gift of land belonging to any family is made, the consent of the leading members of the family must first be obtained, as amongst Egboes land is possessed by inheritance.

The Egboes are generally copper-coloured, but on the eastern border a very small tribe is darker than the rest; the majority possessing blue eyes. They are of a determined nature, and, when uncivilized, fierce in their appearance and boisterous in their quarrels. Captain Burton regards them as one of 'the most ferocious and dangerous of the African tribes.' When exasperated they would coolly and quietly do the most determined act, regardless of the consequences. They would as soon run a knife through anyone as blow out their own brains. A case may be cited as an example of the wanton determination of this tribe. An Egboe man at a certain village in Sierra Leone, not long ago, was exasperated by some domestic disturbance. He deliberately smashed his skull, by violently butting his head against a wall. 'Yet no sooner is the storm pacified, than they are again extremely quiet and yielding; even in common transactions,' writes Bishop Crowther, ' as buying and selling, &c., they get so warm at a little difference or misunderstanding in settling the price between them, that I often imagined they were going to give blows; but they soon settle it, and all is calm and quiet again.' The Egboes cannot be driven to an act; they become most stubborn and bull-headed; but with kindness they could be made to do anything, even to deny themselves of their comforts. They would not, as a rule, allow anyone to act the superior over them, nor sway their conscience, by coercion, to the performance of any act, whether good or bad, when they have not the inclination to do so; hence there is not that unity among them that is found among other tribes; in fact, everyone likes to be his own master. As a rule, they like to see every African prosper. Among their own tribe, be they ever so rich, they feel no ill-will toward them. A poor man or woman of that tribe, if they meet with a rising young person of the same nationality, are ready to render him the utmost service in their power. They give him gratuitous advice, and ' embrace him as their child;' but if he is arrogant and overbearing, they regard him with scorn and disdain wherever he is met. When half-educated, the young men are headstrong and very sensitive; they take offence at the least unmeaning phrase, and become very impertinent.

Although there are considerable dialectic differences among the Egboes in the different parts of this extensive country, such as those between Elugu on the north and Ebane or Bonny on the south, yet still in their country or in Egboeland ' each person hails, as a sailor would say, from the particular district where he was born;' but when in a foreign country or when away from their home all are Egboes. The Bonnians and Eluguans are hailed by one national name. In some districts of Egboe, in Ndoko and Ngwa, the inhabitants are cannibals; but they generally eat the flesh of their enemies slain in war on some great festive occasion; this is connected with some religious rites.

We come now to the consideration of the most important subject relative to the Egboe race—viz., *their religion* and *probable origin.*

The religion of the Egboes is Judaism, intermixed with numerous pagan rites and ceremonies. They believe in the existence of one Almighty, Omnipotent, Omnipresent Being, whom they worship as such, and regard as the Omniscient God who concerns himself with the affairs of man. He is known by the name of *Tshuku*, contracted sometimes into *Tshi*. They also admit the existence of another God, or a superior being, who, in one part of the country, is called *Orissa*, and in another *Tshuku-Okeke*, or 'God the Creator,' or 'the Supreme God,' thus showing that the nation believes in the division of the Godhead—in two beings each equal in power and influence, yet differing in the Godhead; but the existence of a third person does not seem to be admitted or known by them.

Tshuku,* the Omniscient God, who is supposed to preserve them from harm, communicates with his people through his priests, who reside in a city set apart as holy by all the nation. This place is called Aro, or Ano, to which pilgrimages are made, not only from all parts of Egboe, including the tribes along the Coast—viz., Oru, Nimbe, and Brass—but also from Old Calabar in the far east. This city, where the holy shrine of Tshuku exists, is extremely populous, and is spoken of with great reverence and respect, 'almost at times with a degree of veneration. The inhabitants speak the languages of the surrounding tribes, which are heard among the crowded pilgrim votaries who throng the shrine,' but they speak principally the dialects of Elugu and Isuama. They are said to be skilful

---

* The Rev. J. C. Taylor gives the following as a propitiatory prayer made by a woman called Wamah, of Abo, to Tshi whilst offering a sacrifice of goat : '*Biko Tshi, mere'm ihoma, ngi wo ndu, biko kpere Tshuku Abiama, gwa ya obi'm dum ma-biko wepo ihinye ojo di na obi'm tsufu Amusu, mekwa akku bia'm, lekwa ehu, ngi.* I beseech thee, my guide, make me good ; thou hast life. I beseech thee to intercede with God the Spirit. Tell him my heart is clean. I beseech thee to deliver me from all bad thoughts in my heart ; drive out all witchcrafts ; let riches come to me ; see your sacrificed goat ; see your kola nuts ; see your rum and palm wine.'—'*Niger Expedition,* 1857-59.' Crowther and Taylor. Page 348.

artisans, and manufacture swords, spears, and metallic ornaments, specimens of which European travellers have pronounced to be very neatly finished. The town is called God's Town—'*Tshuku ab y a ma,*' or 'God lives there;' and the inhabitants God's children, or *Omo Tshuku.* The very fact of their residing in the town makes the people to regard them with reverence, as being near the presence of the holy deity.

The shrine of Tshuku is placed in the centre of the town. 'When a man goes to Aro to consult Tshuku,' writes Dr. Baikie, 'he is received by some of the priests outside the town, near a small stream; here he makes an offering, after which a fowl is killed, and if it appears unpropitious, a quantity of red dye is spilt into the water, which the priest tells the people is blood, and on this the votary is hurried off by the priest and is seen no more, it being given out that Tshuku has been displeased and has taken him away. If, however, the omen is pronounced to be favourable, the pilgrim is permitted to draw near to the shrine, and, after various rites and ceremonies have been gone through, the question, whatever it may be, is propounded, of course through the priests, and by them also the reply is given. A yellow powder is given to the devotee, who rubs it around his eyes, which powder is called in Egboe '*edo.*' As tokens of a person having actually consulted the sacred oracle, little images, called '*Ofo Tshuku,*' meaning images of God, are issued to him, which he keeps as holy. After returning home from the sacred city a person is considered sacred, or *djudju,* for seven days, during which time he remains at home, speaking to no one, and the people dread to approach him.

Both Bishop Crowther and the late Dr. Baikie encountered one of these pilgrims. He went to Aro to inquire why his wife had no children, and had just returned; and, consequently, was djudju, or sacred, but being strangers they were permitted to visit him. He was, however, unwilling to give any full account of the ceremony, but said that Tshuku was only to be heard through his priests. The account of his journey was the following: He embarked in a canoe from Agbene, in Oru, to a creek nearly opposite Abo; on entering it he proceeded to a place called Igbema, whence he finished his journey by land. On his arrival at Aro, the priest gave him some yellow powder, telling him that if his heart was bad it would kill him. According to his account, at Aro there were people from far in the interior, as well as from Old Calabar and Ibibio, consulting the sacred God—indeed, the UNKNOWN GOD.

Sacrifices are made to Tshuku, consisting of fowls, sheep, goats, and bullocks; but human sacrifices, as such, are never made. There is, however, one propitiatory sacrifice, which is practised to a considerable extent in the interior towns, and which is decidedly Judaistic in its origin. At the end of every year two important sacrifices are made ; the first, done in secret (in thick bush), to take away the sins of the king during the past year; and the second, publicly performed, to take away the sins of the whole people. Unlike the Jews, human beings are procured for the purpose ; none of the inhabitants of the towns where it is performed are selected. A special fund is raised by a contribution of twenty-eight *ngugus* (equal to our 2*l.* 0s. 7½d.) on all who, during the past year, were guilty of gross sins—such, for example, as incendiarism, theft, fornication, adultery, witchcraft, &c. The amount is taken into the interior, and two persons are bought expressly to be offered for the sins of all the inhabitants, and especially for those who have committed those abominable sins. An individual from the neighbouring country is specially hired to perform the deed, and is variously paid, at an average of about twenty ngugus, or 1*l.* 12s. 6d.

The Rev. J. C. Taylor, Church Missionary agent at Onitsha, witnessed one of these sacrifices, which was made to take away the sins of the people and the land during the past year ; and from his account we gather the following : A young virgin of from eighteen to twenty years of age was selected. After several ceremonies had been performed, by which the chiefs and people supposed that the sins of the land were transferred to the poor victim, her hands were tied behind her back, and her legs fastened together with a rope. She was decorated with the young palm leaves, and, with her face to the earth, drawn from the king's house to the river, a distance of two miles. ' The motley group who accompanied the procession cried as they drew along the unfortunate creature, victimized by the sins of their land, *Aro ye! aro! aro!*—*i.e.*, Wickedness ! wickedness ! This alarm is given to notify to the passers-by to screen themselves from witnessing the dismal scene. The body was drawn along in a merciless manner, as if the weight of all their wickedness were carried away, whilst the life was still beating in the palpitating bosom of that unfortunate girl.' On reaching the bank of the river, the lifeless body was received in a canoe and paddled with all haste to the deepest part of the river, and then drowned. This they do believing that by that means they could ' atone for the individual sins of those who had broken God's law during the past year.' and thus, exclaims Mr. Taylor, ' these unhappy creatures fared like Jehoiakim of old—they were buried with the burial of an ass, drawn and cast forth beyond the gates of the city.' The Egboes believe implicitly in the transmigration of souls, that after death the individual appears in various forms, according to his actions whilst on earth, either as wild beasts or human beings; so that slaves, when ill-treated by their masters, generally console themselves that after they have quitted this present tenement they will appear again in another form among their friends and relatives from whom they have been forcibly separated.

The existence of the devil, or evil spirits, is also among their beliefs. The greatest and worst of these they call ' KAMALLO,' which is equivalent to ' Satan,' the literal meaning being ' one going about everywhere and in all directions.' In some parts, however, a more impressive and characteristic name is given to it, distinctly pointing it out as Satan the fallen angel; it is called ' IGWIK ALLA,' which is derived from the two words, ' *Igwik*,' signifying ' *one who lived above before coming down*,' and ' *álla*,' the ' *ground*,' or earth. He is worshipped, and ' persons make inquiries of it if they wish to commit any wicked action, such as murder; bringing presents of cowries and cloth to propitiate this evil being, and render him favourable to their design.' They speak also of lesser evil spirits, the angel of Kamállo, whom they call *Mondjo*.

Do not these religious rites and ceremonies remind us forcibly of the Jewish Dispensation, when sacrifices were made to atone for the sins of the people? And does this not present an emphatic proof of what Mr. Locker wrote, that apart from the native religion of Africa, Judaism forms an element which enters Africa by the natural current of nations from the north-east, from Egypt, Ethiopia, and Northern Africa; that though there are comparatively few Jews south of the Sahara and Abyssinia, still, by the connexion of the Jews with African countries since the days of Moses, Abraham, Joseph, Solomon, as well as the destruction of Jerusalem, and the consequent scattering of the Jews all over the globe, the influence of Judaism on Africa is greater and farther diffused than that of the Jews and their geographical extension. If we take, for instance, the race under consideration, I will go still further, and assert that the more we study them in all their various relationships, the more shall we be convinced that they form a portion of those lost tribes who disobeyed the command of God and were dispersed, but are now mingled with the original inhabitants of the country, and so degenerate in the form in which they now appear.

But to prove this further we must admit the acknowledged and every-day fact that the moving passion of men's minds, even from time immemorial, is a disposition to change their abode; thus the children of Israel, directed by some supernatural influence, migrated from Egypt to Canaan, expelled its inhabitants, and became sole masters of the land.   The Phœnicians of ancient date were characterised by their spirit of enterprise, and they formed colonies in various quarters of the eastern hemisphere.   Adopting the views entertained in Northern Africa, we should conclude that migration was the natural effect of a far greater or more important cause.   It is affirmed to be an immutable and essential decree of the Creator, who, when he placed the sun and stars in the firmament, and directed their diurnal and apparent courses from east to west, ordained that mankind should not be an exception to a law which was intended for all the earth.   Under these considerations we see that the opening line between Egypt and Arabia—between Africa and Asia—known as the Isthmus of Suez, plays an important part in the history of Africa, as it formed the gateway for Asiatic emigration, and, consequently, at various times, numerous occidental tribes poured into Northern Africa through Egypt, either peacefully as emigrants and settlers, receiving special licence, as at the time of the Abaside monarchy, or by force of arms.   We find amongst the earliest tribes who tread the soil of Africa, the Babylonians, the Arabs, the Ammonites, and the greater part, if not all the Canaanites, which last were doomed to destruc-

tion by the hands of Joshua, and, if we believe the account of Pro-
copius, ' while the army was on its march in pursuit of Gillimere
who was afterwards led captive to Justinian by his general, Belli-
sarius, it halted near the Numedian frontier, where a sculptured
stone was found, whereon was written or engraved in Punic—*i.e.*
Phœnician—characters, which nearly correspond with the Hebrew,
" We are the remnants of those tribes who fled before the robber
Joshua, the son of Nun." '

In those early days Africa was known and famous amongst the
then civilized portion of the world, and the Assyrians and Babylonians were among its earliest conquerors, so that about sixty-seven
years after the destruction of the Temple, we are told, in Esther i. 1,
that Ahasuerus, the king of Assyria, reigned from India unto
Ethiopia, over one hundred and seven and twenty provinces. And
since the King of Egypt was considered lord of the people of
Ethiopia or Soudan, we read in Isaiah that the ' king of Assyria
led away the Ethiopians captive, young and old, naked and bare-
footed, to the shame of Egypt.' Northern Egypt then was the most
known portion of the globe, and into it vast immigration took place
from time to time, even to the most remote period. The ten tribes
of Israel, after they were left to follow the dictates of their own
mind, and during the commotion and destructive warfare which
ensued, to escape utter extermination, migrated, according to the
usage of the times, in vast numbers into various countries, but
principally into Northern Africa, as it then presented the safest and
easiest route. Once settled, every commotion and intestine war had
the most powerful effect of inducing these migratory bands to shift
their abode still further,* and so lose all connexion with the other
branch of the tribe. As hundreds of years pass on, and generation
after generation roll away, they lose a great many of their habits
and customs, becoming more amalgamated with the population with
which they associate. But when Mohammedanism overspread
Northern Africa,† destroying by fire and sword all those of

---

* The Romans penetrated through the Northern Desert. *The Jews had a
powerful kingdom* in Abyssinia.—' Burton's Abeokuta and the Cameroon
Mountains,' p. 176.
† Of the ascendancy of Mohammedanism in Central and Western Africa we

another religion, the Israelitish descendants, or the inhabitants occupying the central portion of Africa, passed forward, seeking shelter to the south and west; a part, namely those from the east central, crossing the Binue or Joliba branch of the Niger, descended gradually southward, and became intermingled with the original inhabitants. Protected from incursion on the north by the Binue River, and quietly settled between the Great Niger and Old Kalabar Rivers, they remained in peace, and grew from one generation to another in idolatry, but still leaving tangible proofs in the form of their religion of the Judaistic origin of the inhabitants.

After this slight digression, we will now proceed to investigate more particulars relative to the tribes under consideration. The language, or the little of it that is known, is full of Hebraisms ; the constructions of sentences, the verbal significations, the mode of comparison,

gather the following from Mr. Kœlle's 'Polyglotta Africana,' p. 18: 'The original home of the *Fulbe* or *Phula* was in Lilubawa, near Futa Loro, whose inhabitants are called Toronko, and where they have been often molested by Kafirs. To escape this molestation they went gradually towards the east, in the capacity of nomadic shepherds, till they arrived at Hausa. . . . After they had been tending their flocks a long time in those forests and grass-fields, without towns, and subsisting simply on the produce of their herds, one of their priests, of the name of Fodie, had an apparition of the Prophet Mohammed, which was destined to form a most signal epoch in the history of Phula, and indeed in the history of the whole of Central and Western Africa. In this apparition Fodie was informed that the whole of that beautiful country around them, with all its populous towns and countless villages, belonged to the believers in the Prophet, to wit the Phula ; and that it was Fodie's divine commission, with the help of the faithful, to wrest all those flowery plains, those fruitful hills, and lovely valleys, from the hand of the Kafirs, and then to bring all the Kafirs into subjection to the Islam, and to devote to the sword everyone who refused to believe. Almost beside himself with enthusiasm, and burning with fanaticism, Fodie summoned the believing Fulbe, from every country to the very coast of the Atlantic, to rally around his banner, and to fight with him the battle of the Prophet for the subjugation of all the Kafir tribes of Africa to the religion of God and his Prophet. And, like an electric shock, this message of Fodie pervaded all the lands where Phula were sojourning ; and with a magical power converted the shepherds into warriors. Soon Fodie was himself surrounded by an army convinced of its own invincibility, and thirsty for the battle. Thus commenced those extraordinary Phula movements in Central Afria, which, though unrecorded on the pages of our universal histories, are yet written in streams of blood on the pages of the real natural history of our race, in which every human action records itself. On the spot where Fodie had his apparition, he afterwards built the town of Sokoto, now the great centre of Phula power in Africa.'

are all typical of the Hebrew. Like the Hebrew, from a single root of verbs and other elementary parts of speech, substantives, adjectives and adverbs are formed; and of the declension of nouns, the Rev. J. F. Schön, Linguist to the Church Missionary Society, whilst writing of the cases, said there are none in the sense they appear in Latin, and consequently there are no declensions; but there are cases in the sense ' in which it is applied in the Hebrew language— namely, that form of nouns to which are appended or suffixed the attributive or possessive pronoun.'   Well might a writer in the *African Times*, when writing on the subject of ' Black, the Original Colour of the White Race,' finish his article with the following addenda : ' The Isthmus of Suez plays an important part in the history of Africa and the Ethiopian race.   Ancient mythology has proved that through it extensive migratory movements took place several thousand years ago from Asia Minor to Africa.   From a little study of the ethnology of the language of Western Africa and the Hebrew tongue, one is involuntarily brought to trace out a similarity in one of them to that of the tribes which, from dis-obedience to the will of God, were dispersed, and the greatest num-ber of them possibly went to Africa—I mean the lost tribes of Israel.   If the rites and ceremonies of the religion of the tribes bordering on the banks of the River Niger be closely examined and compared with the religion of the Hebrews at the earliest period— viz., Egbo, Ebo (Heber, Eber) tribe; if the Egbo (Heber, Eber) language, with all its corruptions, be compared with that of the Hebrews, and if the peculiar disposition of the Hebrew tribes, as detailed in Scripture, and that of the Egboes be properly investi-gated, there will be *à priori* reasons for a serious inquiry whether the Egbo tribe, which is but a branch of the Galla tribe in the interior, is the offspring of the lost tribes of Israel, driven down from Central Africa, and forced to cross the eastern or Binue branch of the Niger, by Mohammedan fanaticism.'*

The Church Missionary Society has commenced to labour among this tribe, under the superintendence of the Right Rev. Bishop Crowther.   The Rev. J. C. Taylor has translated the whole

---

* *African Times*, Vol. v., No. 51, p. 29.

of the books of the New Testament into the Central or Isauma dialect of Egboe, with a copious vocabulary. The people are now gradually being taught to read. Many have been converted from heathenism to the true light of the Gospel. At Bonny, the people who formerly considered the *inguanas* as sacred to the gods, and consequently worshipped them, had, by the latest account, taken a decided step against the superstitious worship; and on Easter-day this year (1867), through the influence of the young king, the chiefs having renounced and declared the animal no longer sacred, it was resolved that the town should be cleared of them. The whole town, men, women, and children, at once set about their destruction, and within a few hours no less than fifty-seven were counted in only one market place. It is certain that if the work of educating, Christianizing, and civilizing the people be vigorously taken up, within a very short time astonishing improvements will be recorded.

The resources of this extensive empire have not yet been developed; at present it is the largest and most constant market for palm-oil on the whole western shore of Africa, and if proper means of transport from the interior be introduced, the present rate of shipment will be quadrupled within a very short time. Besides palm-oil, the land produces abundantly shea butter, yams, Guinea corn, kola-nut, cocoa, beans, banana, plantain, ground-nuts, and many other important plants. An important mineral has been discovered within this region, large lumps of lead-ore containing silver have been brought to the market and sold for a trifle. According to the native statement, they are abundantly obtained near Arufo, and found near the surface. A specimen of the ore was analyzed in London, yielding the following result : ' Galena, or lead ore, sixteen hundredweight of lead (equal to eighty per cent.) and three ounces of fine silver to the ton of twenty hundred weight.' Camwood ivory, native-made cloth, and impure carbonate of soda are abundantly found in the interior. In many places large blocks of quartz rock are found. Dr. Baikie described some near Bird's Island ' composed of mica slates, partly altered by the action of fire; the top covered with scales of mica, reflecting beautifully the rays of light, causing a shining silvery appearance.' Where quartz and other silurian rocks are found, as in the Gold Coast and interior regions of Sierra Leone, it is almost admitted that gold enters into the composition of the soil. May we not, therefore, advance the opinion that if the geology of this part of the Coast be properly examined, gold might be found in the composition of the earth?

In the foregoing we have seen that the Egboe nationality is divided into numerous independent tribes, governed by their own laws, but having one national sentiment; that they are still barbarous, unlettered, unchristian, and imbued with a vast idolatrous superstition. The question arises how is it possible to form an independent, united, Christian, and civilized nation, having the same laws and governed by one imperial head. This at once presents a question of vast importance and great difficulty. In the first place, the seat of the *ab initio* Government should not only be near to, or on, the sea-coast, but also be a place of commercial importance. Bonny, having all the advantages above described, is most adapted for the commencement of such an important undertaking; but there are serious prejudices among the neighbouring tribes, which would present great obstacles to their union under the leadership of its king. The chiefs composing the different sections in that country are very jealous of one another, and particularly of the reigning dynasty, and to effect an agreement on this point an individual from without should be elected by the universal vote of not only the kings and chiefs of Bonny, but also the kings and chiefs of all the neighbouring towns.* The elected individual must of necessity be well acquainted with the different departments of a political government, and capable of introducing such institutions, with such modifications as would suit the conditions of the governed. A treaty of unity, or of alliance offensive and defensive, should, in the first place, be entered into by all the various kings and chiefs in the neighbouring provinces.

The next, and most important, consideration would be the raising of a sufficient revenue to carry out the various improvements which it will be found absolutely necessary to make, and this

---

* A step similar to, but differing, however, in details from, the Egba United Board of Management now established in Abeokuta.

he must do by giving the greatest encouragement to trade, by facilitating through every means in his power an increase of the trade of the country, and a trade in new articles of commercial value; thus pouring into the country an increased amount of capital.

Education on a large and comprehensive scale should be made the base of the future progress of the Government. Whilst the alphabetical system of Professor Leptius, of Berlin, adopted by the Foreign Missionary Society for the translation of African and other unlettered languages, is both comprehensive and useful, I think it answers more for philological researches than for an easily-written language. The numerous accents with which it abounds for conveying different sounds, is a great barrier against its general adoption, and for a system which will be applicable for correspondence, the French Alphabetical Standard, with slight modification, and sufficient prac‑ tice to familiarize one's self with the peculiar gradation of sounds, will be the easiest and most advantageous. In the meantime, how‑ ever, the labours of the Revds. Schön and Taylor should receive due consideration and attention. Education should be made compulsory, by a convention, signed by all the chiefs, that every child between the ages of seven and fourteen should attend school. This would materially improve, not only the present, but particularly the future generation. From the very commencement, great attention should be paid to the education and civilization of the female population. Their position in society should be well defined, and no arbitrary in‑ fringement on their rights should be tolerated; for it is they who, in their respective spheres, would become the best expounders of civi‑ lization to the subsequent generation, and by their immense influence on the growing population, would greatly assist in advancing educa‑ tion and in breaking down the barrier of ignorance between the different masses of the population. In every town there should be one or more schools, according to its extent and amount of population, and every facility should be given both to teachers‑ and scholars.

The education of the people should not be limited to those small schools thus established, but advantage should be taken of the civilization of the age, and arrangements be made with the various civilized governments to bring up intelligent natives of the country in mechanics and manufacturing arts. The elementary, but useful, mechanical arts should first be patronized. A number of young men should be sent to Sierra Leone, under the protection of the Local Government, to be brought up as carpenters, painters, shoemakers, tailors, masons, coopers, and sawyers; to Senegal, as wheelwrights and shipbuilders. The king elect should communicate with the Secretary of the Church Missionary Society, through the Bishop of the Niger, respecting the best means of enlarging and making their establishment more efficient; and also invite that most indefatigable body—the Basle German missionaries, whose admirable works on the Gold Coast have been chronicled in another place—to form establishments in the country, with this understanding, that although at the present the parent committee of each society will be required to bear the expenses of their respective establishments, yet still the greatest endeavour of the State would be to unite the two (which differ only in slight forms) into one Church, and make them entirely independent and self supporting. Every encouragement should be given to the Basle missionaries to form efficient mechanical and industrial institutions.

Agriculture should be encouraged in every particular, a fixed plan laid down by the Government, and in every large town a model garden of plants established, where the art of cultivating scientifically should be taught by proper agriculturalists. Facilities should be offered to the population at such a rate as to remunerate them for their labour, and, at the same time, create a demand for the articles. Consequently, it will not only be necessary to introduce new commercial plants, but also of great value to improve and extend those either indigenous to the country or already naturalized. For effectually carrying out this plan, good roads must be made throughout the country, and mechanical contrivances must be resorted to for communicating with and carrying away the produce from the interior to the point of export.

But to ensure the establishment of a firm central Government in such a primitive state of existence, it will be found necessary that

the responsible power should in a great measure be vested in the
king elect for at least a time, although a representation of all the
chiefs in the bond should take place at certain fixed periods to discourse on State matters.   This Government should be the starting-
point for the regeneration of the interior of the Egboe tribe.   The
more firm, strong, and conciliatory are its measures, the greater
influence would it exercise over surrounding tribes, and the more
easily would they rally around it. Let the civilization of those tribes
near the seaboard be well secured, and those small divided states in
the interior would of themselves seek protection from the stronger
Government.   If we see this accomplished in bloody Ashantee and
Dahomy, both of whom rose from a trifling state, how much more
shall we see it in a kingdom based on religious principle and on the
civilization of the nineteenth century !

When once established, the king's authority should not be easily
gainsayed by any turbulent and refractory chief. He must make
himself powerful enough to be feared, whilst at the same time
respected—in fact, he must be supported by a small, but strong,
standing army, composed of every grade in the country, and
armed with the latest improved weapon.   This body would be the
nucleus for the formation of an efficient army.   The neeessity
of such an establishment is sufficiently evident, because without
it he will find it impossible to govern the several wild and
lawless tribes, to curb down the turbulent spirit which the natural
tendency of their minds seems always to point to, and to keep
in union the different heterogeneous but dissimilar elements which
enter into the composition of his kingdom.   But the military
should not be of such a number as to embarrass the financial
condition of the country, nor of the type which the poet thus depicted :—

> Mouth without hands, maintained at vast expense;
> In peace a charge, in war a weak defence ;
> Stout once a month they march, a blustering band,
> And ever, but in time of need, at hand.

By the assistance of the energetic Basle missionaries and discharged
soldiers, a form of drill would easily be drawn up in the native

language, and the men taught accordingly, who might ultimately prove of great service in the organization of local militia throughout the country.

Another very important consideration should not be overlooked —viz., the encouragement, as much as possible, of emigration from without. Nothing tends more to the civilization of a barbarous country than the immigration of civilized individuals into it; they give greater impulse to the industry of the country, and offer examples to the mass of the population; and among so imitative and emulative a people the result would no doubt be very good. Every means should therefore be encouraged to ensure their proper location. It is impossible for a nation to civilize itself; civilization must come from abroad. As was the case with the civilized continents of Europe and America, so it must be with Africa; which cannot be an exception to the rule. Lately, when the argument has been raised to leave Africa to itself, it was surmised, even by men who took great interest in its welfare, ‘that possibly mercantile intercourse would be sufficient to civilize the savage races of Africa’—a doctrine which has been disproved in every part of the world where the merchant’s sole purpose is to acquire a fortune, and where he is not restrained in his actions by a civilized Government. And so we find them adopt the habits—whether good or bad—of the inhabitants with whom they commingle and trade, or, as Captain Burton has it, ‘the white man, after a certain length of residence, grew black, not in complexion, but in disposition, and becoming a perfect dupe to charms, necromancers, &c., put more trust in such things than the wiser sort of natives.’ And where trade is carried on in the mere exchange of goods for produce, as in these parts, the intercourse, although it may continue for several centuries, will not have any material effect in the civilization of the people.

But to prove more conclusively the statement that civilized merchants in a savage country, without the influence of a civilized Government to correct their action, rather retard than encourage civilization, I will quote an example from the work of Dr. Baikie, the particulars of an ordinary occurrence in the Brass River, leaving unnoticed any such cases as have been brought before the

Bench at Liverpool, and published in public journals : ' As an example of the conduct at times of these civilized people, I will relate what had occurred in Brass River very shortly before this period. A white trader, then agent for an English house, had, out of a mere freak, ordered a native who came on board his ship one day to be seized and flogged. This lad's father, however, was a man of consequence on shore, and, on hearing of this outrage, he summoned his friends, and in two large canoes attacked and boarded the ship The white captain armed his Kruboys with muskets, but they, unwilling to quarrel with the natives, or to fight in a bad cause, gave way. The captain then retreated towards his cabin, but just as he was entering it, violent hands were laid on him, and in the scuffle he had one of his thumbs nearly cut off, was put into a canoe, taken on shore, and fastened to a tree, where he was left for twelve hours, and the natives said openly they would have killed him, but that they feared a visit from an English man-of-war. This same individual trained his Krumen to fight with the Krumen of the other trading ships in the River, and, in short, endeavoured to carry on his trading by brute force. Such transactions as these were formerly of daily occurrence, but now, fortunately, they occur but rarely; but *what can be expected of native tribes who see before them deeds which would disgrace a very savage, committed by so-called civilized men ?* ' It must be remembered that the English are considered the mildest of all civilized nations in their dealings with savage nations; but if among them we find men capable of such barbarity, what civilization must they expect from other nations, and how many centuries will it require for their civilization by merchants ?

One of the things to be established as early as possible is a fixed currency for the kingdom. Nothing binds the different commercial elements of a country so much as a common national currency, so that the erection of a mint, by which the inhabitants could have a determined and regular copper, silver, or gold coinage, would certainly lead to paramount results.

In the foregoing pages I have endeavoured to point out the best and only means of bringing a savage, barbarous race into the employments of civilized Christian life, and, in particular, the best mode of effecting the unity and civilization of the tribes within the boundary of the Egboe empire ; but to form a permanent union, accommodated to the opinions and wishes of the inhabitants of the various states, differing provincially in habits, manners, and internal government, would be found a work of such magnitude that nothing but time and reflection, together with a disposition to conciliate, could mature and accomplish it.

PART III.

REQUIREMENTS OF THE VARIOUS COLONIES AND SETTLEMENTS.

CHAPTER XIV.

REQUIREMENTS OF SIERRA LEONE.

1.—*The first Improvement which is loudly called for, is the extension of the Franchise of the Colony.*

The Government of Sierra Leone is *de facto* a self-supporting Government, and the amount of improvement exhibited by the inhabitants entitles them to have a voice in their administrative establishment. 'Nothing in defence could be urged that this or that measure is in advance of the Colony; the Colony was quite ripe for such improvements, the revenue was large, and the intelligence of the people advancing. The time had arrived for an extension of immunities; other Colonies of later years and with a much less revenue and intelligence were politically in advance of this; they had their representatives in the legislative halls of a sufficient number to represent their interests. . . . With respect to an extended franchise, it is most desirable that the Legislative Council of the Colony should be opened to three or four members from the people, made eligible for their seats by being elected and sent there by the people as their representatives. It should be remembered that the people were ready and willing to keep up taxation in order to support the institutions of the Colony, and I do not see why they do not have a voice in the administration of affairs. In short, it was the very principle of the British Constitution that those who were liable to be assessed should have a voice in the administration.'*

At present almost the whole of the members of the Legislative Council are Government officials; there are only two who may be regarded as independent members, one alone of whom represents the people. His single vote would not upset any obnoxious ordin-ance introduced into the Council, which might affect the well-being of the Colony. In his position he is almost a cipher; he might give his vote, but it would prove ineffectual for the purpose. There ought to be more representatives, nominated by public votes of the citizens, to represent their (the tax-paying inhabitants) in-terests in the Council, who should endeavour to turn the expenditure of the revenue to the material advancement of the Colony. The whole Colony should be divided into districts, and each should be repre-sented by one or two members.

There are, at present, insurmountable difficulties in the formation of a General Legislative Assembly for the whole Coast at Sierra Leone. It has been argued that it will defeat the general plan of the head of the Coast Government; that the administrators were merely lieutenants of the Governor-General, and were strictly to follow the instructions, whether they be good for or detrimental to the interests of the several Colonies; that the Colonies were poor, and consequently whatever bills might pass the Assembly would be difficult to carry out, simply on account of the want of sufficient revenue; that, in fact, it would be removing the power from the Governor-General and transferring it to a number of mer-chants. Again, the time of the opening of the Assembly would more or less interfere with business, as it is well known that those who would be nominated would be connected personally with busi-ness. If the appointed time be during the rains, it would be found that the merchants in the palm-oil districts would be too much oc-cupied to be called away, and that at that season Freetown is too unhealthy to encourage visitors. If, on the other hand, it is opened during the healthy or dry season, from December to March,

---

* Speech of Alexander Walker, Esq., in the Chamber of Commerce, Sierra Leone. Published in the *Observer*, vol. i., p. 163.

it will be found to interfere with the trade in ground-nuts, and no one in that region would think of sacrificing his business to attend it, as competition in that trade is very great. Thus, therefore, a general Legislative Assembly for the whole Coast is, for the present, not feasible; but the time will come, if every opportunity is taken to improve the country, when it will be more acceptable.

It stands to reason, however, that the inhabitants of Sierra Leone who are heavily taxed should have a voice in the deliberation of the Legislative Council, and the regulation of the revenue.

II.—*General Improvement in the Educational and Ecclesiastical Department of the Colony.*

It cannot be denied that the greatest regenerative influence in this department is the Church Missionary Society. They support at present a college at Fourah Bay, a grammar-school in Freetown, and a large female educational institution, besides several village schools. They have, infinitely more than the Government and than any other religious body, laboured earnestly for the diffusion of useful knowledge in the Colony, and to their untiring exertion is due that degree of improvement which is now to be observed in the Colony of Sierra Leone. It is evident from their yearly report that they could not continue this support for a much longer period, whilst the Colony has grown to be self-supporting, and a large field is open to them elsewhere to do good; and therefore it is necessary that the people and the Local Government should take up the work they have so admirably done.

We want a University for Western Africa, and the Church Missionary Society has long ago taken the initiative and built an expensive college, which should now be made the focus of learning for all Western Africa. The yearly expenses of that Society for education are now 4,700*l.*,* which falls short of their former expenditure, whilst the total sum expended by the Local Government for this purpose is not far above 400*l.* The result is that the educational department of the Colony is greatly on the decline every year, and more support is consequently required; but the local authorites re-

* Col. Ord's Report on the Condition of the British Settlements, West Coast of Africa—Sierra Leone.

fuse to give this, although they liberally spend 14,000*l.* yearly merely for police.

A superficial consideration of the theory of the Local Government for the limitation of its efforts in this important direction— viz., that extensive funds have long been, and still are being, appropriated for that object from other sources, and, consequently, it could not be so until the aid is withdrawn, as reported by Colonel Ord—is so alluring and attractive that it requires a long residence in the Colony to prove that it is most unsound; and should the recommendation of the Chamber of Commerce, that a portion of the revenue be yearly voted for general education, not be adopted, it will be one of the greatest barriers to the general improvement contemplated by the Imperial Government.

Fourah Bay College should henceforth be made the University of Western Africa, and endowed by the Local Government, which should guarantee its privileges, and cherish the interests of literature and science in the Colony. A systematic course of instruction should be given to the students, and regius professors appointed; for it is high time to abolish that system of Lancastrian schoolboy teaching, and a professor should be appointed to one or two subjects, and should give lectures on the results of extensive reading and research. The subjects will be better mastered by the teachers themselves, and the students would reap largely the benefit. Lectures should be given in the theory and practice of education, classics, mathematics, natural philosophy, mensuration, and bookkeeping; English language and literature; French, German, Hebrew, history in general, mineralogy, physiology, zoology, botany, chemistry, moral and political philosophy, civil and commercial law, drawing and music, besides the various subjects which might be included under the term of theology.

But the study of the physical sciences, which are closely connected with our daily wants and conveniences, should form an essential part of the curriculum, as they cultivate the reasoning faculties Algebra, arithmetic, differential calculus, trigonometry, and geometry, besides being useful in every day life, remedy and cure many defects in the wit and intellectual faculties; 'for if the wit,' as remarked by Lord Bacon, 'be too dull, they sharpen it; if too wandering, they fix It ; If too inherent in the sense, they abstract it. So that, as tennis is a game of no use of itself, but of great use in respect it maketh a quick eye, and a body ready to put itself into all positions, so with mathematics, that use which is collateral and intervenient is no less worthy than that which is principal and intended.' The Commissioners of Public Schools in England, referring to the study of physical science, justly remarked in their report that 'it quickens and cultivates directly the faculty of observation, which in very many persons lies almost dormant through life, the power of accurate and rapid generalization, and the mental habit of method and arrangement; it familiarises them with a kind of reasoning which interests them, and which they can promptly comprehend; and it is, perhaps, the best corrective for that indolence which is the vice of half-awakened minds, and which shrinks from any exertion that is not like an effort of memory, merely mechanical.'

In fact, the whole Colony should be divided into educational districts. In each there should be a free grammar-school, where scholars should be prepared either for a foundation school, to be established in the city, or for the University. Each district should tax itself according to its capabilities for the support of these free schools; and boys who have shown a good degree of intellectual progress in a parochial school should be sent there.

In every village there should be a parochial establishment, assisted by the Government, and not dependent entirely on the paltry sums collected at the school. The schoolmasters should be better paid, so that a better class of men might be obtained as teachers, and the schools visited yearly by Government agents, to see that the rules and regulations are properly carried out.

The Government should also establish a preparatory school at Freetown for the express purpose of training up teachers, or forming a corps of well-trained teachers, who should give instruction both in the theory and in the practical application of the sciences; if very proficient in studies some might be transferred to the University. But before admittance as Government or gratuitous pupils, they must bind themselves to remain in the preparatory school for a stated time and pass a rigid examination. This school could be made to receive paying pupils also, the Government only supporting those who are

intended for teachers in the public schools, and who should undertake to devote themselves for ten years at least to public instruction; and thus a set of well-trained and educated teachers would be
obtained, which would supply the schools of the whole of Western
Africa. It will not be out of place if a minister or officer of public
instruction be created, with suitable councils, to regulate and improve the educational branch, not only of the Colony of Sierra
Leone, but also of the other Colonies in Western Africa; he should
form one system of education for all the public schools, and should
see that the instructions for the guidance of teachers are properly
carried out. In these schools prizes and certificates of honour
should be offered to the most meritorious and deserving students.

The neglect of the West African Colonies as regards the education of the natives by the Government, as the Rev. Henry Venn remarks, 'contrasts unfavourably with many of the British Colonies,
which have established grammar-schools and colleges for the purpose of securing a high standard of education. The Colony of the
Mauritius, in addition to such establishments, has annually granted
an exhibition of one thousand pounds, open to competition by all
races, to enable the successful candidate to proceed to England, and
graduate at one of the Universities. Had this principle been
ádopted at Sierra Leone, and natives of promising abilities been
sent over to complete their education in England, it would only
have given the native race their fair chance of achieving a high
position in the service of the Crown.'

The native pastorate* constitutes the Established Church, at least

---

* The native pastorate has unfortunately been placed in a most difficult condition by its parental head, and it excites the wonder and admiration of every one who studies its working how it has been able to exist.
It is most likely that the parent committee had the idea that the pastorate
would begin under hard and trying difficulties, so that when a greater
laxity of privileges should be granted, the whole working of the system would
go on with ease and success. At present, with the exception of Kissy and
Regent parishes, all the most flourishing churches are under the supervision
of the parent committee, and are not included in the pastorate; it has no
representative church in Freetown under the immediate control of the
bishop of the diocese; and as the whole of the wealth of Sierra Leone is at
Freetown, it is a great drawback to its financial success. Having no immediate interest in that body, we find that the wealthy merchants are luke-
warm and sparing in their donations; Kissy-road, Pademba-road, Wilberforce, and Waterloo are still under the parent committee. But we hope

of Sierra Leone, and the Local Government should now bring it into the same pale, and allow it those grants and privileges which are necessary to keep up the Church of the State.

They should divide the Colony into parishes, recognized by the Government, and should appoint vestrymen, who would guard the interests of the Church, and there should be a yearly assemblage or convocation of all the ministers for the purpose of discussing measures for the benefit of the Church.*

The sum of 4,000*l.* voted yearly would even scarcely be sufficient to supply the wants and requirements of the ecclesiastical and educational department of the Colony, but it could be made to answer for the present—viz., 1,000*l.* for the native pastorate, and 3,000*l.* for educational establishments. Of the latter, 1,000*l.* would be ample for the part payment of principals and regius professors, who should be selected by the Church Missionary Society, and should also derive a fractional amount from their lectures. Two sections should be formed, and the lectures delivered during each of them, and the students pay a certain sum for their tickets to each lecture, as is done in other universities.

III.—*The Formation of a Municipal Council.*

The time is perfectly ripe when Sierra Leone should have a town corporation, since the existence of such a body in a country is a true sign of advance in political matters, and we hope that no narrow-minded prejudice will prevent its immediate establishment. The Gold Coast once formed themselves into a corporate body, through the recommendation of Sir Benjamin Pine, which did a

that ere many months have elapsed the committee will adopt the wise and all-important step of handing over one or other of the two parishes at Free-town to the native pastorate. At present that venerable society has voted 250*l.* for the erection of a native pastorate church in the city, but it will require about 1,500*l.* at least for its completion ; we have, therefore, to look to the liberality of the merchants and the inhabitants generally for its speedy erection.

* Since writing the above a local ordinance of great importance has been passed in the Legislative Council, bearing date July 3, 1867, by which a Board of Education has been formed. The Colonial Government granted towards education, at least for the time, 800*l.*, which is a decided advance on the preceding years ; but how has it been applied ? 300*l.* went towards the payment of Inspector of Schools, 150*l.* towards the clerk, and most likely 50*l.* towards stationeries, office-boy, &c., leaving a balance only of 300*l.* towards the subject matter of the ordinance.

great deal of good amongst the population, but which was made null and void by Mr. Andrews, during his short career as Governor of that place. Sierra Leone, from its rate of mortality and the necessity for a vigilant sanitary police, requires a town council and a medical registrar. These would root out the pernicious causes of the diseases in the Colony, relieve the police-court of a great many of its cases and officers, and, consequently, save the Colony a fair sum of money. The benefit derived from the summonses, fines, &c., after paying all expenses, should be used entirely for renovating the town, clearing it of filth and dirt, &c. We hope that this will be among the first measures taken by the executive authorities.

It is almost impossible to understand why each successive Governor shuts his eyes against the formation of a municipal council; it is the very first step by which a people can be made accustomed to manage their own affairs. The charter of the Colony has always provided for it, although, virtually, the local Government has never acted on it. (See *Sir Benjamin Pine's Evidence in Parliamentary Committee*, 1865. *Quest.* 3,052.)

IV.—*The Transfer of the Registrar of Births, Marriages, and Deaths from the Legal to the Medical Profession, and the Establishment of a Health Officer.*

The beneficial result which will arise from this transfer cannot be overrated. Ever since the formation of this office, the population have been kept perfectly ignorant of the *rationale* of the registration —viz., the rate of mortality, the different causes of death, the proportion of births to deaths, the amount of legitimate or illegitimate births, the causes of periodic endemic diseases; in fact, there has never been a generalized summary published, weekly, monthly, half-yearly, or yearly, for the benefit of those for whose interest the office is established. At present the office is in the hands of a legal gentleman, and it is certainly impossible for the legal mind to classify diseases, to trace their causes, and to point out their remedy. This truth is acknowledged in England, where none but medical men have the appointment. The books in the office, as it now stands, are almost a dead letter to the population, but which might hereafter be used for reference, and may serve as a means for drawing up a comparative statement of the health of the Colony at various periods.

Lately a Board of Health has been formed, composed of the leading merchants and officials in the Colony, presided over by the colonial surgeons.   A non-medical gentleman (!) is appointed Inspector of Nuisances, to report to the board the necessary improvements that ought to be made in the sanitary condition of Freetown. But the city is so large that it is impossible for only one man, or one board so constituted, to bring a sufficient pressure on different localities so as properly to clean it of filth and dirt.   The city ought to be divided into parishes, and each parish appoint its own board, which should receive full authority from the Government to act, and each board should appoint its own inspector of nuisances, who should report to it the state of the parish, and recommend various improvements, which, being sanctioned by the Government, would certainly be carried into effect.   According to the present arrangements there is very little hope that an effectual sanitary reform would be the result; and the present ordinance, so far as the general good is concerned, is a stepping-stone to a more enlightened ordinance.

V.—*The Extension of Colonial (British) Protection to the Merchants in the Rivers in the Neighbourhood of Sierra Leone, and consequently the Extension of the Custom-office to those Places.*

It must be very provoking to think that nearly within gunshot of the barracks at Freetown, British merchants could receive no protection from the Government; that they could be tried and flogged by the natives, and their goods confiscated, without receiving any redress from the local authority, as is exemplified in the late outbreak in Mellicourie River.   Proper steps should now be taken to prevent such disturbances, and the merchants, I think, are perfectly ready to pay into the Colonial coffer duties on goods landed in those Rivers, should they be guaranteed protection.

Most of the chiefs of those places have broken faith with the Government, have maltreated British merchants, have been conquered by our arms in different engagements, and have asked protection from us.   Will it not be right that we should give them that which will be a boon to the Colony?   I think it is time that these trading ports should be made an integral part of Sierra Leone, since the merchants do more extensive business there than in the Colonies.

But we find that after all the letters and petitions of the merchants at Mellicourie, the Local Government would have nothing to say in the matter, although, as we have observed in page 98, this country has made a most rapid advance in improvement and civilization since Sierra Leone traders have made it a port. Many of the French merchants residing in the Colony have large interests in Mellicourie, and finding that they receive no redress from the natives for the losses they sustained, and that no representation to the local authorities in the Colony would move them to make a pressure on the marauders, they, after waiting for nearly two years, were compelled to apply to their Government for the desired assistance, which immediately took the matter in hand. It is certain that Mellicourie will ultimately become a French station. Unless the Foreign Office assumes its rights, the merchants of the Colony will gradually be turned away from it, and, being in close proximity to the Colony, we shall thus, through excessive *inertia*, allow a European Power to be established so near to our doors as to enact those inconveniences which we are now crying against and endeavouring to remedy in our settlements on the Gold Coast with the Dutch Government. This very occupation of the French is against all treaty, as in the archives of the Colony of Sierra Leone, vol. 2, p. 305, Ordinances, Royal Charters, Treaties, &c., we have the full text of a treaty signed by the Acting-Governor of Sierra Leone, and the kings and chiefs of the Moriah Land, and entered into on the 18th day of April, 1826, by which the latter ceded over ‘ the full, entire, free, and unlimited sovereignty, right, title, and possession, in and over all the seas, rivers, harbours, &c., of their respective territories, from Conta in the South to Ferighna in the North;’ and yet in the face of this the Government of Sierra Leone could rest quietly, unheeding all remonstrances from the chiefs of the district, and allow the French to come and quietly seat themselves, and afterwards, through their protective system of trade, turn away the British merchants who have laboured to improve the trade. The following is the full text of the treaty :—

' *Treaty between his Honour Kenneth Macaulay, Acting-Governor of
the Colony of Sierra Leone and its Dependencies on behalf of His
Britannic Majesty, and the Chiefs of the Soumbuya Soosoos with
their allies the Tura Family.*

' The Tura Family, to whom the throne of the Mandingo (now
called Moriah) Country belongs, and the chiefs and headmen of the
Soumbuya Soosoos, anxious to put an end to the war which has
been carried on for the last twelve years between Amurat (Omaru),
the present chief of the Mandingo Country and the Soumbuya
Soosoos, and to draw closer the ties of amity and friendship which
exist between them and the Colony of Sierra Leone, have deputed
for that purpose the Soumbuya chiefs, Alimamy Dalla Mahammadu
(Dalla Momadoo) and Sankie Brama (Sankie Brahima) and the
Tura Family, Amurat the head thereof, and his Honour Kenneth
Macaulay, Acting-Governor of the Colony of Sierra Leone and its
Dependencies, being willing on the part of His Britannic Majesty
to contribute to so desirable an object, the said parties have agreed
as follows :—

' There shall continue to be, as heretofore, friendship, amity, and
free intercourse between all His Majesty's subjects and the inhabitants of the Soumbuya and Mandingo Countries subject to the said
chieftains.

' Provides for free permission to British subjects to form trading
establishments and factories in all parts of the Soumbuya and
Moriah Countries, to exempt them from the imposition of all duties
and exactions, under whatever plea the same may be made, and that
all such may carry on their trade in such manner as they think
proper.

' Provides and guarantees to the Acting-Governor of Sierra
Leone and his successors, on behalf of His Britannic Majesty, free
roads to all British subjects, strangers, merchants, &c., through
their respective countries, and for them to pass and repass " with
their retinue, goods, wares, and merchandise, &c., between the
Colony of Sierra Leone and the interior countries of Africa," and
that they " shall not be called upon or made to pay any duties,
customs, or sums of money, on any pretence whatever, except for
such expenses as they may actually have incurred."

P

' Provides against the export of slaves, or the entrance of any slave-craft in the " rivers, bays, creeks, or waters," of their respective countries.

' For the purpose of rendering the provisions of this treaty more effectual, the said Soumbuya chiefs and the Tura Family give, grant, and cede over to his Honour the Acting-Governor of Sierra Leone and his successors for and on behalf of His Majesty the King of the United Kingdom of Great Britain and Ireland and his successors the full, entire, free, and unlimited sovereignty, right, title, and possession in and over all the seas, rivers, harbours, creeks, inlets, and waters of their respective territories, from Conta (the town where Mr. Rosenbush's factory has been established) in the south to Ferighna in the north, and in and over one mile inland from the seaboard of the same.

' It being necessary for the coasting trade that the Island of Matacong should be a neutral and free resting-place for the canoes and craft belonging to all the surrounding tribes, notwithstanding any wars which may exist among them, the Soumbuya chiefs, to whom the same belongs, have requested his Honour the Acting-Governor to accept the cession thereof, and have granted, ceded, and transferred over to the said Kenneth Macaulay, Acting-Governor of Sierra Leone, and his successors, for and on behalf of His Majesty the King of the United Kingdom of Great Britain and Ireland and his successors for ever, the free, unlimited right, title, possession, and sovereignty in and over the said Island of Matacong, with all the rivers, bays, creeks, harbours, and waters thereof.

' Provides for the cession of further parcels of land inland, should the same at any time be required, on " fair and equitable terms."

' His Honour the said Kenneth Macaulay, for himself and his successors, Governors of the said Colony on the part and on behalf of His Majesty the King of Great Britain and Ireland, his heirs and successors for ever, agrees to accept the sovereignty of one mile inland from the seaboard and of all the seas, rivers, harbours, creeks, inlets, and waters of the Mandingo and Soumbuya Countries from Conta in the south to Ferighna in the north, for the more effectual performance of the obligations of this treaty, and also to accept the sovereignty and possession of the Island of Matacong, and to preserve the same as a neutral and free resting-place for the craft and canoes of all the surrounding tribes whilst in amity and friendship with His Britannic Majesty.

' Provides for closing the rivers of such parts of the two countries as shall not discontinue the war and make peace.

' Nota Bene.—This ninth article was abrogated and the trade opened by treaty (No. 24, Compiled Ordinances of the Colony of Sierra Leone, vol. 2, page 313) between his Excellency Sir Neil Campbell, Captain General and Governor-in-Chief in and over the Colony of Sierra Leone and its Dependencies, &c., &c., &c., and the chiefs of the Soumbuya Soosoos, with the Tura Family, dated at Wonkafong, 25th May, 1827, signed by Sattan Lahie, chief of all the Soumbuya Countries, and by Michael Proctor, as Commissioner of the Governor of Sierra Leone, and witnessed by Issiaka Rogers and J. J. Robinson.

'In witness whereof the said parties have hereunto set their hands and affixed their seals this eighteenth day of April, in the year of the Christian era one thousand eight hundred and twenty-six.

' Signed,   ' ALIMAMY DALLA MAHOMODU.
         ' AMURAT.
         ' SANKY BRAMA.
' Signed,   ' K. MACAULAY, Acting-Governor.
' Witnesses, Wm. M'Vicar, Lieut. 2nd W. I. Regt.
  ' W. Lardner, Ensign 2nd W. I. Regt.
   ' and three Arabic signatures,
   ' Suleimani, Omaru, Mohamodu Brahima.'

It is necessary that the Gallinas, the Searcies, and Mellicourie, should be united to the Colony, whose territorial boundary would then be considered properly remodelled, and the administration of the Government would be more efficient and economical ; the colony could guarantee the merchants there sufficient protection if a plan like the following be adopted :—

Let a constabulary force of 100 men be enrolled, and paid by the Colonial Government at the rate of 1*l.* 10s. per month, for the express purpose, which should include all necessaries ; let them be properly officered, and distributed at the rate of thirty to each station; let the officer who would be the commandant be properly paid, and be made also the Custom-house officer in those Rivers, with strict orders not to interfere in the native quarrels, but to protect British property. Each vessel as it proceeds up the River should hand over its manifest to the safe care and keeping of the commandant—should give him also an inventory of the goods in the vessel, with their true value, and a written declaration attesting their truth, and a bond signed that, should it prove false, they were to be liable to a heavy fine. They should be required to pay an *ad valorem* duty on all goods, with specific duties on tobacco and rum; it should be made optional to those who are well known in the Colony to pay to the commandant in cash the amount of the duty, or give an order to their principal at Freetown, and all vessels coming within the territorial boundary to trade should be made to pay the *ad valorem* duty.

The communication with these different places would be very easy; a boat or a schooner could be sent from one place to the other; and, as there is always a colonial steamer at anchor, periodical visits to these places can be ensured.

Granting that the Governor-General has at his disposal an intercolonial steamer, according to the resolution of the House of Commons Committee on Western Africa, the steamer should be sent monthly to these stations for the conveyance of letters and orders, and for the collection of the revenue from customs. The very fact of this monthly visitation would check any outbreak amongst the natives.

What would be the result of these measures?—

1. That the revenue of the Colony would be greatly increased and probably doubled.

2. That the British merchants would have proper protection.

3. That the influence of the Colony would be greatly extended.

4. That merchants who have hitherto been afraid to venture on the River trade would at once undertake it.

5. That the resources of the country would be better developed.

6. That the political situation of the Colony would be greatly advanced.

VI.—*The Abolition of the System of Sending the Liberated Africans to the West Indies, and the Re-introduction of the Apprenticeship System.*

According to the present system of the Mixed Commission Department, the recruits, as soon as they are landed from the slave-ships, are sent to the Government yard at Kissy, where they are kept for two, three, or even four years, until they have escaped three chances of being sent to the West Indies. In the Government yard they are kept in total ignorance and idleness, although they are fed and clothed. They are not permitted to go to any school, nor are they taught any useful mechanical works in the establishment; the consequence is that when they leave they are seldom of any use to themselves or anyone else. This system requires a radical change, and the Colony requires their recruits more within the Colony than out of it.

There should be formed an industrial establishment at the mountain village of Gloster, under the supervision of the Church Missionary Society, paid from the imperial chest, where paid carpenters, shoemakers, masons, blacksmiths, wheelwrights, &c., should be continually kept at work. The superintendent should be a practical German mechanic, a type of those of the Basle Missionaries at Accra. The recruits should first be sent to the Normal School at Kissy, where, after learning to read and write for one year and a-half, they should be sent to the Industrial School at Gloster to be put to a trade, and be kept there for four or five years; many of these useful arts would thus be taught with great advantage to the Colony.

The establishment might be made partially self-supporting by each department of trade being made to receive work from without, through the superintendent; the tailors should be made to sew the gaol clothes; the carpenters could be put to Government building and repairs, &c. The female recruits should be placed at Charlotte School, and, after a year and a-half of training in needlework, reading, and writing, be distributed amongst different families.

The Rev. Henry Venn, in his pamphlet on the West African Colonies, whilst questioning the policy of removing liberated Africans from the African Coast, as materially checking the civilization of Africa, and retarding the grand scheme of extinguishing the slave-trade by substituting native industry, justly remarks: ' The present advancement of Sierra Leone is wholly due to the liberated Africans located there upon their release from slave-ships. Separated from all their old heathen associations, and brought under civilizing and Christian influences, they have proved, as a body, tractable and industrious. The testimony of Governor Ferguson, and of others, establishes the truth of this. Bishop Crowther, and many of the most wealthy native merchants, were liberated Africans. Many hundreds of this class, after acquiring the Christian and civilized habits of a British colony, have migrated to different parts of the Coast as traders. The European traders, their rivals, are too often accustomed to speak of them with bitter contempt and vituperation. But the evidence of the naval officers, and of the better class of European traders, gives a very different account of their character, and of their influence with their countrymen; and represents them as a hopeful element in the civilization of Africa.' With all these evidences before them, the authorities have stopped the supply of liberated Africans; and vessels with captured slaves, after being condemned by the Mixed Commission Court, are sent to the West Indies. ' This policy is more to be regretted as the Colony of Sierra Leone has lately obtained a large accession of territory in the Quiah and Sherbo Countries,' to which immigration is very much wanted for agricultural purposes.

VII.—*The Formation of a Dry Dock in Freetown.*

The material for forming a dry dock is abundant in Freetown, and as there are no docks in the whole of Western Africa, I think that if a proper one were formed it would be well patronised, and bring a good revenue to the Government. This would of course require a large outlay, which would, however, be returned to the Local Government in kind in the course of a few years.

Krew Bay would be the most fitting place that could be selected, and a yearly grant of 3,000*l.* or more would soon erect an extensive dock which would be serviceable to men-of-war and merchant vessels, and which would increase the knowledge of shipbuilding in the Colony. But it is not only on account of position and fitness that I should urge the necessity of forming a dry dock there, but particularly as it is the hotbed of malaria—the Golgotha and Gehenna of the western portion of the city. Consequently its formation would lessen the high rate of mortality and destroy the miasma which has devastated the population of the Colony. A Government dockyard would be a most advantageous undertaking for the city and the Coast. The French Government is building a similar dockyard at Dakar, on the mainland of Goree.

VIII.—*An Improvement of Buildings at the Sea Front of the City.*

There is no town on the Coast in which the sea frontage gives so dull and unhappy an appearance as Freetown, especially during the rainy season. We find here a tumble-down building, there a half-finished store; here broken rocks and upheavals of the earth, there an inroad of the sea into the town. We find nothing in a regular form, but everything pell-mell.

In a former edition I proposed that an agreeable promenade should be erected along the sea frontage of the city of Freetown, but this would be a most expensive undertaking; an improvement, however, can be made in the buildings. The Legislature should step in and compel all holders of lands bordering on the River and facing it to make proper repairs, or build according to a regular plan furnished by the Government.

IX.—*A System of General Supply of Water to Freetown should be Adopted.*

This must either be done by Government, or by a private company, but as the former is better able to do it, we hope that it will not be long before it will make a beginning. In dealing with the subject of the water supply in the Chamber of Commerce, Mr. Walker remarked that it would not only be ornamental, but extremely useful in a sanitary point of view; it would supply the wants of the thousands who weekly attend the market, and would more effectually clear the cesspools of their filth and dirt, and consequently improve the general health of the Colony. It is a project that could be most easily accomplished, as Freetown is on a gradual slope from the hills, and several beautiful streams run down through the town from the mountains. With very small outlay, reservoirs, with pipes, could be easily laid down, and the water conducted into the different parts where it might be required.

It is inconceivable that so large and flourishing a city as Freetown, with a population of nearly 20,000 inhabitants, should still suffer from the want of the supply of one of the most material elements of existence ; the outlay would be comparatively small, and within a very short time it would produce a standing revenue to the Government. The numerous prisoners which infest the gaol could be advantageously employed for laying down the pipes or building masonry reservoirs, which would immensely lessen the expense. The authorities it is said have had for some time in contemplation the carrying out of this most useful suggestion, which we hope will soon become a fact.

X.—*The Introduction of New Plants in the Mountain and other Districts, which might become Sources of Profitable Commerce to the Colony.*

In the description of the inhabitants of the Mountain and Sea Districts of the Colony, I have shown that they are the poorest and most contented in the Colony ; that their means of making money is most limited ; that they are principally agricultural in their habits—cultivating the common necessaries of life and supplying the markets of Freetown with vegetables, &c.; that at one time arrowroot was extensively cultivated by them, but on account of the low prices offered for it in the market, it became unremunerative. The aged population is fast dying away, and the young generation, finding nothing profitable to occupy their time in the district, either change their residence to the capital or emigrate to other parts,—and thus a yearly depopulation to a fearful extent is going on. The country on the mountains, which once was cleared and dotted with plantations of various sizes, is now covered with thick jungles, and those places which twenty years ago were covered with low trees, form now thick forest, so that gradually the open plain fields of Sierra Leone are being converted into forest lands. The only means by which this can be arrested will be the introduction of new plants into the Colony (by the local authorities,) which will be remunerative to the planters. Not only should the best specimens of native plants be ascertained and cultivated, but specimens of plants growing in other tropical regions should be introduced. The Curator of the Kew Gardens, the late Sir W. Hooker, had always urged the necessity of introducing new plants in Africa, and was ready, and so his son also now is, to supply the specimens; but ' there is no record of any such attempts on the part of the Government to develop the natural resources of Africa, although the native races are in that stage of civilization in which helps are most needed, and they have proved themselves apt to take immediate advantage of new sources of profit.' The Government should therefore introduce such new plants, and encourage the cultivation of the best specimens of such native plants, as would, in course of time, be remunerative to the planters.

The following plants might be amongst those which, if introduced, would be beneficial to the country and inhabitants:—

Theobroma Cacao, or the chocolate plant, which grows spontaneously in the West Indies and in the central regions of America, and which has been introduced and cultivated in the Mauritius and the French Island of Bourbon, as well as lately in the Aquapim Mountains of the Eastern District of the Gold Coast by the Basle Missionaries, should certainly be one of the first plants introduced by the Government, as the climate and soil of the Mountain District is well adapted for its cultivation. This will at once bring into the market of Sierra Leone an article of high commercial value, and also the richest and most nutritive kind of vegetable food for the inhabitants of the Colony.

The *Nopal Plant*, or *Opuntia Cochinellifera*, which affords nourishment to the cochineal insect, will be highly profitable. It grows within the same latitude of the colonies in Western Africa— viz., in Peru and Mexico—and has been successfully introduced in Teneriffe. Such is the value of the cochineal that at present more than 500,000*l.* worth of the insect is annually exported from South America. The introduction would be easily accomplished, as the Governor of Teneriffe, if applied to, would certainly supply the Governor-General with specimens.

Virginian Tobacco.—The fact of tobacco growing wild in the Mountain District is a certain proof that it will be very easy to cultivate it, but the people should be taught the mode of properly preparing it. An improvement should be made in the mode of cultivating, and in the preparation of the numerous *fibre* plants and the indigo plant, which grow spontaneously in the forests of the country. Full description and the mode of preparation should be supplied to the people.

The above are only a few examples of new plants which might be advantageously introduced into the Colony; but there are others which grow in the East and West Indies, part of Mexico, and South America, which might also be made the subject of inquiry, and the action of a paternal Government might thus be profitably used in encouraging an infant trade.

XI. *Proper Measures for the Encouragement of Agriculture should be Introduced in the Colony.*

It is true, as remarks Mr. Venn, that although the Parliamentary Committee of 1842 pointed out the neglect of the Colonial Government in not promoting agriculture and establishing model farms, yet up to this day it has never been attempted. 'The neglect of agriculture in these Colonies,' he says, ' is the great drawback upon their prosperity, and is often alleged against them as a flagrant reproach. One fact may be stated in proof. Sierra Leone is supplied with rice, the staple article of food, from the surrounding countries. When war breaks out, the supply fails. For the last two or three years, in consequence of internal wars, rice, which had been imported into England from India, has been again sent out from England to supply the market in Sierra Leone, though any quantity might have been grown in the Colony itself! This neglect of agriculture arises chiefly from the taint of African slavery. Agriculture in other parts of Africa is carried on by slave labour. The free men of the British Colonies, therefore, prefer any kind of trade or barter to agricultural labour. Here, then, the Colonial Governments should have supplied the remedy by establishing model farms, by prizes to successful producers of agricultural produce, by public warehouses, where small farmers might store their goods for shipment, and by various other modes of instruction and encouragement.'

Mr. Rosenbush, in a letter to F. Fitzgerald, Esq., remarked that the greatest requirement of the Colony is agriculture, and he recommends the establishment of a model farm by convict labour; but, for this to be of service, botanical gardens should be attached to it. ' At present,' he said, ' the characteristic feature of the inmates of the gaol is to make the institution a kind of refuge.' Availing themselves of the ' temporary leave of absence,' they go out, but invariably soon return, on account of being worthless for honest employment. In a model farm they would first work to maintain themselves, and, secondly, become acquainted with agriculture, which might induce many to remove to parts where they were not known, and endeavour to regain an honest position in life. The expense of one farm could scarcely be more than the amount which the establishment of the Colonial Government now costs, and it would very soon become self-supporting. It should be open for the inspection of everybody, in order to stimulate others to follow the useful employment of agriculture.*

I have stated above that this neglect of agriculture has been alleged against the African peasant as a flagrant reproach by many Europeans who visit this Coast. These very calumniators of the African peasantry, who have closely observed how laboriously the peasantry of their country are obliged to work for their livelihood, always forget that the position, wants, and requirements of the two classes are extremely different. Their general saying runs thus : ' At home a peasant would labour for a whole day and would do ten times the work these lazy fellows do. Your people are too lazy ; they have lands in abundance, which would soon make them rich if properly cultivated.' It is a fact which cannot be doubted by anyone, that European peasants do by far more work than the African peasant, but the conditions of the two people are vastly different. In England, for example, the lands are most un-equally divided; the aristocrats are masters, and the peasants more like mitigated serfs; in Africa the peasants are masters of the lands, and can cultivate any extent for their own private purpose without restriction. In England the number of the labouring class exceeds the number of workmen required to occupy the various necessary callings, and, consequently, those who have secured an employment are obliged to work hard to keep their place and credit; in Africa the contrary is just the case, the population is insufficient

---

* *African Times*, August, 1865, p. 14.

to cultivate the vast extent of lands by which they are surrounded, and they have no credit to keep up nor place to lose. In England the labouring class is compelled to work hard before they can be supplied with the necessaries of life, if not they must starve; in Africa if a labouring man is unable to work, his neighbours supply him with food, or go out and work the field gratuitously for him, or if well, he goes for a few weeks to his plantation, and without much labour obtains in a few months from the fertile soil his year's stock of provision. In fact, in England the labouring class has always great external pressure to bear upon them, demanding both their moral and their physical strength; whilst the same class in Africa has little or no external pressure to bear on them. In England the food of the peasant is compound, expensive, and very scarce; in Africa the food is simple, cheap, and plentiful. In England the peasant is compelled by the state of civilization and the necessity of the climate to procure clothing, which entails a greater outlay and a necessity for increased labour; but in Africa the climate is so hot and uniform that the peasants go about half-naked, and therefore have little or no expense for clothing.

Now with all these local advantages on the side of the African peasantry, can it be a matter of surprise that they confine themselves almost entirely to the cultivation of produce sufficient for their yearly consumption? Can it be a matter of surprise, I say, that the English peasant labours infinitely more than the African peasant? In the one case, the land supplies the peasant abundantly, whether he works hard or not; in the other, starvation awaits him if he does not work hard, and should he not pay dearly with his strength and skill, he is sure to fall to utter destitution. To the English peasant the words of Mr. Thomas Carlyle, in his inaugural address as Lord Rector of Edinburgh University, echo loudly. 'If a man,' says he, 'gets meat and clothes, what matters it whether he have ten thousand pounds, or ten million pounds, or seventy pounds a-year? He can get meat and clothes for that, and he will find very little real difference intrinsically, *if he is a wise man.*'

There is a plant now growing abundantly in all the villages in the otherwise barren Mountain District, and, in fact, in every part of the Colony of Sierra Leone, which, if properly cultivated and worked, would lead to a mine of wealth to the destitute inhabitants. The Local Government should take it in hand, offer prizes for the best manufactured articles from it, and should depute representatives in the villages to teach the inhabitants the mode of cultivating it. This plant has been noticed in a letter in the *Cavalla Messenger*, printed at Cape Palmas, which gives the mode of planting, preparing the fruit, and preparing the fibre. The following is the letter *in extenso* :—

'I take the liberty, in the following communication, to call the attention of your readers to the growth of the plantain for its fibre.

'In the first place I would remark that it is easily cultivated. In preparing the ground for the crop in this country, we meet with one grand difficulty—the want of the plough and team. Yet this is less felt than in many parts of the world. The constant fall of rain in the growing seasons softens the ground, and conveys to the root of plants the soluble parts of the decaying vegetable and mineral matter composing the soil as perfectly and thoroughly as if the land were ploughed and otherwise cultivated by a team. But in the growth of the plaintain we are less dependent on the plough and oxen for success than in the management of most other crops. This is a fact very strongly recommending it to the attention of the farmer.

'To put out a field of plaintains, the ground should be prepared much as it is for cassada roots. The ground then should be laid out in rows about twelve or eighteen feet apart each way. At the point crossed by these rows the soil should be thoroughly dug up, and a healthy root set in the centre. The plant usually does best when laid down so as to sprout from the side. This will give from three to four hundred plants to the acre.

'For the first year or two cassada, cotton, pepper, ginger, corn, arrowroot, sugar-cane, or some other crop, should be grown with it. The third year will give seven suckers to each plant, which will make 2,400 to 2,800 stalks, with as many bunches of delicious, healthy, nutritious, fruit. This gathered when fully ripe may be easily preserved for food or export. In England it takes the place of dried apple, and commands a price that will richly repay the farmer for all the labour of cultivation and curing for market.

'The process of drying is simple. The ripe fruit is laid in the hot sun on mats elevated from the ground. After it becomes wetted, it is taken from the skin and replaced upon the mats till dry, when it is found coated with sugar, like figs. This process might be shortened by kiln-drying.

' The fruit when full grown, before the process of ripening commences, is very rich in starch, and when dried and ground makes an excellent meal. To make plantain meal the plantain must be removed with a bamboo knife, so as not to discolour the fruit. Then cut in thin slices and dry in the sun, or on a kiln, which is better; when brittle, grind into a meal.

' The fact that the fruit for home consumption or the foreign market will richly pay for cultivation is an item of importance. For this purpose is plantain chiefly raised. The stalk is by many regarded as valueless. Yet it is, by the addition of a little labour, worth 3d. a stalk.

' An acre of well-matured, thrifty plantains will produce 6,000 lbs. of fibre, at a cost in labour of 3*l*. per ton; and with an additional cost of 7*l*. per ton it may be placed in an English market. Plantain fibre, after patient, varied, and repeated experiments, has been proved to be equal to hemp for all the purposes of cordage, and now commands the same price as good hemp, say from 30*l*. to 35*l*. per ton, giving a clear profit to the grower of more than 20*l*. the ton.

' To convert the stalk into fibre it is cut into lengths of three feet long and quartered. This should be done as quickly as may be, so as not to blacken the fibre with the iron instrument used in cutting.

' Furnished with a mill like a horizontal sugar-mill, having wooden rollers, four feet long and one foot in diameter, turned by horse power, the quartered stalks are passed between the rollers longitudinally, so as not to strain the fibre. Then the crushed stalks are washed thoroughly (which process separates the fibre from the pulpy matter of the stalks), and the fibre is hung on poles under a shade to dry The sun discolours it. When dry, it is combed or hackled, as flax or hemp, when it is fit for the market. The tow, or waste from the combing, is beaten and prepared as half-stuff for paper, at a cost of 8*l.* per ton, and is worth as much as linen rags for paper, say from 16*l.* to 20*l.* per ton.'

Miss Waldren, of Cape Coast, forwarded to England some years ago a large quantity of Cape Coast-made plantain fibres, the market value of which did not pay a tenth part of what she laid out. This at once put a stop to the people of Cape Coast attempting its exportation; but in this case the mode of preparation was at fault, which makes it perfectly valueless, and which should act as a caution to those who again attempt to prepare it for the English market. It was cut carelessly with an iron knife, which of course blackens the fibres; it was crushed in the sun by pounding, which discolours the fibres, destroys their texture, and weakens their strength. It was exposed to dry in the sun, the fibres were not placed in layers, but were entangled into a meshwork, so that the ends could not be easily traced, and consequently they were never combed. These facts will at once explain the cause of the failure. A proper experiment should now be instituted by the Hon. George Blankson, in his large plantation at Acherobuanda and Framangue.

XII.—*The Erection of Substantial Batteries on Signal Hill and on one or more of the Elevations in its Neighbourhood.*

The greatness of a country is not merely calculated from its riches, its extent, and its commerce, but intrinsically from its power of defence. No part of Sierra Leone would be of any material use to an invader but Freetown, the capital, which could be made completely impregnable by a comparatively small outlay. The entrance into the harbour of Sierra Leone is by a very small channel, situated near Cape Sierra Leone, and overlooked by Signal Hill and a few eminences, with plateaus on their summits, in its neighbourhood. From the experience of byegone years it is certain that the Colony is by no means safe should war be declared against France or America; and now that the political horizon seems peaceful, it will be the better part of valour if suitable fortifications be erected in these elevated positions which completely overlook the harbour, by which every foreign vessel would be debarred from entering the port and bombarding the town. The French are strongly fortifying their settlement at Senegal, without the least regard to expense; but so open and defenceless is our principal

Colony on the Coast, where there is scarcely one gun fit for use against the heavy armament of men-of-war now-a-days, that, within a few hours, a French or an American sloop-of-war could level the town to the ground. Let us, therefore, begin in time to prepare ourselves, and not wait until our enemies are on our heels. Three good earth batteries, made tenacious in their slopes by the planting of the Bahama grass, so common in the streets of Freetown, and supplied with heavy Armstrong guns, would be all that would be required.

XIII.—*The Raising of a Sufficient Amount of Money for Rapidly Carrying out those Improvements which are Essential to the Health and Industrial Development of the Colony.*

It will be observed, from the reading of the above pages, that the Colony will require a large amount of money at once to carry out these useful improvements, over and above the present revenue. A loan has been suggested by many, but the Colony will be obliged to pay a large interest until the capital is paid ; and this will necessitate an increase in the taxes. In my opinion this can at present be dispensed with if the amount required be not far over 100,000*l.*, and let the Colony be her own debtor.

Let a colonial paper currency to that amount be issued, and made equal in value to the specie in circulation, and redeemable in ten or more years ; let the Legislature be stringent in preventing any depreciation of its value ; let the large mercantile establishments take it up and have it circulated, and let the Government redeem every year from two to four thousand pounds ; and in a few years those large improvements indicated will be made, which, in the course of a short time, will pay their own expenses without any outlay from the colonial chest. A similar plan was, some years ago, adopted in the building of a large wharf (if my memory be correct) in Jersey with great success.

It might be remarked that whilst I condemn the practice in Liberia of a wholesale issue of paper currency,* I recommend the same thing at Sierra Leone. But there is a great difference

---

* *Vide* above, Liberia, p. 17.. I am glad to be informed that Liberia is now making an effort for the redemption of her paper currency.

between the two countries. The former, having a very small revenue, issued an amount of this medium far above her capacity for redemption; and this not for the building of any public works which would pay their own cost, but to avert a crisis. The latter, on the contrary, has a large revenue, which is above her expenses, and a few years ago she had in her chest about 15,000*l*. over and above her expenditure. The paper currency, if adopted, will be for building public works, which will be made to pay their own expenses, without costing a farthing to the Government. Thus, if water be conveyed to the town and supplied to the different houses, the people will be taxed for it, and the money derived from it will go towards reclaiming the paper currency, until it becomes an independent source of revenue. I shall, therefore, recommend the adoption of this measure as the most practical that could be found suited for the Colony of Sierra Leone, and not to venture at present on a loan for these improvements. I shall, however, in another place point out where a loan might with the best advantage be contracted.*

XIV.—*The Enrolment of the Militia Force.*

An act was passed at Sierra Leone, not very long ago, by which all the male inhabitants of the Colony, within a certain age and not suffering from any physical disabilities, were enrolled as a Militia; they were drilled at stated intervals, and reviewed yearly by the Governor. The Militia Force had an expensive band, and there was really a military air and gait observed among the rising generation of the Colony. It was a most useful establishment, as they were employed in many cases as sentries in the different guards when the soldiers were engaged in active service. As auxiliaries, they were employed without pay on active service, as in the late Quiah war near Sierra Leone. But when it was decided that the Coast was to be garrisoned by a whole West India Regiment, with its headquarters and band stationed at Sierra Leone, the local authorities began to find fault with the Militia Force; they were not considered sufficiently disciplined and subordinate, and ultimately they were disbanded, and the national band was superseded by that of the West India Regiment. But if the truth be told, the fault of the

* *Vide* below, Gold Coast.

Q

want of discipline and subordination must lie at the door of the local authorities. By some false ideas at the formation of the force, they appointed merchants between the ages of fifty and sixty years as captains and lieutenants, who could only just read and write, whilst the young men of education and buoyancy, who would give their time and interest to it, were placed in inferior grades, unless they purchased their commissions. It was supposed that these old men would buy out their freedom by paying the sum of ten pounds to the Government, but they held fast to the commission, which was given them, although incapable of learning the drill. The authorities there outdid themselves. Inefficiency was the consequence, which ultimately led to the disbandment of the whole force. It is necessary that the Militia Force be re-established on a better footing, as a time will certainly come when they will be found of the greatest service to the Local Government of the country.

XV.—*The Formation of a National Bank at Freetown.*

The growing wealth of the city of Freetown necessitates the formation of a Government, and consequently a responsible, bank in it. A bank at Sierra Leone, formed and supported by the Local Government, and placed in connexion with a safe bank in England, will furnish a most important lever to the merchants and small traders in the Colony; which benefit would ultimately extend to the other Colonies on the Coast. In commercial circles the importance of a good, reliable banking establishment is well known and appreciated. Even in this Colony, where there are only small private banks, so greatly are they appreciated that, at the approach of the mail steamers, the banks have sometimes to close their doors against business men.

It would be a very important savings bank for the poor, who now bury their small savings in the ground; they would thus obtain good security and a premium. It would supply the merchants and traders with money during the trading season, when ready cash is much required; and, by some arrangement, it might be made to supply the military and naval department on the Coast at a certain rate of premium. So that whilst it will be advantageous to the commercial and other inhabitants of the Colony, it would also be serviceable to the local authorities and the Imperial Government.

XVI.—*The Formation of an Intercolonial Post throughout the Colony in Connexion with the Present Post-office.*

This is one of the growing wants of the Colony; and its non-existence is so inconvenient that it is a wonder that the subject has never yet entered into the consideration of the authorities, as its establishment would greatly increase the revenue. It will require, in the first place, that the houses should be properly and legibly numbered, as at present the streets are all named, excepting those in the villages. The payment for letters should not be more than one penny for each half-ounce; the delivery at Freetown should be twice a-day at the commencement—viz., at 8 A.M. and 6 P.M.—and in the villages twice or three times a-week. The expenses, after the stamp machine is obtained, would be to increase the pay of the present Postmaster of Sierra Leone, which should be graduated yearly according to the probable increase of the undertaking, and the appointment of additional post-office clerks; the formation of various sub-offices in the town, and the erection of waterproof post-boxes in conspicuous places; the appointment of village postmasters, and, last, the post carriers. In the villages the various ill-paid schoolmasters would be the most eligible persons to fill the appointment of postmaster; their pay of course would be commensurate with the importance of the village. If properly arranged and centres formed in districts—viz., at Regent, Waterloo, and Kissy—there is no doubt that the undertaking would, whilst of great convenience to the Colony, add a great deal to the revenue of the Colony.

XVII.—*The Necessity of Introducing by the Legislature a Strict Vaccination Act, for the Purpose of Protecting the Community against the Yearly Ravages of Small-pox.*

The prevalence of small-pox every year in Sierra Leone, and in the other Colonies in Western Africa, should be an immediate incentive for the Government to interfere and introduce a remedy to an evil which vitally affects the public health. The prevalence of the disease is most discreditable to those who can prevent it, since it is well known that the remedy—viz., vaccination—is 'specific and infallible.' The protection is only temporary and limited, it is true, but during the time it lasts it completely protects the system. On the subject of vaccination these two points should always be borne in mind—viz., first, that when performed it should be thoroughly done, presenting three or four permanent deep scars on the arms. This should be done a few weeks after birth. Second, that the vaccination should be repeated after the age of puberty, or the twenty-first year.

In places like the Colonies of Western Africa this can only be established by the Government, who should make it compulsory on everyone to have the operation performed. I should, therefore, urge upon the authorities the appointment of properly paid vaccinators, both for vaccination and re-vaccination, as well as the appointment of inspectors of vaccination, who should make periodical inspections of the various districts, and report on the degree to which the operation has been performed, not only in districts, but also in individual cases. Every individual, parent, or guardian, who refuses to be or to have their child or ward vaccinated should be prosecuted by law.

XVIII.—*The Supply of Medical Men or District Dispensers to the various Villages of the Colony.*

That it is the duty of a paternal Government to look after the health of the poor inhabitants of the country is undoubted; but we find that whilst there are two colonial surgeons in the capital, the districts are left unsupplied. The poor inhabitants get sick and die without the chance for life being given them; there are now on poor-law boards and no poor-law medical officers attached to each village or district; in fact, no public organization for succour of the afflicted poor. The consequence is that the death rate is still constantly high, and the authorities take no means for effectually diminishing it.

On this account a medical school attached to the University of Western Africa will be fraught with the best advantage, and then the Government would have at their disposal able dispensers, who would understand, to some degree, medicine and surgery, and great relief would be given to the poor, who are dying away uncared for and unattended.

XIX.—*The Laying Out of Certain Lands as Pleasure Grounds for the People and Ornaments to the Town.*

It has been admitted as a just maxim that appearances exercise a vast influence in producing effects whether pleasurable or otherwise. The valuable effect which the laying out of lands in the tropics produces on the inhabitants, especially the European population, cannot be overrated; for we find that where every piece of ground around a dwelling is properly cultivated with beds of flowers of various descriptions there is afforded a healthy exercise to the mind, a pleasurable enjoyment to the senses, a useful employment of the body, and a destruction to rank vegetation which makes the abode unhealthy—all which benefits would be derived if such an undertaking were carried out on a grander scale. In Freetown it cannot be said that there are no spots which can be usefully converted into pleasure-grounds and parks; for, surrounding the Governor's residence and Fort Thornton, and at the base of the table-land forming the military barracks, are open lands, in the very centre of the town, where now nothing but rank vegetation grows; and where, in the two unhealthy periods of the year, in the beginning and ending of the rains, the decayed vegetation emits deadly effluvia in every direction to greet the highest official on the Coast, imperilling his life, and inducing him to escape those two epochs by leaving the seat of his Government. Yet it cannot be accounted for that the Governor himself, whose life is in danger, can look down every day on these waste spots, without putting into execution measures for averting the evil.

The question arises, what remedy should be recommended to put a stop to the danger? I answer, make that spot into a park, and well-arranged pleasure ground. To do this will cost the Local Government scarcely a farthing, as it possesses numerous prisoners who can be employed for this express purpose, and, consequently, the hackneyed excuse, 'want of money,' cannot be advanced. Plant trees in regular lines, supplant the rank vegetation by the green healthy Bahama grass, place seats in proper positions, and make proper walks. Government House will thus be freed from its poisoned atmosphere, and the inhabitants greatly benefited. At the race-course, and at Kingtom, there are places where, by a little ingenuity and expenditure, parks or pleasure-grounds can be made.

CHAPTER XV.

REQUIREMENTS OF THE GAMBIA.

In the Committee of 1842, of which Viscount Sandon was chairman, Mathew Forster, Esq., in his evidence on the importance of the trade of Western Africa to England, which he considered susceptible of very great augmentation as soon as internal anarchy ceased, and a habit of industry and civilization was introduced and extended, remarked that ' the rapid success of the Colony on the Gambia, on which so little money has been spent, and that little not at all in the most advantageous way, proves how much more may be done, even in Africa, by judicious selection and prudent conduct of a settlement. Patience; the determination to await the slow, but certain, development of the resources of the neighbouring population, which will follow a demand for their produce, is the first requisite. And from the want of this so many zealous and apparently well-planned attempts at civilization, but which all bore the fatal error of a desire for immoderate, and therefore impossible, success, have failed.' He considered the Gambia the most important of the three Colonies (Sierra Leone and the Gold Coast), from the great length of its river communication, the vast resources of the country, and the commercial character of the people in its neighbourhood. Three years after this statement was made—viz., in 1845, the ground-nut trade was introduced; in that year the value of its export was only 199l., but the inhabitants went zealously to work at it, and so greatly did they employ their time and energy to the trade, that thirteen years after its introduction— viz., in 1858—the value of the export was 188,000l.

But the great drawback to all improvement in the Gambia and its neighbourhood is the ascendancy which the Marabout bigots have now gained over their former masters, the Soninkies; whilst they were under this rule trade and agriculture prospered, but now that they have gained the upper hand, anarchy, slave-hunting expeditions, insecurity of life and property, are the inevitable results. These Marabouts are ambitious, overbearing, and very covetous. Since their ascendancy they have destroyed the most flourishing towns along the River, which supplied the merchants of Bathurst with large quantities of wax and ground-nuts. ' Where are the towns of Sanding, in Vintung Creek? of Yanemaroo? of Tendabah? and a hundred other large towns? Have they not all been pillaged and burnt down? and have not the men, women, and children, who were not able to escape, been captured and sold as slaves?' Now that the Marabouts' supremacy is an accomplished fact, to ensure the prosperity of the Gambia, it is our place to look to our own interest and employ those means which may be conducive to the strengthening of British authority throughout the River. To this end, therefore, all our policy must tend, and the following suggestions will aid a great deal in accomplishing this most desirable result.

I. *The Reduction of Most of the Small Hamlets in British Combo into One or More Large Towns.*

The old maxim, union is strength, is nowhere more evident than in the towns on the banks of the River Gambia, where the people are constantly exposed to the brutal inroads of petty chieftains. I have, (on the consideration of the self-government of the Gambia), entered into some details relative to the exposure of Upper Combo to the descent of their treacherous Marabout neighbours whenever a favourable opportunity offers itself. The towns or hamlets in this district consist of the congregation of a few ill-constructed cane huts, very thinly populated and exposed in every direction. Separately they are incapable of withholding for a few seconds the impetuous attacks of the Marabouts, who would destroy village after village, killing the male population and carrying the females and children into captivity. Collectively they could withstand, and perhaps force the Marabout army to retreat, and gain a complete victory over them. Grants of land should be given to each man, and they should be made to build in concentrated centres, and the people should be restrained from putting down here and there one or two huts and calling it a town. They might have farms at any distance they liked, but they should be compelled to congregate in large towns at convenient distances from each other for residence.

II. *The Building of Block Houses or Defensible Walls with Port-holes on the Frontiers of British Combo and in Albreda, and other British Territories opposite to the Hostile Marabout Neighbours.*

The appearance of good physical force is the only means of check-ing the warlike tendency of a savage race. From the accounts which I have given in another place, it is evident that the neigh-bouring tribes in the Gambia are a restless, mischievous, and cunning people, who look lustily after the British possessions, and would seize the first opportunity of making themselves tem-porarily masters of a portion of them.* Our chief object should be to defend our frontiers as best we can; and one of the best means would be to form blockhouses on the frontiers, to make one or more stockades consisting of well-planned brick walls, with portholes and outside ditches, so placed as to defend any part of these large towns, and to teach the inhabitants properly to defend these stockades, which would give strength and support to the other-wise timid inhabitants; be a safe rendezvous for military opera-tions on the frontiers whenever required, and would more particularly serve as a moral check to the Marabouts, who would not on the face of it attempt to make an open raid on the country.

These enclosures, if built of stones or bricks, will require only the first outlay; and as these Marabouts fight only with small

---

* Referring to the late disturbed state of the River Gambia, by the neighbouring tribes in the River Gambia, and the warlike and menacing at-titude of Mabba, the late formidable King of Badiboo, a writer in the *African Times* made this sensible and homely remark : ' The real cause, to all those who have studied the character of these Marabout inhabitants of the River Gambia, is to be found in that ambitious, overbearing, and covetous disposition of the Mussulmans, who view with discontent the rich prize they would obtain, could they have an opportunity of making one midnight raid on the rich Babboo Christian merchants at Bathurst. The toleration of this overbearing disposition of the Marabout chieftains in the River Gambia will always lead to serious complications. They must be made to understand that the British Government, although desirous of peace, yet still will never tolerate any nonsense from them.'—*African Times*, Vol. vi., p. 134.

firearms, these simple walls would withstand any of their attacks. One or two such walls would be a sufficient defence for Albreda against any attacks of the Marabout neighbours at Neomy or Barra. The wooden stockade, which was lately commenced by Governor d'Arcy, is almost worthless, as, within a few years, it will fall to the ground, and in fact the power of the Marabouts in over-coming difficult wooden stockades, surrounded with thorns and ditches and protected by equally fierce Mandingoes, should lead us to adopt a better means of defence; consequently it will be necessary for the authorities to give this suggestion a serious con-sideration.

III. *A Standard of Building, Inexpensive in its Construction, should be insisted upon in Combo by the Executive Authority, and the Poorer Inhabitants should be compelled within a certain time to to imitate it in the Construction of all their Buildings.*

In no place on the whole Western Shores of Africa do the huts of the poorer class of natives present such a low, squalid, miserable, filthy, unhealthy, dark, and disagreeable appearance as the Mandingo huts on the River Gambia. They are so low that one has almost to go on all fours, or stoop to a very inconvenient degree, before he can enter the huts, where he is in most cases surrounded with filth of every description.

We will take for example the town of Baccow, in the immediate vicinity of the invalid station of Cape St. Mary. The Mandingo huts are small circular buildings, without ventilation; and the in-habitants, who crawl in, sleep with their sheep in almost the same room. Filthy in the extreme, these huts in the British possession remain a standing disgrace to the Gambia Government. It is about the first object that strikes the observation of a new visitor of the Cape. This kind of building had existed without improvement ere Baccow was ceded in 1840 to the British throne, and it will still remain so for centuries to come if the Government does not interfere in the matter. It is the duty of a civilized government to endeavour as much as in it lies to civilize the natives under its rule; and the local authorities in the Gambia will be remiss in their duty should they allow this state of squalor to continue in the Mandingo towns in British Gambia.

IV. *Improvement in the Educational Branch of the Colony.*

I have dealt so much on the subject of the education in Sierra Leone, and of its non-existence in the Gambia, that I have only to impress on the local authorities the necessity of taking in hand the education of the young generation of the Colony. The Gambia is infinitely worse than Sierra Leone in this most important branch of civilization; the inhabitants, being Mohammedans, heathens, and Christians, and the schools being under the direction of the Wesleyan Missionary society, and the Roman Catholics, most of the children, from the exclusiveness of the teaching, do not attend the schools.

There should be established all over the country, Government schools with a uniform system of discipline and instruction regulated by schemes planned by the Government. They should have 'the same books, the same rotation of lessons, the same method of communicating instruction, the same hours.' Besides the ordinary course of instruction, Arabic should be made a part of the studies of the pupil; and Arabic teachers from Senegal should be engaged for that express purpose. The necessity for this is obvious, since the Governor frequently gets letters in Arabic from the Marabout chieftains in the neighbourhood, and he has to go about the town to get them interpreted; whilst in Senegal, the French Governor receives from the independent kings letters in Arabic, and communicates with them in the same language. The Government should make it compulsory for every child above and under certain ages, to attend in one or other of the schools in the Colony. An inspector of schools should be appointed, whose duty would be to see that strict uniformity is observed in all the schools, and that the masters and teachers attend properly to their work. The parents should be made to pay a certain amount, however small, as 'education, like other objects of attainment, is not to be duly valued, especially by those who are unable to comprehend its ultimate uses, until it has the price of money put upon it; until some sacrifice is made to obtain it; and the party making this sacrifice thereby acquires, as it were, a property in it. Given for nothing, it is regarded as little more than nothing, and as what may be had at any time; but so soon as a payment is made, the regular attendance of the children becomes a question of profit and loss, and the parent takes care to enforce it.' The children in the Gambia are most backward in their schooling. The computation will be probably correct if we say that in the British Territory in the Gambia, only one in every fifty children attends school, and yet still the local authorities take no stringent steps for ensuring more general educational advantages to the people. True it is that both the Wesleyans and the Roman Catholics receive 100*l.* each for schools, but what is that amount for such a large extent of country and population. We leave it for the consideration of the Council whether a more uniform system of Government schools should not be established throughout the country, and the children be regularly taught.

V. *Proper Means used for the Development of the Natural Agricultural Resources of the Country.*

The rapid growth of the ground-nut trade on the River Gambia should lead the Government to endeavour to improve the other natural agricultural resources of the Gambia. There are several plants which grow in their natural strength and luxuriance in the Gambia, and which, with little labour and attention, can be made useful exportable commodities. The cotton-plant, which is indigenous to the country, is extensively cultivated, and since the American war is largely exported from the Gambia. To encourage the growth, Mr. Thomas Brown, one of the leading merchants of the Colony, has got out a steam cleaning machine for the cotton business, and his establishment has always had enough to do. The cotton crop of the Gambia, unlike that of other parts of Africa, from the peculiar nature of the climate, is annual.

The indigo plant is also indigenous in the Gambia and grows in great luxuriance during the rainy season ; the natives cultivate and manufacture it for home consumption, and they produce dyes not surpassed by the best Indian or Manchester baft. The trade, if opened, will be a paying one. It will commence in the latter part of the rainy season, after the ground-nut is planted, and would give the people remunerative occupation for the time and the merchant a good exportable commodity during the rainy season. It will not be out of place here to call upon the leading merchants of the Gambia— to Mr. Brown especially, whose praiseworthy zeal in offering any new articles of trade is well known—to give a little more of their time and attention to the introduction of this trade, which in a few years would be a commercial blessing to the Gambia.

Fibres.—There are a great many fibrous plants in the Gambia; some are specially cultivated by the natives for making ropes. In the *African Times** a 'Constant Reader' has given a few but important instructions on the cultivation and preparation of certain useful fibres for the English market. The fibres of Africa, if opened to native exertion and commercial enterprise, will be found to be a great 'mine of productive and commercial wealth.' The plant which is cultivated by the natives in the Gambia yields fibres almost equal in value and texture to that produced from the China grass, and it only requires to be properly cultivated, cropped, retted and prepared for exportation in order that it might take its place in the European market with fibres of other countries.

Indeed, for the agricultural resources of the Gambia to be developed, the Government must have shows at intervals of three or four years, and good prizes offered to the exhibitors of the best native manufacture.

Colonel D'Arcy, the late Administrator of the Gambia, in his Blue-book reports, writes, under date of November, 1866, respecting agriculture in the settlement:—

'My successors will be wise if they support agriculture in every way; it is the sheet-anchor of this settlement. Unfortunately, remonstrances alone are not sufficient to detain the natives from baneful war, so tempting to the savages, who risk death and famine for the chance of abducting human beings, whereby they are suddenly enriched. The old leaven of slavery is the curse of Africa. . . . Much of the cotton crop, grown from the Egyptian seed the Government imported in 1862, was spoilt from the simple fact that the natives planted it in June instead of August. It is a sun plant, which, even at birth, requires two month's rain, not four. The printed monthly report of the discussions in reference to the best time and most approved mode of planting rice, indigo, ground-nut,

---

* *African Times,* Vol. vi., No. 63, page 26, September 22, 1866.

cassava, beniseed, &c., would, I am convinced, be read by the people of the West Coast with as much eagerness as the Parliamentary debates are in England.'

VI.—*The Formation of a Savings Bank for the Mechanics and Labouring Classes of the Colony.*

From the description I have given of the spendthrift nature of the young generation of the Gambia population, it will be obvious that such an establishment would produce universal good, not only to the mechanics, sailors, and labourers, but also to the small traders, whose small savings are squandered in trifles before the commencement of another season. On the importance of this subject the late Mr. T. Ingram remarked that at St. Mary's, ' the labouring natives, such as mechanics, sailors, &c., suffer great inconvenience, and not unfrequently heavy losses, for want of an establishment wherein to deposit their savings with a certainty of having them at command when needed.' If a savings bank be formed, all the surplus money of the Colony can be deposited in it, ' which would save the temptation and risk of keeping it in huts, where it is so frequently stolen, and could always be made available when required ; and once the sum of four or five thousand dollars was deposited, guaranteed bills of short dates might be discounted, which would be an accommodation to strangers and persons desirous of making payments in a useful convertible medium, and a benefit to the inhabitants, as affording a small return in interest for capital not otherwise required ; ' the small traders would immediately take advantage of it, and would gladly transfer from the hands of their employers to the bank, any surplus money that might be due to them after the season is over.

But to give it the fullest confidence it must be under the supervision of the Government, though immediately conducted by a Board of Directors, yearly elected, composed of officers and merchants, with a paid secretary, whose salary should be a commission on the business done.

VII.—*The Establishment of a Good British Station at Fatta Tendah, about Four Hundred Miles in the Interior, on the Banks of the River.*

M'Carthy's Island was bought from the King of Calabar for the express purpose of protecting and encouraging the trade in the upper portion of the River. It is about 175 miles from Bathurst. But it is well known that most of the trade in the River Gambia comes from the Upper River, where the nuts are superior in quality and in marketable value to those in the Lower River. Around M'Carthy's Island but a very small quantity of nuts is obtained; the largest quantity comes from a distance of about 175 to 200 miles further up the River, of which Fatta Tendah is the centre. If at all, a colonial station must be formed up the Rivers, to be of service to trade and commerce, it must be where the most business is performed; and had Fatta Tendah been a British station, Baccary Sardah the King of Boondoo, would not have destroyed the property of British merchants in 1866 to the amount of 50,000*l.*

Against the native force M'Carthy's Island is a natural fortification; its impassable barrier, the River, will always be a check to the proud Marabouts. With two or three constables, and a few special constables when needed, and a sub-manager to administrate justice, it can be left to take care of itself. But our main force up the River should be concentrated at Fatta Tendah, a place superior in every respect to M'Carthy's Island. It is dry, healthy, and high above the swamps, having in its neighbourhood elevated grounds and high lands. It is situated on the banks of the River, and about thirty to forty feet above its level. Being in the centre of the trade in the upper Rivers, its occupation will give confidence to the traders and native chiefs in the kingdom of Woolie, whose king has always regarded the British Government, who are masters of the waters, as his ally.

The establishment need not be expensive; a good wall, built by prisoners, assisted by a few masons, enclosing on three sides a large piece of ground forming the town, and protected by the River on the fourth side, furnished with four bastions and portholes, mounting eight six-pounder howitzers, surrounded by a deep ditch, will be all that will be required to check any progress of the Marabouts. From twenty to thirty Militia, with a civil manager, who should command the sub-manager at M'Carthy's Island, should be stationed there; they should receive the same pay and be treated exactly the same as constables; they should be properly drilled, and every man who takes his abode in the town, be he Mandingo, Jollof, Sarawoolie, European, or Colony born, should enrol himself as a volunteer, and should be ready to fight against any intruder. A system of this kind would materially improve the trade in the Upper River, would give confidence to the traders, and prevent the natives from committing those acts of base treachery to the traders which have led to their ruin.

VIII.—*The Support of a Colonial Sailing Schooner, Equipped to a small extent as a Vessel of War, ·and Properly and Inexpensively Manned.*

Now that the Government of the Gambia has been deprived of the small steamer, which was most essential but too expensive for the River trade, the local authority, with its improved revenue, should step in and itself assist in maintaining a small, fast-sailing vessel (schooner), which would completely answer all the purposes required, for giving support and assistance to the trade in the River. The schooner can be made to pay its own expenses, as when not immediately required by the authorities, it could be freighted by the merchants. When sent with despatches to M'Carthy's Island or Fatta Tendah, or wherever occasion may require, it might take freight to and from these places; so that whilst serving the purpose of the Local Government, it would pay its own expenses and ultimately its cost. From 400*l.* to 800*l.* will purchase in England or America a strong, well-built schooner, which can carry three or four light guns. To make it inexpensive, it should be commanded and manned entirely by a native captain and crew, which would reduce the expenses to nearly one-half. All the small, and many of the large vessels belonging to the merchants in the Gambia, which sail up and down the River, and down the Coast to Bulama and Rio Pongas are supplied with native captains and crews, which, so long as the vessel remains on the River, would answer infinitely better than having a European captain, who would occupy a nominal position in the vessel, always requiring a native captain to pilot the ship.

I do not see why a measure of this kind should not be undertaken by the Local Government, independent of the Home Government, and even the Central Government at Sierra Leone. It will, I am certain, meet with the hearty support of all the merchants in the Gambia, and would, within a very short time, repay the outlay.

IX.—*The Formation of a Municipal Council at St. Mary's.*

This would have a most satisfactory effect on the general population, and would tend to improve the general health of the Colony; a town mayor is very much needed at Bathurst.

The appointment of a Municipal Council would be useful in clearing out the rubbish from the town; in completing the different drains; and in making proper roads to the different villages.

A Sanitary Board has been formed by Colonel D'Arcy, the late Governor of the Gambia, but its operation has been most limited; it has scarcely effected any good. The improvement of such a small place should be left to the working of a Municipal Council and its town inspector, who should receive every support and assistance from the local authorities. The Governor could put a pressure on a respectable body thus constituted, while prisoners should be employed principally for drainage and other sanitary purposes. It would take years and a large sum of money to drain Bathurst sufficiently; but by small and repeated outlay, according to the capabilities of the country, we might be able in years to come to effect some tangible improvement which would diminish the frightful mortality of the Colony.

X.—*The Building of Winter or Rainy Season Residences at Cape St. Mary's, in Combo, or in other parts of British Combo.*

The most unhealthy period in the Gambia is in the rainy season, when the breeze is from the south, south-west, and south-east, blowing over a tract of mangrove swamp, several miles in extent, into the town, carrying with it the deadly miasma which is generated from it. On the east and south-east point of Bathurst there is an immense swamp, ' extending even to the outskirts of the town, over which the high tides flow, depositing a compound of mud and animal and vegetable remains carried down by the river. When this filthy mass, impregnated with diseases, is acted upon by the tropical sun a most offensive effluvium is brought forth, so destructive to human health and life ' that it is deadly even to the natives. With such a topographical sketch of the insalubrious state of the neighbourhood of Bathurst, it is no wonder that the merchants, on the approach of the rainy season, escape for their lives to Europe, leaving their clerks to feed on the deadly miasma.

But much of this mortality might be avoided if the merchants were to spend a little amount in building villas at Cape St. Mary's, which is the most healthy spot in the whole of the Gambia, and the superior sanitary condition of which is unquestionable. Whilst the principal merchants make their escape from the pestilential hole to England, is it not just for them to think of the best means of preserving the health of the European clerks whom they brought out, especially when the means are so simple and so much within their reach?

So early as 1840, Dr. Robertson, then Colonial Surgeon of the Gambia, gave the most flattering account of the salubrious state of Cape St. Mary's and the country in its neighbourhood, which all subsequent writers have, and which I, from personal observation, must confirm *in toto*. 'Cape St. Mary's,' said he, 'is situated on the lee-shore at the mouth of the River Gambia. The land in the immediate vicinity of the coast is fifty feet above the level of the sea. The soil is a dry loam, superincumbent on a bed of granite.

'The country for several miles along the coast is clean, and almost clear from wood; it descends in a gentle slope from the sea towards the interior, consequently, the great quantity of water that falls during the rainy season is rapidly carried away from the vicinity of the Cape, and flows into the creek situated some distance in the interior, and through this channel finds its way into the sea.

'The Cape, being so near the sea-shore, enjoys at all times the full advantage of the sea-breeze, which, combined with its elevated situation, gives it a continual atmospherical temperature several degrees cooler than the Island of St. Mary's.

'The Cape has been for some years resorted to by invalids, and the great improvement in health, universally experienced after a short residence there, is a sufficient proof in itself that the atmosphere possesses a degree of salubrity not often to be found on the West Coast of Africa.

'There being no swamp in the neighbourhood, the land breeze brings with it a cool air, devoid of that pestilential effluvium which poisons the atmosphere of St. Mary's.'

R

The natives enjoy excellent health here, and live to a stage of longevity seldom, if ever, witnessed at Bathurst; and when it is remembered that the Cape is only seven and a-half miles from Bathurst, and that there is a good road to it, it is paradoxical to believe that such liberal firms as Forster and Smith, Thos. Brown and Co., Murrell et Cie., and T. F. Quin, which employ a large staff of European clerks, should not long ago have adopted this most desirable and inexpensive step.

XI.—*The Erection of a Bridge over Oyster Creek.*

Situated between the Island of St. Mary's and the mainland, or British Combo, is a small muddy stream, the banks of which are thickly studded by mangroves, called Oyster Creek. This stream is ferried by a huge boat, moved by paddle-wheels, which is continually out of repair. The ferry costs the Government nearly 50*l.* a-year. With an outlay of from 300*l.* to 400*l.* a good substantial bridge could be built over this stream, which would at once relieve the Government of the yearly outlay, and the population from the great inconvenience which they now experience. It should be done by contract, as the Government will find this to be the least expensive and more certain mode of effectually erecting it.

I have often heard some of the merchants remark that had there been a bridge over Oyster Creek, so that they could drive with ease and at any hour over to Cape St. Mary's, they would at once remove from the pestitential air of Bathurst. It is a plan that would relieve both the merchants and the labouring class of the population from the very great inconvenience which is caused by the ferry. It would improve trade, and encourage the well-to-do merchants to erect country residences in British Combo.

CHAPTER XVI.

REQUIREMENTS OF THE GOLD COAST.

THE Government of the Gold Coast has always been regarded as the most difficult and intricate of all the Governments on the Coast; but if it be closely and quietly investigated it will be found that most of the ado which has from time to time been the cause of these misunderstandings between the natives and the Government, has been occasioned by the executive authority exceeding the charter of the settlement.

The British Gold Coast is merely a Protectorate, the natives having their own kings, using their own laws, and performing their time-honoured customs; beyond the Fort-gate we have not a foot of ground in the country. After the turbulent period previous to 1830 and the peace proclaimed between Ashantee and the natives through British influence, the inhabitants submitted themselves to the British Government, not as subjects, but as independent nations, in alliance with, and protected by, the United Kingdom of Great Britain and Ireland, without any stated laws respecting their Government; and the chiefs have always looked upon our Sovereign as a kind of feudal superior, against whose enemies they were bound to fight when called upon, and who was in turn bound to aid them in case of trouble from within or without. The treaty between the British Government and the native chiefs distinctly stipulates that the natives are to be governed by their own laws, except in certain cases plainly specified.

But according to the decision of Lord Carnarvon (1866), the late Secretary of State for the Colonies under Lord Derby's administration, all the towns on the sea-coast in the vicinity of the Forts are to be regarded as British Colonies, entirely independent of native influence and power—viz., Cape Coast, Anamaboe, and Accra.

The present condition of the Gold Coast is worse than ever it was since the days of Doodoowah. Formerly there was a close, compact union between all the kings of the Protectorate under the English authority; the very name of the Governor of Cape Coast was a spell to bring any refractory king to bay. His power in the Protectorate was only limited by the boundary of the territory of the King of Ashantee. No one dared gainsay his orders, as severe retribution was certain to follow. British authority was respected and loved, and commanded implicit obedience; but now the people have been plainly made to understand that the Government will not stir a foot beyond the towns in the neighbourhood of the Forts were their country to be overrun and conquered by the enemy; that the Governor will not interfere in any of their palavers; that beyond fifteen miles of the sea-shore the inhabitants were to attend to their own domestic affairs and settle their own palavers; that anarchy and disorder may run riot in the interior without the Governor having the least power to interfere or of compelling them by force to desist. Tantalized by the orders continually received, and by the heterogeneous elements under his rule, we find that in some cases the action of one governor entirely contradicts his proclamations; whilst he informs the tribes that, beyond fifteen miles, he would give them no protection, he fines them heavily, and compels them with threats to pay the amount for crimes not to be regarded beyond a misdemeanour. Again, each governor has his own particular policy to follow. One prides himself for having undone the policy of his predecessor, whether it tends to destroy the proper development of the country or not. Another carries on the Government with such vigour that the very name of the British rule is regarded as tyrannical and hateful; and a third, on assuming the reins of Government, endeavours by firm, yet pacific measures, to regain the lost name of authority, using well-considered and well-planned measures for the development and extension of the commerce of the country, and thus gains a general celebrity for firmness and conciliation.

In truth our relations with the native chiefs in the vicinity of the settlement have been unstable; the rapid and successive changes of governors leave no room for any fixed plan to be entered into for the general good of the place. The Gold Coast Government is considered as a trying ordeal for the ability of individuals. The man who governs there must either rise to eminence or fall to a nonentity, and thus we find that within the short period of five years no less than seven different governors have exercised the supreme power over the Gold Coast—viz., from March, 1862, to March, 1867 *—how, then, can we wonder at the disgraceful state of the Protectorate, and that our relations with the natives in the interior and with the powerful kingdom of Ashantee are so unsatisfactory?

It is on this ground that we must impress on those who are opposed to the formation of a Central Government, the infinite benefit that the whole Coast must derive from the introduction of such wise changes in the Coast Government. The administrators are now no more than the lieutenants of the Governor-General, whose fixed views on the policy to be pursued by each successive administrator will necessitate the adoption of one line of policy for a period sufficiently long to manifest its advantages or disadvantages. His Excellency the present Governor-General, Sir A. Kennedy, C.B., loves Sierra Leone, the seat of his Government, where he formerly served, and was much esteemed by the inhabitants. He is a thorough statesman; and his policy, if we may judge by his antecedents, will most probably be advantageous to the Coast, which has been allowed to fall into an almost unparalleled disorder through the most flagrant maladministration. It is to be hoped that he will not feel himself bound to follow the late policy, which has unsettled all the previous relations of the natives with the Government; and as he is thoroughly conversant with the nature of the Government on the Coast, having acted previously in the capacity of governor in the oldest of the West African Colonies, —and his antecedents are such as to insure confidence in the intentions of the ruling power—there seems just reason for believing that in his hands the concentration of the Coast Government under one head may prove less injurious. Sir Benjamin Pine, now Governor of St. Kits, in the West Indies, was one of the most efficient

* Viz., Messrs. Andrews, Ross, Pine, Jones, Mockler, Conran, and the present Administrator, Mr. Ussher.

of the local Governors on the Gold Coast.* He was a man most competent to elevate the condition of the Coast Government under his charge. He first proposed and enlarged on the desirability of forming a Central Government in West Africa. For years he held various appointments on the Coast—as Chief Justice and Queen's Advocate at Sierra Leone, and afterwards administered the Government for nearly two years. After acting as Governor of Natal for nearly six years, he, at the end of 1856, was appointed Governor of the Gold Coast. At Sierra Leone his measures were found to be most salutary. He took a lively interest in the education of the rising population; visited and examined the schools and colleges, which had a most beneficial effect amongst the general public. On the Gold Coast his measures were still more deserving of great praise. He established municipal councils in the centres of the Protectorate Territory, encouraged and trained up the people to self-government, took up the claims of the educated natives, whom he supported with all his influence, and advocated measures for the general benefit of the country. I must be excused for thus recording here the merits of Sir Benjamin Pine, because I feel that every native of Sierra Leone and the Gold Coast is deeply indebted to him.

Hitherto the greatest drawback towards the efficient Government of the Protected Territory of the Gold Coast was the mixing up of the Dutch and English possessions; the Dutch having small towns dovetailed in the English Territory. They declined to levy any duty on import or any direct or indirect taxation, so that our Government was compelled to limit its import duties, because if much increased the whole trade would have gone to the Dutch. A purchase of the Dutch possessions out and out would have been the most

---

* It is necessary that I should say a few words more relative to Sir Arthur Edward Kennedy, who has been appointed Governor-General of the West African Colonies. He had been in 1852 Governor of Sierra Leone, and the lively interest which he took in the education of the young and in the advancement of the Coast augurs well for the present unsettled state of the West African Colonies. His firmness and decision in dealing with refractory chiefs in the neighbourhood of the Colony of Sierra Leone will prove, we hope, a sufficient guarantee that decisive measures will be taken, as occasions require, to bring the British rule under proper respect in the various Colonies. From our experience of him we may safely say that he understands *suaviter in modo*, as well as *fortiter in re*.

profitable thing that could have been done, as it would have insured the material advancement and Christian civilization of the country ; but all negotiations on the subject have hitherto failed, from the incompetency, it is said, of the Dutch Government to alienate any Dutch land except for an equivalent in land. More recently negotiation had been resumed for the exchange of territories, and the consolidation of the Coast Government by the two Powers by establishing a uniform fixed rate of Import Duties; and by a line to be drawn from the Sweet River, near Elmina, into the interior to as far as the Praah, making Dixcove, Appolonia, Wassaw, Commendah, British Secundee, and Awoowen, Dutch ; whilst Cormatine, Assam, Mouree, Barracoe, and Dutch Accra become English. This treaty was to come into force on the 1st January, 1868.

The following is a *verbatim* extract of the treaty, which was signed in London, March 5, 1867; and the ratifications exchanged in the same place July 6, 1867:—

' Article 1.—Her Britannic Majesty cedes to his Majesty the King of the Netherlands all British forts, possessions, and rights of sovereignity or jurisdiction, which she possesses on the Gold Coast to the westward of the mouth of the Sweet River, where their respective territories are conterminous ; and his Majesty the King of the Netherlands' forts, possessions, and rights of sovereignty or jurisdiction, which he possesses on the Gold Coast to the eastward of the mouth of the Sweet River, where their respective territories are conterminous. The boundary between the possessions of Her Britannic Majesty and those of his Majesty the King of the Netherlands will be a line drawn true north from the centre of the mouth of the Sweet River as far as the boundary of the present Ashantee Kingdom, but with such deviations within three English miles of the Coast as shall be necessary to retain within British Territory any villages which have been in habitual dependence on the British Government at Cape Coast, and within Netherlands Territory any villages which have been in habitual dependence on the Netherlands Government at St. George d'Elmina.

' Article 2.—The two high contracting parties agree that the following tariff of duties of Customs shall be enforced in their respective possessions upon the Gold Coast :—

'In the British Possessions.—Ale, beer, wine, and all spirits or spiritùous liquours, per old wine gallon, sixpence ; cigars, snuff, òr tobacco in any shape, per pound, one penny ; gunpowder per pound, one penny ; firearms of every description, each one shilling ; on all other goods of every kind, an *ad valorem* duty of three per cent. on the invoice price.

'In the Netherlands Possessions.—Ale, beer, wine, and all spirits or spirituous liquors, per litre, eight cents; cigars, snuffs, or tobacco in any shape, per kilogramme, ten cents ; gunpowder, per kilogramme, ten cents ; firearms of every description, each sixty cents ; on all other goods of every kind, an *ad valorem* duty of three per cent. on the invoice price.

'Article 3.—In order to prevent frauds in the importation of goods, the high contracting parties engage to empower the officers of the respective customs on the Gold Coast to require the masters of vessels to make declaration of the nature, quantity, and value of any goods which may be allowed to land. If the officers of customs shall be of opinion that the value, so to be declared, is insufficient, they shall be at liberty to take the goods on public account, on paying to the importer the amount of his valuation, with the addition of ten per cent. thereon, and returning any duty which may have been already paid.

'Article 4.—The tariff of Customs Duties, specified in Article 2, shall be put into operation from and after a day to be agreed upon between the two Governments, and shall remain in force for a period of ten years ; and, further, until the expiration of twelve months after either of the two contracting parties shall have given notice to the other of its desire for a revision or termination thereof.

'Article 5.—The tariff of Customs Duties may be enforced or relaxed by the local authorities at their own discretion, or according to the orders of their respective Governments, in respect to articles imported for the use of those authorities or for the personal use and consumption of officers in the actual service of the Government.

'Article 6.—The mutual transfer of forts, possessions, and rights of sovereignty or jurisdiction, stipulated in Article 1 of the the present Convention, is dependent upon and subject to the establishment of the proposed tariff, and shall not take effect until the

Government of each country shall have procured the enactment of any laws or regulations necessary in order to establish that tariff for the term and under the conditions hereinbefore described, and shall have actually put the same into operation.

' Article 7.—After the transfer alluded to in the foregoing article shall have been made, a map shall be drawn of the new boundary division according to the terms of Article 1. Two copies of the said map, duly attested by the Governments on either side, shall then be appended to this Convention, for the purpose of showing the boundary, which shall undergo no alteration, even should any of the villages mentioned at the end of Article 1 be subsequently abandoned, or the tariff be modified or withdrawn.

' Article 8.—The present Convention, after receiving, so far as may be necessary, the approval of the legislative authority, shall be ratified, and the ratifications shall be exchanged at London within a period of four months, or sooner if possible.

' In witness whereof the respective plenipotentiaries have signed the same, and have affixed thereto the seals of their arms.

' Done at London, the fifth day of March, in the year of our Lord one thousand eight hundred and sixty-seven.

' CARNARVON,   ' BENTINCK,
' STANLEY,   ' C. J. M. NAGTGLAS.'

In this treaty the Dutch are decidedly the gainers, as the British authorities were pressed to make it ; but it ought to be an advantage to the natives of those parts, especially those under British rule. In the first place the Dutch ceded a few old, dilapidated, uninhabitable, stone piles, misnamed forts, containing some worthless, honeycombed, unserviceable iron guns, which have been over 100 years on the seaboard of Western Africa, for the lately repaired fort at Dixcove, which, in 1863, was manned with new heavy ordnance, at enormous expense, from Woolwich.

Secondly, a few sea-coast towns, not ten miles distant in the interior, hemmed in on all sides by British Territory, the area of which put together does not measure, at its maximum, five hundred square miles form the ceded territory of the Dutch ; whilst we gave them in exchange countries extending into the interior to the utmost boundary of the Coast Government, and occupying, at the least calculation, one hundred thousand square miles (Apollonia, Wassaw, Awoowen, &c.).

Thirdly, the population in the ceded territory of the Dutch is less than 10,000 souls, whilst that in the English, whose destiny we have handed over to the Dutch, and who would rather be anything but Dutchmen, numbers over 150,000 souls.

Fourthly, the Dutch ceded barren, rocky lands, containing neither mineral resources nor anything of commercial importance; whilst we ceded the vast gold-mines of Wassaw and Apollonia, which, if the Dutch should undertake to develop them, would repay them a hundredfold.

The Convention, therefore, was in every respect advantageous to the Dutch, but it was imperative that it should be concluded—

Firstly, because the two Governments are now distinctly separated from one another; each having its line of territory distinctly marked.

And, secondly, because a uniform tariff is now enforced by both Governments on articles imported into the country, while

Thirdly, a good and substantial revenue will be insured, and consequently there will be no excuse for the neglect of the local authorities for not making adequate improvement in the social wellbeing of the people.

But it has always been remarked, with great truth and justice, that of all the Governments on the Coast of Africa none is more inimical to the moral and intellectual improvement of their subjects than the Dutch Government; and whilst valid improvements might be traced in the even neglected English and late Danish possessions, the Dutch subjects are in total ignorance, and are left entirely to follow their own superstitious ideas. No missionary is permitted to live amongst them, nor are there any schools worth noticing for the benefit of the rising generation.

It is to be hoped that this new arrangement, which will free the Dutch Home Government from the annual expenditure of 12,000*l.* for its maintenance, would lead them to open new institutions for the improvement of the people, or allow the assistance of those select bodies who have made it their earthly mission to propagate Christianity and educate the otherwise untutored heathen.

The British portion of the Gold Coast may now congratulate

itself that from the Sweet River to the Volta, at least, it is one compact whole, no longer intersected by Dutch Settlements, the European influence exercised in which was uniformly hostile to all improvements; and only served to impede the march of Christian civilization, by preserving in immediate contact with it centres of demoralizing barbarism in which the worst excesses of heathenism were not only tolerated but encouraged. If a good understanding be established between the chiefs and the ruling power, if cautious and well-studied plans are carried out, and no precipitate measures employed, the future of the Gold Coast may be a satisfactory one. As it is there are a great many measures required to be enacted before the settlement can run a well-organized race with the other colonies on the Coast, which I must here briefly consider.

I.—*An Assemblage or a Congress of Kings should be held at Cape Coast, and one at Accra, for the Consideration of Matters relative to the Good of the Protectorate.*

The great difficulty found in the Gold Coast is caused by the Executive ignoring the authority of the kings; thus, during the Government of Mr. Andrews, a king of an important district was heavily fined, and almost imprisoned, through the misrepresentation of one of his subjects ; a petty commandant had power to summon a distant king from any part of his imperial rule, have him brought to his petty police-court, and fined heavily for some charge his subjects might bring against him. Mr. Pine acted better in this respect; and such treatment to the kings everyone must acknowledge as most injudicious, unreasonable, and impolitic, as well as most damaging to the British influence on the Coast. The effect is that the Administrator, instead of being loved, is hated and abused, and his proclamations are trampled under foot.

But his Excellency Sir Benjamin Pine, during his wise and able rule, made distinct regulations for the guidance of all magistrates in the district courts, providing for proper treatment of the kings, and the mode in which complaints were to be brought against them. These rules were promulgated in an ordinance dated Cape Coast Castle, March 15, 1858, and were to the following effect :—

1. Before any subject of an important king or chief in the interior makes any complaint against him to our courts, he is to

inform the king or chief of his intention to do so; the king or chief is immediately to send a proper messenger with him to the Court, in order that both sides may be heard at once. This rule is to be enforced as far as practicable.

2. No summonses are to be issued against any such king or chief at the instance of their subjects; but in important cases, where there is reasonable grounds for not enforcing the preceding rule, a letter is to be sent to the king or chief, stating the cause of complaint, and desiring his attendance, or that of one of his headmen or messengers, as may be most convenient to him.

3. Petty and frivolous complaints against any such king or chief are to be discouraged. In most of such cases it will be sufficient to send a letter to him informing him of the cause of complaint, and desiring him to do justice, and also if necessary desiring him to report how he has settled his case.

4. In cases between the subjects of such king or chief, it will frequently be desirable to remand them for his decision in the first instance, cautioning him against making large and exorbitant charges for doing so, and desiring him to report how he has decided the case, and the amount of fees he has charged. All parties must be clearly informed that an appeal will lie to the Court.

5. In cases of a decidedly political nature, such as disputes as to the succession to the stools, and differences between great chiefs, the Judicial Assessor and the commandants are, in general, not to interfere, further than by taking evidences and referring the matter to the Governor for his instructions. In cases of emergency, however, the commandants are to act according to the best of their judgment, taking care to report their proceedings to the Governor by the earliest opportunity.

The 6th and 7th rules refer to cases to be heard by commandants, and the reports necessary to be forwarded to headquarters for the Governor's information.

A congress of kings in the Protectorate is more necessary now than ever, seeing that, according to the decision of the Home Government, they are to be left to fight their own battles; and nothing would tend to keep them in amity and union, as well as in good faith in the Local Government, so much as such yearly meeting, with a friendly discussion on topics that would be essentially beneficial to the Protectorate. One should be held at Cape Coast, the head-quarters of the Western District, and the other at Accra, the head-quarters of the Eastern District.

At Cape Coast should assemble the Kings of Denkera, Assin, Mansoo, Anamaboe, Abrah or Abacrampa, Mankasin, Agimacoo, Western Akim, Essicoomah and Akiunfudie, presided over by the Administrator; at Accra, the Kings of Crobboe, Aquapim, Aquamboe, Adda, Eastern Akim, Goomon, and Winnebah, presided over by the Administrator.

I shall here only detail the subjects for consideration, without attempting to enlarge on their necessity:—

1. That one of the kings be nominated head of all the kings of the Western District.

The advantage of this is that in cases where there is an obstreperous king of the Western District the Administrator has only to apply to the nominated head King, who could more easily see his instructions carried out with less expense than the Administrator of Her Majesty's Forts and Settlements.

2. That a similar selection be made in the Eastern District.

3. That the kings should bind themselves to defend one another against a common enemy.

4. That should any quarrel arise amongst themselves, the aggrieved party should inform the king-in-chief, who should, if necessary, call together the other kings, and the guilty party should suffer the penalty inflicted by their decision, subject, however, to the approval of the Administrator of Her Majesty's Forts and Settlements.

5. That the extradition of all political offenders and political refugees of the King of Ashantee be strictly enforced.

6. That there should be made a broad road from one town to the other by the male subjects of each town, in default of which a fine should be inflicted.

7. That the kings should be prevented from executing capital punishment; but when anyone has shed innocent blood, he should be forwarded to the British authority, to undergo his trial, and, if found guilty, to be forwarded to the place where the crime was perpetrated, and there hanged.

8. That the commandants be prevented from sending a summary summons against a king to appear in their courts, such being derogatory to the regal authority. That in any case of complaint they should report the same to the Governor, who should give it his early attention.

9. That the king's person should be regarded as sacred, and that he should on no account be arrested by any warrant, either from a commandant or from the Supreme Court, except he rebels against existing authority.

10. That immediate obedience should be required of every king to the Administrator's summons, or that of the king-in-chief, in default of which a heavy fine be inflicted.

11. That the inhabitants should have a right of appeal from the King's Court to the Commandant or Stipendiary Magistrate Court, but no judgment of the King's Court to be set aside unless the case is thoroughly sifted, and a report filed in the King's Court.

In such a case the appellant should be required to deposit a certain amount for costs, unless he pleads *in formâ pauperis*.

12. That the kings should forward to the Administrator the names of their magistrates or other officers of their court, as well as whatever changes they might make from time to time, as circumstances may render necessary.

13. That proper means should be adopted to keep intact a friendly relationship with their powerful enemy, the King of Ashantee.

II.—*That there should be Placed a Resident Consul from the Gold Coast Government at Coomassie.*

The frequent disputes which have arisen between the Ashantee potentate and the Administrator of Cape Coast have shown clearly that the best means for keeping the two powers in peace and amity is to have a consular agent at Coomassie; and none but a native of good education who could speak the language fluently should be appointed. Hitherto the policy of the Governors with the king is generally carried by the former sending a letter by an interpreter, who understands very little English, and in many cases could scarcely understand the language made use of in the letter; he therefore interprets it according to his own idea of the sentence, and in a great many cases puts an entirely wrong meaning to it.

These mistakes of interpreters are of everyday occurrence in the court, and great palavers on the Coast when the interpreters are unlettered, and are generally corrected by the educated natives. The consul should be allowed a clerk; should be handsomely paid; should have four months' leave of absence at the end of every three years, with his expenses paid to the Coast. He should be paid out of the revenue of the Colony, and his actions be under the immediate control of the Administrator of the settlement.

At such a time as at present it is of high importance that our Government on the Gold Coast should keep on the most friendly terms with the Kingdom of Ashantee, and that no bellicose attitude should injure the relationship between the two Governments. The present unfriendly state is mischievous to the trade of the British Gold Coast, since the treaty of cession came into operation. Previous to this treaty, we commanded all the countries to the boundary of Ashantee—the Dutch, who have always been the ally of Ashantee, were limited to the sea-board—and, consequently, the Ashantees could never show themselves on the sea-coast towns when there was a misunderstanding between them and ourselves. The case is now different; the Ashantees will have an open pathway from Coomassie to Elmina through Wassaw (without passing through English territory) where they could trade freely and independently of Cape Coast and Anamaboe.

The British merchants in British territory and the local revenue will suffer the disadvantage if our line of policy with Ashantee is not changed; the former will certainly transfer their business into the Dutch territories, which are always opened to them. It was on this point of territorial limit that the negotiation for an exchange of territories in 1858 met with a hitch, when we showed a determination to retain Wassaw. The negotiation went on smoothly up to the time when Captain Coulon, an experienced Dutch officer, arrived from the Coast of Africa at the Hague. He raised the objection that if Wassaw were retained by the British Government the Dutch would be confined only to the sea-board, would be prevented from communicating with their allies, and that the Ashantees would stop their opening trade with interior tribes. This at once broke up the negotiation. But that point being now conceded, we have given up our power of moderating and governing the trade between Ashantee and the Coast, as the Ashantees will now be able to show themselves on the sea-board, trading freely between Elmina and Apollonia, independently of Cape Coast and Anamaboe. It is a great triumph to Ashantee, and proves most conclusively the force of my recommendation in the first edition of this work, that we should purchase out and out the Dutch Territories, which they were ready at that time to sell, were we willing to pay down ready cash for them. Hitherto, we have always boasted that we can shut out the Ashantees from the Coast; can prevent them from being supplied with guns, powder, and salt; can limit their trade, and can force them to submit to our terms by effecting a complete land blockade of their Territory. By the treaty which came into opera- tion on the 1st of January, 1868, we have lost all these advan- tages, as no one would believe that if we choose to go to war with Ashantee, the Dutch would blockade their forts against them, to the ruin of their merchants and subjects, for our benefit. At present their intention is to make a good, durable road from Elmina, through Wassaw to the borders of Ashantee.

III. *That the King of Coomassie be induced to Send a Resident Consul to Cape Coast.*

His chief business will be to seek after the interest of the Ashantee traders on the Coast; to attend immediately to any complaint they may bring to him of being maltreated by any of the kings or their subjects. The result of these two acts will be that trade will be greatly increased; that there will be greater faith and cordiality between the two Governments, and that the social and political ad- vancement of the Colony will be greatly enhanced.

The governors should always bear in mind this Latin maxim: *Cessante causâ, cessat effectus*, or, *Sublata causâ, tollitur effectus* (withdraw the cause and the effect is destroyed).

IV. *That an Improvement should be Made in the Educational De- partment of the Government.*

At present the Colonial Government only supports a small school at Cape Coast, where the boys learn scarcely anything more than to read and write. In former years they gave the children a very good education, having efficient masters, but those now-a-days employed do not even know the rudiments of grammar ; the pay is so trifling that the educated would not think of offering themselves for the post.

So degenerate has become the head Colonial School, supported and overlooked by the Local Government, that the following account of it (which I have taken every pains to verify) cannot but be read with pain at the neglect of the local authorities in such an important matter as that of education : ' For some few years Cape Coast was much commended as to the education given in the Government School. But things are sadly changed. This same Government School, which is the only school except the Wesleyan Missionary's on the Gold Coast, is now *a play-house.*' The teachers are undeniably ignorant of the first rudiments of the English language, although the pupils, who had previously a fair master, are very smart. ' These boys are now suffering under the hand of an unqualified master ; a man of dull apprehension, who, fearing his scholars would shame him if they continued in the school, threatens their expulsion. His assistants were once astounded to find him arguing with a boy as regards the word *efface.* When the boy used the word he told him he never heard it before, and that it was not an English word, and continued arguing till the boy proved the existence of the word by an English dictionary.'* Such, then, is the educational element of the only school supported by the Cape Coast Government ; it is superfluous for me to say another word as to the necessity of a radical reform ; except, perhaps, recommending that Government schools should be established at various districts, with properly-paid educated teachers from Sierra Leone or elsewhere, and a central Government Academy established at Cape Coast.

The Wesleyans should extend and improve their educational establishments, and teach mechanics and agriculture, so that the boys after leaving school would not become loafers, but of real use to themselves and their friends. I have, in the chapter of the Self-government of the Gold Coast, considered at length the labours of the Basle missionaries, but I think it will lead to greater industry and laudable emulation if the local authorities would pass an act, by

* The *African Times.*

s

the assistance of the Legislative Council, making it binding, to a certain degree, on future governors that the most advanced pupils in these schools should be employed to fill up vacant posts.

V. *That there should be Formed an Industrial School at Cape Coast.*

The Gold Coast is greatly wanting in good mechanics. There are no good carpenters or masons to be found; nor are there any shoemakers, grainers, painters, tailors, joiners, coopers, or wheelwrights, in the proper acceptation of the term. The Basle missionaries have endeavoured to supply the deficiency and teach some of these branches, but they are wanting in funds; and therefore it should be taken up by the Government, and a large establishment formed at Cape Coast, with one of these German mechanics at the head.

A number of young persons should be sent to the French settlement in Senegal to learn shipbuilding, as it will supply a great desideratum to the working portion of the Gold Coast. At present whilst a costly boat (from 30*l.* to 60*l.*) is serviceable on the Gold Coast for only three, and the utmost five years, in the Gambia one of inferior quality, from the superior workmen which the merchants keep, who have been taught in French Goree, or Senegal, would last from ten to fifteen years; whilst on the Gambia workmen are able to build small craft from forty to eighty tons burden, on the Gold Coast the people are unable to repair properly a leaky boat, and their rivers are consequently unsupplied with those small craft which are of such importance to the Gambia trade. I have seen several good and expensive English-made boats, unserviceable from being slightly out of repair, lying in the court-yard of many of the merchants on the Gold Coast, and allowed to rot, which in the Gambia and Senegal would very easily be put in proper working order, and made useful for many more years. But the Gold Coast is not in close proximity to Senegal.

VI.—*The Abolition of Slavery in the Towns on the Sea-coast in the Vicinity of the Forts which, according to the late Secretary of State for the Colonies, are British Colonies.*

By Geo. IV., cap. 113, sec. 2, all dealings in slaves are pronounced unlawful, and the tenth section makes all such dealings a felony punishable with transportation for life. By 3 and 4 William IV., cap. 73, sec. 2, it is further enacted that, from and after the 1st of August, 1834, slavery shall and is hereby utterly and for ever abolished and declared unlawful throughout the British colonies, plantations, and possessions abroad.'

From the above it is clearly proved that if the despatch of Her Majesty's Secretary of State for the Colonies be worth its weight, slavery, in the form of domestic slaves, should on no account be tolerated on this Coast; especially when it is considered that within twenty yards of the Governor's residence slaves can be and have been (1866) bought and sold. I have, in the Self-government, endeavoured to point out the position of the slaves as regards their masters; that it is an institution which engenders the most indolent habits; that it deteriorates the vitality of the male inhabitants; that it is in every way the most destructive element in the Gold Coast politics. It is probable that the slaves may prefer to remain with their masters, who are generally kind and indulgent to them, and on whom they depend for support; but this should not be permitted.

Hitherto the British authority had peculiar rules in dealing with domestic slaves on the Gold Coast. It was enjoined by Order of Council, dated 4th April, 1856, sec. 3, to the judicial functionary of the settlement that, in the administration of justice to the natives, he should pay equitable regard to the local customs, so far as the same shall not be repugnant to Christianity or to natural justice, and that in a country where slavery pervades society from the heir to the throne to the meanest servant, and where every man has been accustomed from time immemorial to look upon his children and servants as the most valuable property he possesses, it is impossible to abstain from entertaining questions between masters and slaves and disputed rights to slaves, inasmuch as claims are frequently set up by individuals to whole families without any just foundation; and if these were not examined and determined, the subject of such claimants would be inevitably reduced to slavery wherever the claimant had sufficient power to enforce his claim. 'Therefore,' remarked Judge Corner, 'rigidly abstaining from interfering to enforce slavery, as I conceive is the duty of every British magistrate, my endeavour is always in dealing with such cases to mitigate as far as possible the evils necessarily incident to the system, at the same time that care is taken not to violate unnecessarily the long-established laws and usages of the country.'

With regard to cases of ill-treatment of slaves, this high authority, who had ample opportunity of forming a just opinion on the subject, said : 'I am proud to say that I have them very much less than, previous to my residence in this country (Gold Coast), I could have imagined to be the case; and I consider it a remarkable circumstance that, in upwards of two years that I have now exercised my office, no case has come before me in which, upon examination, I have found such a degree of cruelty or severity as to justify me in exercising the power of emancipation.' The complaints of ill-treatment, he avers, were mostly of a frivolous nature; in those cases where the masters had punished the slaves, the punishment was merited by gross misconduct on the part of the slaves.

In those cases where he had to decide against claims to slaves, the slaves received from him certificates of their freedom; thus preventing a renewal of the claim in some future period. 'In accounting for this state of things, the fact of the total cessation of the foreign slave-trade on this part of the Coast, consequent upon British occupation of it, must not be forgotten; but independently of that I must say that the conduct of masters towards their servants generally is such as I could earnestly recommend as an example to be followed (sub modo) by some of our friends at home, for they are commonly looked upon and considered as members of the family, more particularly in the rural or bush districts, working side by side with their masters, eating from the same dish, and constantly addressing each other by the titles of father and son. The master usually provides a wife or a husband for his slaves, and frequently, if it be a female, takes her to wife for himself or his son;' which forms the utopia of savage bliss, but ought not longer to be permitted in British colonies, the British Constitution forbidding its existence. Its continuance now on the Gold Coast, where a portion of the British Army serves, gives a false idea that England supports and protects that unlawful traffic; whilst beyond mere toleration this is not the case. If, in the newly-acquired Colony of Lagos, Governor Glover is able to abolish domestic slavery, I do not see why it should not be attempted on the Gold Coast.

Let it be proclaimed that Cape Coast, Anamaboe, Accra, including Christiansborg, are for ever to be regarded as free towns. That slavery, under whatever shape or form, should no more exist there; and everyone residing within five miles of them shall be free men. That none of their inhabitants should hold or sell slaves ; and that anyone violating the law should be rigidly prosecuted by law, and, if found guilty, severely punished. That any slave coming within these free towns from the interior, or whatever place, should repair to the Forts, and there receive his manumition, and become thenceforth a free man. In these free towns the lands should be divided into lots amongst the people. All lands should be registered, and proper grants issued out to landowners. No claim of land hereafter should be recognized without such a grant, all unregistered lands being made Government property. Each slave on being freed should have a portion of land given him for building and cultivation, and the authorities should take steps to encourage location, and thus by degrees concentrate the interest of the whole of the Protectorate on these free points. Liberal institutions should be granted to the people, and every means adopted to elevate them.

There are, of course, many objections that would be raised to the abolition of a custom which time and habit has honoured. Thus the slaves, not being accustomed to live independently, might make their escape to the interior tribes, and then resell themselves, so that, after being freed from one master, they might become enslaved to another. This is a difficulty which must occur, and will be hard to obviate ; but if the Local Government, with its improved revenue, makes itself strong and respected by the interior tribes, if there is union and friendship between the interior kings and the Local Government, this practice will soon be put down by the Government making it distinctly known and generally proclaimed that any case of traffic in man between themselves and any of the inhabitants of the free towns would be met by the authorities with severe punishment. At the commencement there will be a few cases, which will rapidly decrease according to the measures of the Government.

The question of compensation may appear to present some difficulty. The financial difficulties of the country cannot allow this to be entertained; and should we have to wait until this is accomplished the Coast will never get rid of this social evil. In fact Earl Russell, in a despatch to the Governor of Cape Coast, dated July 14, 1844, sufficiently silenced this question; he stated that it could not be entertained—first, 'because in no case has compensation been given' in a British Colony, 'except for the enfranchisement of slaves duly registered; and, secondly, because Her Majesty's Government do not admit that it was even lawful to hold any person in slavery in Her Majesty's dominions on the West Coast of Africa, although the existence of slavery there at a former period may, as a mere matter of fact, not be capable of contradiction.'

VI.—*The Establishment of a Permanent Commandancy at Accra.*

It cannot be doubted that the Eastern District of the Gold Coast is the most important on this whole Coast both as regards revenue, resources, capabilities, and I must also say extent, although it occupies a secondary post.

The commandancy of this district has within the last few years been filled by officers commanding the detachment in the station, but in the last appointment a change has been made in this routine line by an officer being appointed from the Central Government at Sierra Leone. He acts *ex officio* as presiding magistrate; and the Accra district being at some distance from Cape Coast, cases of importance and great intricacy are of frequent occurrence; it is therefore absolutely necessary that the Commandant should know something of law; mere common sense has proved entirely insufficient, and in many cases ridiculous, especially when he has to withstand the criticism of acute and clever attorneys. Again, it is necessary that the commandant should be acquainted to a certain degree with the native customs and laws, since frequently cases arise among the natives in which the laws of England are inapplicable, and he has to arrive at his decision entirely by the guidance of native laws. Especially of late years the necessity for a permanent commandancy has been most keenly felt. Within the short space of two years it was calculated that there were no less than seven different officers appointed as Commandants; the result was that not one of them had time to become well acquainted with his duties, and everything went "wrong," and the Accras were the sufferers.

Alive to the benefit of such an establishment, Sir Benjamin Pine appointed a permanent civilian commandant to succeed the venerable James Bannerman, but he was soon deprived of the office after Pine left. For the benefit of this part of the coast it should again be established, the post should be made remunerative, a solicitor be obtained to fill it, or an independent person who is subject to no orders but that of the governor, and who understands something of the law.

VII.—*There should be established Itinerant Commandants styled District Commandants, one for the Eastern and the other for the Western District. Each District should be divided into Sub-Districts, and Clerks, styled Clerks of Districts, appointed, who should receive their orders from the Itinerant Commandants.*

This will be a very important step in the government of the whole territory; it will keep the supreme authority well informed of all that is going on in every part of the country, and enable the executive to employ stringent and quick measures in stopping at the bud any outbreak or disturbance that may disturb the peace and commerce of the country. Secondly, it will enable summonses to receive immediate attention. Thirdly, it will prevent intestine wars between neighbouring chiefs. Fourthly, it will make the inhabitants feel that the Government takes some interest in them. Fifthly, it will make them pay a greater respect to their kings, giving them power over their subjects, and at the same checking any barbarous custom they might be inclined to practise.

The District Commandants should be made Justices of the Peace, and should make a tour of inspection through each sub-district, settle all disputes, issue summonses, hear cases, see that the roads are properly kept in repair and make annual official reports on the state of the district, and their progress. Each Clerk of District should have two constables attached to his post, and he should have all cases in readiness prior to the arrival of the District Commandant; the whole establishment should be made self-supporting by the summonses and fines.

VIII.—*Good, open, and properly laid Streets should be made in at least the principal Sea-port Towns.*

There is no town or village in all the Colonies of Western Africa in which there is such a great want of good streets as on the Gold Coast. Whilst all the British towns in the Gambia, Sierra Leone, and more recently Lagos, have been properly laid out with open streets, the Gold Coast, as in many other things, has never received the slightest attention in this particular. Here, where Europeans have resided for more than a hundred years, where we have a good military force and a large colonial staff, the native huts are placed in such confusion as to be equalled only by towns in the far interior where civilization has never reached. Even in the newly-built towns on the sea-coast such as the new Christiansborg, there is no control whatever exercised by the local Government to prevent this helter-skelter mode of building. The huts are all huddled together, leaving irregular narrow lanes, interrupted here and there by piles of fermented mud or deep excavations containing stagnant water. In some places these lanes are kept in the most revoltingly filthy state. It is said to have been lately in contemplation to pass an ordinance to rectify this evil, and form open streets in the various parts of the town. This would necessitate a revision of the tenure of lands already referred to. It is the wish of all those who have the interest of the Gold Coast at heart that some such plan as this should be carried into effect.

IX.—*To Encourage every Means tending to Work the Gold Mines of the District properly.*

This is a subject of intrinsic importance to the wealth, prosperity, and good government of the Gold Coast. In the chapter on the self-government of this part of the Coast I have endeavoured to point out the numerous rich mines which abound in various districts, and the imperfect manner in which they are worked. Something should be done to remedy this, a company should be formed for the express purpose of digging these mines; and the Government should guarantee its protection against any molestation from the native tribes. If Clerks of Districts as well as District Commandants be established, this can be very easily done, and a well-organized company with a trifling capital would within a very short time so open these vast resources of the country, that before long we should find men from every part of the world 'ploughing the ocean and digging the mountain sides' after it, and then the Government of Cape Coast would be of some importance to the British throne. Dr. Robert Clark, late Colonial Surgeon of this Coast, in a paper read before the Ethnological Society, has given a most lucid account of the gold-digging by the natives in the extensive gold-fields of Wassaw, which we have lately transferred to the Dutch Government.

The natives in the gold districts are very much prejudiced against having any one who wears European clothes, or who can speak a European language, in the gold districts. They are afraid of the gold being worked by civilized men, and consequently make religion the scapegoat for their resistance. They maintain that the inexorable Fetish forbids any white man—or 'black man in white man's clothes,' to use Captain Burton's phraseology—to go near the mines, and consequently veto every effort in that direction. Mr Thomas Hughes, an intelligent native of Cape Coast, commenced mining operations some years ago in the rich field of Western Wassaw. He was promised support by the Local (Andrew's) Government, so that he imported expensive machinery for that express purpose, and had it transported by labourers to the locality selected, and commenced digging. Within a short distance his diggers came to a thin stratum, and by continued digging they met with a fine, rich vein. During this time, although residing within a few yards from the diggings, the king of the district strictly prohibited him from going near it, as being against the demands of Fetish. Mr. Hughes was compelled to obey, on the alternative of instant expulsion. This, however, came in due course of time; no sooner was it known that he had met a fine vein, and that he was likely to succeed, than he and his people were ignominiously turned out of the country and his machinery destroyed. He proceeded to Cape Coast (this was in September, 1861) and reported the circumstance to the local authorities, and requested the promised assistance. His importunities met with a deaf ear; no effort was ever made to recompense him for the loss he had sustained, and he was interdicted to enter the country. From that time he became a ruined man.

No good will be obtained from the gold-mines of the Gold Coast except—

1. Civilized agency with proper machinery be employed to work them.

2. The Local Government take proper effective means for supporting their efforts and protecting them.

At present the British Gold Coasteans depend entirely for their gold trade on their inveterate enemies the Ashantees, whilst their country is replete with mines. Having ceded those of Wassaw and Apollonia to the Dutch, we have those in Denkera and Akim. A good road to these districts will be the first thing to be attempted; and I must here leave the subject for the attention and consideration of the local authorities and the well-to-do inhabitants.

X.—*The Placing of a Small Steamer in the River Volta.*

Unquestionably, at present, the Eastern District is the most important in the British Gold Coast; rich in the most exportable commercial articles, palm-oil, palm kernel, and cotton, it is unfortunately surrounded by tribes who know how to make themselves disagreeably felt by panyarring loaded canoes and carriers passing through their country, and quietly retreating into their mountain fastnesses. It is, therefore, of great importance to the merchants of Accra, to the development of the country, and for the increase of the (all-important) revenue, that the Volta should be properly protected by a small steamboat. For the last three years the commercial condition of this district through the River has been interrupted by the causes above enumerated, the merchants almost reduced to bankruptcy, and the Local Government cannot raise a revenue. A small steamer placed on the Volta to protect the trade, to cost from 200*l.* to 500*l.*, will be of paramount value to this part of the Coast, and might be employed for towing rafts of palm-oil puncheons down the River. The oil from the district of Crobboe can be brought down in small puncheons to Amedica, as the River between those places is shallow, rocky, and unsafe. Here the merchants can transfer them to large butts, then to be towed down the River. By these means the little steamer would pay its own expenses.

XI.—*Alteration in the Currency of the Country.*

The *cowry* currency is as cumbrous and inconvenient as the Spartan iron bars of Lycurgus; it is full time to change the system. It has been successfully changed in some parts of the world where it was once prevalent, and if on the authority of Captain Burton,* the late Sayyid Said of Zanzibar and Muskat found no difficulty in changing the system, I do not see why we should not attempt the experiment. Substitute a copper currency for cowry, and I am certain that it will very soon take amongst the people. At present even the oil-men in the interior, who demanded, in years gone by, a large quantity of cowry, are now too happy to receive silver, for which they are ready to give a very heavy discount. They have discovered that the cowry shell was too bulky to keep, and consequently prefer silver, several thousand pounds of which yearly pass through Accra, and yet still silver coin is always scarce. The bush people, as the interior tribes are called, receive them in exchange for produce, take them in the interior, and then bury them, and they are therefore lost sight of. Many of my readers who have never seen nor know the value of the cowry shell will be astonished to hear that its possession is really inconvenient to the rich. The weight of 2,000 of the blue shells is computed at from 80 to 90 lbs., which is scarcely equal to four shillings and sixpence. Lieutenant Forbes complains that to carry fifty dollars he had to employ five women. Copper coin should be effectually and compulsorily introduced, as it would save time and expense to the merchants, and would lead to a great improvement in the trade.

XII.—*The Formation of a Good Constabulary Force.*

The present constabulary force of the Gold Coast is very poor, whilst the police at Sierra Leone cost the Local Government about 14,000l. a-year. On the Gold Coast it scarcely costs 1,000l., although the latter has an area of territory more than fifty times that of the former. From the turbulent and ruffian-like state of the interior tribes, it is necessary that there should be a good and efficient police force in the Gold Coast. Sir Benjamin Pine, through this, recommended the formation of a good constabulary

---

* 'Abeokuta and the Cameroon Mountains,' pp. 320, vol. 1.

force, placed under the immediate control of the Administrator, which would enable him to carry out a firm administration of the law. It would be more serviceable to keep order than the soldiers of the West Indian Regiments, who have no stamina for bush operations, and who cannot be easily moved by the Administrator. The Administrator of the Gold Coast should be a man with a mind capable of exercising an inflexible adherence to resolutions once formed for the vindication of the law, as such a course would always command support, and 'involves less danger than a weak submission to clamour.'

The recruits for the constabulary should not be entirely from the Gold Coast, as their connexion by relationship would never permit them to carry out any important orders effectually. The majority should therefore come from without—e. g., the Hausa of Lagos, or men from the other Colonies. They should be well cared for, properly drilled, and placed under the immediate control of the Administrator. Two hundred men so enrolled would be of more use to him than three hundred West Indian soldiers within the Castle of Cape Coast, and then, like Nelson, although in a different manner, he could afford to leave his despatches unopened when about to enforce any measure for the good of the country.

CHAPTER XVII.

REQUIREMENTS OF LAGOS—SOME REMARKS ON THE REPUBLIC OF LIBERIA.

WE have in Chapter XII. considered at some length the physical geography of the interior countries of the Colony of Lagos, their capabilities, the manners and customs of the people, and now we have to remark on its requirements; but not having had sufficient opportunity during my brief stay there to make a full investigation of the subject, my remarks will be but few and of a general nature.

1. Every improvement should be made in the drainage of the town.

2. The various rivers already detailed should be properly, carefully, and systematically surveyed.

3. Every facility should be given to the inhabitants for the transport of their produce from the interior into the port of Lagos.

4. A good tram-road should be made in various directions to the interior, commencing from Lagos and other British towns—one from Ikorodo to Makun, to be pushed forward to Ipara. Another from the mainland of Lagos to Munsho, to be carried to Otta, a third from Worro to Igbessa, and a fourth from Badagry to Addo.

With these few observations, I must dismiss the subject of Lagos, with the hope that I may hereafter get sufficient opportunities to make it a subject of close examination and report, and shall now pass on to a few remarks on the Republic of Liberia.

My friend Professor Blyden, of this republic, in an oration delivered in Syria not long ago, made the following remarks respecting the neighbouring British Colony, Sierra Leone, the seat of the British Government in Western Africa. 'Sierra Leone,' said he, 'strikingly exemplifies the inefficiency of European legislation as a

civilizer of the black race. Under British rule, crippled by monarchical restraint, the African element, so essential to African civilization
in Sierra Leone, is rendered subdued and silent, and hence that
province has been, and under like circumstances will continue to be, of
no marked avail as a pioneer of intelligent progress. Even if
it should not be possible for the Republic of Liberia to acquire them
in the course of time in an honourable and quiet manner, still they
will never rise to sufficient importance to cause us internal uneasiness.'
Whilst we cannot endorse this qualified statement of Professor
Blyden, as it is not our intention here to discourse on the subject,
Liberia will no doubt allow Sierra Leone to point out certain defects
in the government of that Republic, which, if remedied, would greatly
enhance social advancement and material progress. In Chapter II.
I have considered certain defects in the constitution and government
of the Republic which are of fundamental importance. Here I intend
to remark on some social defects which should engage the immediate
attention of the Legislature.

First, appearance aids considerably in our diagnosis of the
character of a person, place, or thing. The entrance to Monrovia,
the capital of the Liberian Republic, reminds one of the entrance to a
purely native town, where the light of civilization has never reached,
and it gives to the causual observer the idea of a want of a
firm government, a want of revenue, a want of developmental
powers, and the existence of great inertia in the municipal authority
of Monrovia. At the very entrance of the town, as one jumps-out
of his boat, he first meets with a number of miserable cane fishing
huts, occupied by an almost naked crowd of kroomen and women;
the children, wretchedly tattooed, squatting about in perfect nudity,
and answering the calls of nature in every direction. Behind these
about twenty feet in diameter, is a thick bush, in which is a narrow
footpath leading to a pile of stones put together helter-skelter,
without any idea of masonry, and forming the commencement of
a bridge, which is so rickety as to require a passer-by to keep
Newton always in memory, as the least loss in the centre of gravity
would lead to a fearful catastrophe. All around this bridge is an
extent of land consisting of mangrove swamp, which is entirely
exposed twice in the course of the twenty-four hours, and which

gives out most deadly miasmata. Such was the condition of the entrance of Monrovia, the capital of the Liberian Republic, when I landed there in January, 1866.

The miserable fishing huts should on no account be permitted to remain where they are; the bush should be cut down, and the land reclaimed from the river, and sold for the benefit of the town corporation, which can be easily done by the building of a river wall along its edge at low-water mark; the rescued land can then be filled up and hardened with materials from without, so that in course of time, instead of being the source of pernicious poison, it might be of gain to the municipality of the town. On the whole, Monrovia was a very unfortunate selection for the capital of the Republic; and the large and open streets are covered with huge basaltic rocks, which entirely preclude a carriage drive.

Whilst we rejoice with the Liberians on their yearly accession of emigrants from America, it behoves us to remind them that unless certain improvements are made among the aboriginal inhabitants whom they meet in the country, in order that they may be brought to the scale of equality with themselves, there will be a poor chance for the prosperous futurity of the Government. These original inhabitants are a firm, able-bodied race, who, unlike the American Indians, would withstand ' wave after wave of destructive and malignant tempest,' were it ever to be brought against them. They are a perpetual race, and the climate is more likely to devastate the emigrants than them —i.e., if the former continue to remain pure and unmixed with the aboriginal inhabitants. The improvement in the position of the coloured population of America would lead à priori to the belief that ere long there would be but very few emigrations from that country and consequently a general diminution of the civilized population. It must always be borne in mind that purely mulatto population cannot exist for any lengthened period; they must either merge into one or other races (black or white), or gradually die out. Among mulattoes propagation is less prolific, and the offspring is delicate and short lived. When, however, propagation has been maintained in purity, within a few generations the whole race dies out. The duty of the Liberian Government should therefore be :—

1st. To interdict all tattooing of children in all the towns and villages where the Government has sufficient influence to do so.

2nd. To make education of the children up to a certain age a compulsory act.

3rd. To pay special attention to the education of young kroo females.

Within a few years, if adopted, this would lead to great improvement in the general population, and then there would be a possibility of intermarriages taking place between the emigrants and the aborigines, and a powerful element in the future government of the Republic be ensured.

Liberia is now recognized by the great Republic of America as an independent nationality, and this happy event has been crowned by that State appointing a consular agent to reside in Monrovia. At the birth of the young Republic, England stretched forth her helping hand to her, and assisted in every way to raise the standard of the population, and to develop the resources of the country; there was perfect harmony between the two Governments; a British consulate was established in Monrovia, which carefully watched over the interests of British merchants. This, unfortunately, has been abolished, although the trading establishments of British merchants in this territory have lately been very much increased. The Liberian Government, through many difficult questions which have lately arisen respecting territorial boundary, have represented to the British Government the necessity of re-establishing the consulate, and we think that it will be a great boon, not only to Liberia, but also to British capitalists, should this be acceded to.

CHAPTER XVIII.

CONCLUDING REMARKS.—ADVICE TO THE RISING GENERA-TION IN WEST AFRICA.

In 1846, Mr. Hilary Teage, a Liberian, delivered a most graphic, eloquent, and touching speech in Monrovia to the citizens of Liberia, in which we find the following passage: ' Upon you [fellow-citizens], rely upon it, depends, in a measure you can hardly conceive, the future destiny of your race. You are to give the answer whether the African race is doomed to interminable degradation—a hideous blot on the fair face of creation, a libel upon the dignity of human nature; or whether they are capable to take an honourable rank amongst the great family of nations.' This is a most valuable admonition, which should be treasured up by every one in Western Africa, but especially the rising generation, bearing in mind that they have a special mission to fulfil on earth; that they are not exclusively their own property, but that by industry and perseverance they might so better their circumstances and position as to give material aid to those less favoured than themselves. It must also be remembered by them that Western Africa in literature and science is among the least of nations. It has been so destined that, with the exception of the aboriginals, no other nation has been able to plant a sure footing in her, and consequently that from her sons, and her sons alone, must her complete regeneration be looked for. The initiative cannot be expected to come from within—it must come from without; and it is certain that 'genius, talent, and virtue will be honoured, whether clad in rags or in broadcloth, and the nobility of a manly nature will not always continue to be estimated according to the colour of the skin.'

Let the younger portion of the population, who are so susceptible and ready to take offence and retort at the least occasion, remember

T

that all Europeans who enter their country, by the higher degree of intellectual and moral cultivation which they, as a race, have received, are entitled to a certain degree of respect as the harbingers of civilization, imitating the good and virtuous, whilst shunning those whose actions are a disgrace to civilization—waiting patiently whilst maintaining an upright and dignified course, for the time when they will see the necessity of modifying their opinions and acting up to them with ideas of loftier and holier order. In the meantime, however, let them be uniformly courteous, cultivate their minds, and strive zealously for substantial worth. Let them seek independence without bravado, manliness without subserviency; and let them put their shoulders to the work, and 'prove by the effort they themselves make that they, too, desire, and are striving, and will strive for the Christian and industrial regeneration of Africa; and do this with the modesty not at all incompatible with manly self-reliance, and a due sense of the innate dignity which should characterize men who have been helped out of their degradation, and brought at once into the ranks of a Christian civilization which has taken eighteen centuries to be developed.'

It must be remembered that there is no royal road to greatness—that it cannot be said that this or that man possesses a heaven-born reputation, greatness, or talent. It must be bought by severe perseverance, by an undaunted courage and industry, by real hard work and application, with a love for the undertaking we have in hand, by an uncompromising, disinterested adhesion to the truth. These, and these alone, will be the keystone for every one to ascend to the altitude of material and honourable success—success that will produce in us primarily real improvement, for real and extensive usefulness to our country hereafter, when the time is ripe. What, may be asked, are the passports to this honourable success? Dr. Rivington, in an admirable address delivered at the opening of one of the London Medical Schools, stated them to be ability, labour, and character—these three are the passports to an honourable fame. 'Ability,' says he, 'is the capacity for acquiring and using knowledge and skill; labour, the means of acquirement and use; character, the direction and control of acquirement and usefulness. Ability without labour is the talent wrapped up in a napkin; ability without virtue will work not for the true end of all talents, all knowledge, and all effort—the use and advantage of men—but for the gratification of a selfish vanity, which would tarnish its laurel wreaths.' That the African race possesses undoubtedly this ability may be further proved by the result of competitive examination in Europe between those who are educated there and their more favoured schoolmates, by the progress they make in different undertakings in their native climate ; and it behoves them, therefore, to labour steadfastly for the regeneration of their country, and to dissipate from the minds of those indisposed to the advancement of their race, the false theory always advanced, that they are incapable of advancement.

They should make it their ruling principle to concentrate their mental powers, their powers of observation, reasoning, and memory, on the primary objects of their engagement. 'Never to observe without thought ; never reason to confident conclusions without a sufficiency of certainly verified facts ; never to acquire facts without submitting them to the test of reasoning and, when occasion offers, to the test of experience,' as it has been conclusively remarked that observation without thought is a hasty observation, and the experience derived from it is wasted; and if we reason without a sufficiency or verification of facts we shall reason into error; and if we remember without comparison the result will be that we shall be a vast storehouse of inconsequential knowledge.

The Right Hon. Mr. Gladstone, in an able speech delivered at St. Martin's Hall, Hanover Street, Long Acre, in July, 1867, most truthfully said 'that each man in his situation should labour for the improvement of his mind earnestly and yet humbly, never thinking that the knowledge which he may acquire is even as a grain of sand in comparison with the knowledge which he cannot acquire, but still confidently labouring that the knowledge within his reach has, first of all, a great value in itself ; and, secondly, that it has a great value beyond itself—viz., its value as an instrument of culture reacting upon the mind, strengthening it, enlarging it, enlightening it, giving it firmness of tissue, suppleness and elasticity of movement, a capacity applicable to all the purposes of life, of raising the human being not in outer circumstance alone—

although it no doubt exercises a most powerful influence in that direction—but in himself, in his character, in those faculties with which he is endowed, and in consequence of his possession of which, that high and noble privilege has been ascribed to him that he alone of all other creatures was made in the image of God.' These remarks should be treasured up in the minds of the rising generation; but it will be my place here to caution those who, having received good and proper education, systematically neglect the powerful means at their command, become idle and vicious—who, forming themselves the supporters of late hours and the patrons of cloths, petticoats, and *payhnes*, virtually constitute themselves the Goths and Vandals of the colony they reside in—to whom

> Thinking is but an idle waste of thought,
> And nought is everything, and everything is nought—

men who look upon their lives not as the public property of their country, and therefore requiring those improvements necessary for its advancement, but as a superlative cope for the whist table, *écarté*, unlimited loo, and unlimited lewdness—not as the time for extending the benign influences of their education to their less favoured brethren, but as a 'fine, though, ah! sad fate! a fugitive opportunity,' for drinking brandy and water, whisky punch, and an unlimited quantity of beer (Rivington). Such men, happily, are few in number, who instead of deprecating in the most unmeasured terms the vices of a class of inhabitants who seize every opportunity of allying them to the anthropoid apes, imitate them in their degrading habits. Let them consider that their own interest is intimately bound up in the interest of their country's rise; and that by developing the principle of public interest they will bring the Government to take an interest in themselves, and thus their interest and that of their Government will not clash, but become identical; and then would it more fully appear that there is no such thing as the real interest of a government 'contra-distinguished from the real interest of a community; no such thing as the interest of a community contra-distinguished from the real interest' of the country. And it will also be found that it is not the interest of all men to be attracted by power, by wealth, by fame, by great place, and by mere book-knowledge, but that, on the contrary, it is the interest of all men to be attracted by virtue, by honesty, by charity, by wisdom, by truth, by happiness, and by peace.

Let the rising generation, therefore, study to exert themselves to obtain the combined attractive influence of knowledge and wisdom, wealth and honesty, great place and charity, fame and happiness, book-learning and virtue, so that they may be made to bring their happy influences to bear on the regeneration of their country ; and then there will be the real exercise of those qualities which will gradually lead to the attainment of the power of self-government, and the contemplated improvement of the House of Commons Committee will go on *tuto, cito, et jucunde.**

* Safely, quietly, and with ease.

FINIS.

INDEX.

LONDON : PRINTED BY W. J. JOHNSON, 121, FLEET STREET.

For EU product safety concerns, contact us at Calle de José Abascal, 56–1°, 28003 Madrid, Spain or eugpsr@cambridge.org.

www.ingramcontent.com/pod-product-compliance
Ingram Content Group UK Ltd.
Pitfield, Milton Keynes, MK11 3LW, UK
UKHW010348140625
459647UK00010B/929